International Perspectives on
Inclusive Education

Simone Seitz
Petra Auer
Rosa Bellacicco (eds.)

International Perspectives on Inclusive Education

In the Light of Educational Justice

Verlag Barbara Budrich
Opladen • Berlin • Toronto 2023

This book is available as a free download from www.budrich.eu (https://doi.org/10.3224/84742698).

© 2023   by Verlag Barbara Budrich GmbH, Opladen, Berlin & Toronto
www.budrich.eu

    ISBN   978-3-8474-2698-1 (Paperback)
    eISBN 978-3-8474-1868-9 (PDF)
    DOI   10.3224/84742698

Verlag Barbara Budrich GmbH
Stauffenbergstr. 7. D-51379 Leverkusen Opladen, Germany
86 Delma Drive. Toronto, ON M8W 4P6 Canada
www.budrich.eu

A CIP catalogue record for this book is available from Die Deutsche Nationalbibliothek (The German National Library) (https://portal.dnb.de)

Cover design by Bettina Lehfeldt, Kleinmachnow – www.lehfeldtgraphic.de
Picture credits: photo: stock.adobe.com
Language editing by Marc Weingart, Werther – http://www.english-check.de
Typesetting by Angelika Schulz, Zülpich
Printed in Europe on acid-free paper by docupoint GmbH, Barleben

Preface – International Perspectives on Inclusion and Educational Justice

Mel Ainscow, Gottfried Biewer, Vera Moser

It has been almost 25 years since the World Conference on Special Needs Education, co-organised by UNESCO and the Ministry of Education and Science of Spain. The conference led to the Salamanca Statement and Framework for Action, arguably the most significant international document that has ever appeared in the field of special education (UNESCO 1994). In so doing, it endorsed the idea of inclusive education, which has become a major global influence in subsequent years.

The Salamanca Statement concluded that:

> Regular schools with [an] inclusive orientation are the most effective means of combating discriminatory attitudes, creating welcoming communities, building an inclusive society and achieving education for all; moreover, they provide an effective education to the majority of children and improve the efficiency and ultimately the cost-effectiveness of the entire education system. (p.ix)

The aim, then, is to reform education systems. This can only happen, it is argued, if mainstream schools become capable of educating all children in their local communities. This suggests that moves towards inclusive schools can be justified on a number of grounds (UNESCO 2017). There is:

- **An educational justification:** the requirement for schools to educate all children together means that they have to develop ways of teaching that respond to individual differences and that therefore benefit all children;
- **A social justification:** inclusive schools are intended to change attitudes to differences by educating all children together, and form the basis for a just and non-discriminatory society;
- **An economic justification:** it is likely to be less costly to establish and maintain schools which educate all children together than to set up a complex system of different types of schools specialising in particular groups of children.

Subsequent years have seen considerable efforts in many countries to move educational policy and practice in a more inclusive direction. Further impetus to this movement was provided in 2008 by the 48th session of the IBE-UNESCO International Conference on Education, with its theme *'Inclusive Education: The Way of the Future'*.

Moving forward, the year 2016 was particularly important in relation to the future of the legacy of Salamanca. Building on the Incheon Declaration agreed at the World Forum on Education in May 2015 (UNESCO 2015), it saw the publication by UNESCO of the Education 2030 Framework for Action. This emphasises inclusion and equity as laying the foundations for quality education. It also stresses the need to address all forms of exclusion and marginalisation, disparities and inequalities in access, participation, and learning processes and outcomes.

Like all major policy changes, progress in relation to inclusion and equity requires an effective strategy for implementation. In particular, it requires new thinking which focuses attention on the barriers experienced by some children that lead them to become marginalised as a result of contextual factors, as opposed to the categories a learner may or may not fall into. The implication is that overcoming such barriers is the most important means of forms of development of education that are effective for all children.

In this way, it is argued, inclusion is a way of achieving the overall improvement of education systems (Ainscow 2020). This means that it is important that inclusion and equity in education are studied, encouraged and evaluated with an intersectional view that covers preschool, basic, secondary and tertiary education (Bešić 2020).

This book makes an important contribution to thinking in the field in respect to this global reform agenda. As noted in the introductory chapter, it provides a range of different perspectives on inclusion-related research in the light of educational justice, as well as different and complementary approaches to further theorising and researching educational justice in the light of inclusion-related issues.

Kurt Lewin, a pioneer in organisational psychology, famously noted that there is nothing so practical as a good theory. A theory is an explanation, a set of ideas about how something works, and the practical application of a good theory can be invaluable. The field of inclusive education has often lacked attention to theory, not least because the most important players, the teachers, have limited time to make sense of complex texts.

Another problem is that different perspectives are often rooted in particular national contexts. As a result, barriers of language can act as barriers to learning from comparisons. The chapters in this book illustrate the benefits that can be gained when learning from national differences. In particular, they bring together different perspectives on inclusive education which refer to or compare various education systems in Europe and reflect on them in relation to notions of justice.

References

Ainscow, M. (2020): Inclusion and equity in education: Making sense of global challenges. In: Prospects 49, 3, pp. 123–134.

Bešić, E. (2020): Intersectionality: A pathway towards inclusive education? In: Prospects 49, pp. 111–122.

UNESCO (1994): Final Report: World conference on special needs education: Access and quality. Paris: UNESCO.

UNESCO (2015): Incheon Declaration and Framework for Action for the implementation of Sustainable Development Goal 4. Paris: UNESCO.

UNESCO (2017): A guide for ensuring inclusion and equity in education. Paris: UNESCO.

Table of Contents

Part III: Doing Inclusion – Doing Difference

Introduction – In the Light of Educational Justice: International Perspectives on Inclusion

Simone Seitz, Petra Auer, Rosa Bellacicco

In the international discourse, there is a broad consensus that inclusion-oriented developments of education systems go hand in hand with an increase of educational justice or even represent an active contribution to it (Ainscow 2020; Seitz et al. 2012). The current debate in this area often refers to international agreements such as the Agenda 2030, which postulates strengthening high-quality, inclusive education and reducing social inequity (United Nations 2015; goals 4 and goal 10).

However, within this context, it is noticeable that different concepts of justice are referred to quite inconsistently, either implicitly or explicitly. First, the concept of *distributive justice* in the sense of equality of opportunities (Rawls 1971; critically Walzer 2006) receives widespread attention, above all, in approaches following the meritocratic principle and compensatory approaches (critically Berkemeyer 2018). According to a concept of distributive justice, it is considered fair if well-performing children assume privileged positions in society once they are adults. The concept thus presupposes the autonomy of young learners since it is up to them to achieve through effort. Equality is therefore also reflected in the provision of compensatory means in case of disadvantage. Such an understanding is criticised since all children are rather dependent on kindergartens and schools, which offer appropriate opportunities to develop autonomy (Stojanov 2011: 22), and the idea of compensation for the "disadvantaged" is framed by hegemonial concepts of normalcy. Therefore, these connections are often discussed with reference to Bourdieu's theory of habitus (Bourdieu/Passeron 1971). Second, reference is made to *social justice* in terms of capabilities (Nussbaum 2006). Following the idea of social justice or participatory justice, according to the Capability Approach, policies should ensure conditions that enable everyone, considering the diversity of life situations, to develop their capabilities with the perspective of equal citizenship in societies (Otto/Ziegler 2010; Terzi 2007). Equity in education is then not simply demonstrated by the fact that as many children and young people as possible achieve measurable, high performance in school – as often postulated in discussions around the international large-scale-assessment studies (PISA; OECD 2019) – but rather by the extent to which they are given the opportunity in schools to develop their personality, considering the diversity of their life situations (Sauerwein/Vieluf 2021). A third perspective is the concept of *recognition justice*

(Honneth 1992; Stojanov 2011; Prengel 2013), which is led by a particular focus on pedagogical relations based on recognition. According to this approach, educational justice indeed shows that recognition, seen as a social practice, opens paths to self-realisation and personality development.

These briefly outlined varying understandings of educational justice are also linked to different perspectives on childhood and youth, particularly in relation to the notion of its temporality: in the context of the above mentioned internationally observable output-orientation of education systems, children are primarily addressed as future adults and childhood is understood as a phase of "becoming". Against this background, the main task of educational institutions would be to achieve systematic competence acquisition in children, whereas a view on childhood and youth as a phase of "being" seems to be increasingly pushed into the background (Honneth 2020.) and, together with this, possibly also the recognition of children as persons who are endowed with biographies and valuable characteristics. Further, it can be noted that this does not yet clarify the extent to which different perspectives on childhood and youth might be linked to hegemonic concepts of normalcy, as might be seen in the above-mentioned preventive and compensatory approaches, which are therefore often criticised (Kelle/Tervooren 2008).

This already indicates that the discourse on educational justice still holds meaningful gaps. In particular, the open question how the tension between societal, institutional, and individual responsibility for education and the view of children and youngsters as more or less endowed with autonomy (Bou-Habib/Olsaretti 2015) can be theorised more precisely.

Given the complexity of the issue, we deliberately place them here in an international context to bring together different perspectives on inclusive education which refer to or compare various education systems in Europe and to reflect them in the light of educational justice. We do so in three parts:

Section I entitled *Conceptualisations underpinning research on diversity, equity, and inclusive education* (Chapters 1–4) contains contributions presenting theoretical approaches or discussing theoretical conceptions, which can be understood as a possible starting point for conducting future-oriented research on the topic. Overall, the single chapters add to a growing repository of theoretical foundations on inclusion-relevant aspects of education and educational justice and offer implications for research and educational practice.

Section II on *Educational justice within different educational systems* (Chapters 5–8) details the findings stemming from studies that present various facets of diversity, normalcy and inclusion and the different characteristics they take across multiple discourses. The comparative studies included in this section offer impulses to reflect cultural-normative as well as structural dimensions of (in)equity in the education systems.

Section III *Ambivalences: Doing Inclusion – Doing Difference* (Chapters 9–11) triggers the debate on dealing with diversity and equity in education seen as a social practice in kindergartens and schools. What follows is an exploration of frictions between regulative level and educational practice as well as hidden rules of normalcy and dynamics of classism, racism and ableism in education and also in scientific discourses.

In the following, each chapter is briefly summarised by highlighting its importance to the readers of this volume.

The entry point for the first section is a contribution that focuses on the political ontologies of difference. As such, Chapter 1 (Boger) arises from the author's theory of "trilemmatic inclusion", which maps concepts of anti-discrimination and/or 'inclusion' through the differentiation of their political ontology of 'otherness/multiplicity/difference'. In doing so, she elaborates three knots, namely, *empowerment, normalisation* and *deconstruction*, three vectors that can be triangulated into contradictory desires, which, however, all aim to end discrimination. In this volume the approach is focused from an international position which the author describes as trans_position.

Instead, Chapter 2 (Tervooren) critically discusses the subordinate role of the socially constructed category of 'disability' in childhood studies in Germanophone contexts. The issue is negotiated in three steps: by drawing upon childhood studies' critique of the developmental paradigm, by showing how 'disability' as social category is debated in research on childhood in German-speaking contexts, and by elaborating the international discussion on 'disabled children's childhood studies'. Building on these, the author concludes by addressing possible challenges of intersectional childhood studies which are related to the complex social category of 'disability'.

Guided by the aim to get a deeper knowledge on children's perceptions of academic performance and assessment, Chapter 3 (Seitz & Imperio) elaborates the state of the art of existing research on the topic. The contribution provides a detailed overview of studies conducted around the globe, taking the perspective of the approach of Childhood Studies and the Student Voice movement, and raises the question what role children play in these studies and how the image of the child underlying research might be reflected in the light of educational justice.

In Chapter 4 (Kaiser & Seitz) the section closes with an analysis of the discourse on achievement and inclusion. Starting from the role of schools in reproducing inequities, on the one hand, and the two international political agendas related to large-scale assessment and inclusion and sustainability, on the other, the authors elaborate the narrative formations and stabilising rules of interpretation of (the) discourse(s) within scientific articles in German language.

The second section begins with Chapter 5 (Seitz, Hamacher & Berti) pursuing the question if all-day schooling can be seen as one way to strengthening educational justice in terms of equity, shedding light on the topic from the children's point of view. Along with findings from an investigation that captures primary school children's perspectives of all-day school, the relationship between formal and non-formal education as well as children's social role (i.e., being children, students, and peers) within both of them constitutes the central point of the contribution.

Starting likewise from the results of an empirical study involving primary school children, which show that the latter differ in the importance they attribute to specific values according to the school system their school belongs to, Chapter 6 (Auer) approaches the topic of inclusiveness of the education system in the Province of Bolzano (Italy), a multilingual region. Taking the perspective of the socialisation of values within the school context and considering the organisation of schools through a tripartite division according to the official languages of the territory, the question is raised how far the latter is in line with a conception of inclusion as *one school for all*.

Chapter 7 (Bellacicco & Cappello) focuses on data on school inclusion in Italy: the critical analysis of different statistics collected at national and local (Province of Bolzano) levels about inclusive education is significant for determining how Italy monitors the quality of education. The study leads to a questioning of different priorities of analysis emerging in different reports and, above all, the missing dimensions which would be necessary to gather data for strengthening inclusive policies.

Through an international comparison of three national cases – Ireland, Italy, and Norway – commonalities and differences of funding models and the related policy contexts are elaborated in Chapter 8 (Banks, Cappello, Demo, Hausstätter & Seitz). Referring to neo-institutionalism (Scott 2014), the authors structure the investigated object on different levels, summarising the interrelationships of governance, funding and pedagogical practice. Reflecting critically on the conception and funding of inclusive education, the authors dare to examine how the idea of funding inclusion is culturally constructed in the three countries.

To reframe policy and practice of inclusive education, an intersectional and interdisciplinary framework focusing on racism and ableism as interlocking systems of oppression in education – the Disability Critical Race Studies (DisCrit) – is discussed in Chapter 9 (Migliarini), which begins the third and final section of this edited volume. The contribution explores the "SENitization" of students with experience of migration and brings it to-gether with a pilot study in a school in Italy that struggled to provide appropriate support to these students who have been labelled as "disabled". Examples of an intersectionally reflected inclusive practice by means of DisCrit are illustrated.

Chapter 10 (Frizzarin) is based on a validation study. The validation of an instrument aimed to measure adolescents' attitudes towards otherness which combines a qualitative and a quantitative approach is detailed. Moreover, the representations of students involved in the study are directly drawn upon concerning their definitions of otherness. The results of the study facilitate a discussion about attitudes that school and classmates hold towards peers identified as "Others" and that likely result in marginalisation and exclusion. A reflection of the issues identified in international literature about Individual Educational Planning in inclusive classrooms and the underlying tensions is provided in Chapter 11 (Bellacicco, Ianes & Auer). Problems where there can be several different and combinable solutions, and dilemmas, consisting of two conflicting alternatives, are identified here as two crucial challenges. The chapter concludes by ways to bring together the two poles of dilemmas highlighting some progress of recent Italian laws that have promoted a new perspective on Individual Educational Planning.

The book concludes in Chapter 12 (Demo) with a reference to the *dispositif* of the dialogic. The author uses it to discuss a possible integration of central antinomies of inclusive education, both on a theoretical level and on the level of educational policies and practices. On this basis, she proposes the image of a border crosser for the role of inclusive education and inclusive research.

Overall, this book offers a rich dialogue of different perspectives on inclusion-related research in the light of educational justice as well as different and complementary approaches to further theorising and researching educational justice in the light of inclusion-related issues.

References

Ainscow, Mel (2020): Promoting inclusion and equity in education. Lessons from international experiences. In: Nordic Journal of Studies in Educational Policy 6, 1, pp. 7–16.

Berkemeyer, Nils (2018): Über die Schwierigkeit, das Leistungsprinzip im Schulsystem gerechtigkeitstheoretisch zu begründen. Replik auf Christian Nerowski. In: Zeitschrift für Erziehungswissenschaft 21, pp. 447-464.

Bou-Habib, Paul/Olsaretti, Serena (2015): Autonomy and Children's Well-Being. In: Bagattini, Alexander/Macleod, Colin (eds.), The Nature of Children's Well-Being. Indicators and Research 9. Dordrecht: Springer, pp. 15-35.

Bourdieu, Pierre/Passeron, Jean-Claude (1971): Die Illusion der Chancengleichheit: Untersuchungen zur Soziologie des Bildungswesens am Beispiel Frankreichs. Stuttgart: Klett.

Honneth, Axel (2020): Die Armut unserer Freiheit. Aufsätze 2012-2019. Berlin: Suhrkamp.

Kelle, Helga/Tervooren, Anja (2008) (eds.): Ganz normale Kinder. Heterogenität und Standardisierung kindlicher Entwicklung. Weinheim, Basel: Beltz Juventa.

Nussbaum, Martha C. (2006): Frontiers of justice: Disability, nationality, species membership. The Tanner lectures on human values. Harvard University Press.

OECD (2019): PISA 2018 Results. Where All Students Can Succeed (Volume II). Paris: OECD Publishing. https://doi.org/10.1787/b5fd1b8f-en.

Otto, Hans-Uwe/Ziegler, Holger (eds.) (2010): Capabilities – Handlungsbefähigung und Verwirklichungschancen in der Erziehungswissenschaft. Wiesbaden: Springer.

Prengel, Annedore (2013): Pädagogische Beziehungen zwischen Anerkennung, Verletzung und Ambivalenz. Opladen, Farmington Hills: Budrich.

Rawls, John (1971): A theory of justice. Harvard University Press.

Sauerwein, Marcus/Vieluf, Svenja (2021): Der Capability Approach als theoretisch-normative Grundlage für das Monitoring von Bildungsgerechtigkeit. In: Die Deutsche Schule 113, 1, pp. 101-117.

Seitz, Simone/Finnern, Nina-Kathrin/Korff, Nina-Kathrin/Scheidt, Katja (2012) (eds.): Inklusiv gleich gerecht? Inklusion und Bildungsgerechtigkeit. Bad Heilbrunn: Klinkhardt.

Stojanov, Krassimir (2011): Bildungsgerechtigkeit. Rekonstruktionen eines umkämpften Begriffs. Wiesbaden: Springer VS.

Terzi, L. (2007): Capability and Educational Equality. In: Journal of Philosophy of Education 41, 4, pp. 757–773.

United Nations (2015). 17 Goals to Transform Our World. https://www.un.org/sustainabledevelopment/.

Walzer, Michael (2006): Sphären der Gerechtigkeit. Ein Plädoyer für Pluralität und Gleichheit. Frankfurt: Campus.

Part I:
Conceptualisations Underpinning Research on Diversity, Equity, and Inclusion

Political Ontologies of Difference and Their Trilemmatic Structure

Mai-Anh Boger

Translating rhizomatic maps is an inherently theoretical act as rhizomatic research aims at connecting spaces, objects, thoughts and subjects by de-centralising one's perspective again and again. The theory of trilemmatic inclusion (Boger 2017) is one of these theories that are based on the method of cartography – following the traces of Deleuze & Guattari (1977; 1992) as well as concepts of situated knowledge (Harding 1986) and standpoint theory (Haraway 1995). It maps contradictory concepts of anti-discrimination and/or 'inclusion' by differentiating their respective (political) ontology of 'otherness/multiplicity/difference'.

The problems of translation start with the fact that this theory has no name which is to be taken serious: in the German original text it is called "Theorie der trilemmatischen Inklusion" (Boger 2019a-d), hence, on the German book covers, you will find the term 'inclusion'. This is due to the fact that *at this moment* in Germany, the word 'diversity' is oftentimes associated with neoliberal concepts of diversity management which have very little to do with anti-discriminatory actions that are worth mentioning from an activist's standpoint. In the wording of rhizomatic research one can say that these (ab)uses of activist's language activate *lines of flight*: some German-speaking researchers coined terms as, for example "radical diversity" (e.g., Czollek et al. 2019) to evade this (ab)use of the concept of 'diversity', whereas others hope that the word 'inclusion' will not suffer the same fate and stick to this label. Some people already renamed the theory "Trilemma of Diversity" (e.g., Auma et al. 2019) which is an equally valid option as one cannot map the spectrum of meanings, connotations and associations of any of these words – inclusion, diversity, anti-discrimination – without knowing the context in which they are used. Ironically and consequently, this fact lies at the heart of theoretical maps that therefore behave like hypersensitive cry-babies in the process of *translation as a form of trans_position*. If one trans_poses a theoretical map by translating it, what is left of it? We'll see at the end of this article.

On the other hand, there is the calming fact that this specific map can be reduced to a logical core that is resistant and resilient towards word games: a trilemma is composed by three basic sentences (or: lemmata) and the dilemmatic relations between them. In this case, if two of the lemmata are

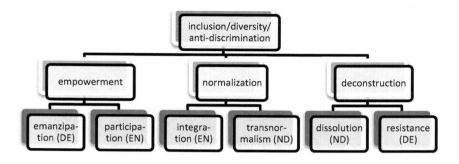

Figure 1:   Different and repeated names of our hopes to counter discrimination
(Examples from German Pedagogy)

affirmed, the third one has to be dismissed. The basic sentences were found
by mapping desires in the field of anti-discrimination (or, as said, what others
call 'inclusion' or '(radical) diversity'): how is the desire to be free(d) of
oppression and discrimination articulated? Connecting various fields of
political activism and their respective academic fields – ranging from gender
(studies), queer (theory), disability (studies) to postcolonial studies, critical
race theory, and beyond – three knots reoccurred. These are loaded by the
desires for empowerment, normalisation and deconstruction which
denominate the three basic sentences of the trilemma. They inspire aims of
political activism that can be found in every discriminated/oppressed group
and that are repeated again and again. Depending on which field they come
from, they can bear different names, making the question of translation even
more interesting as it shows that concepts are trans_posed not only between
languages in the stricter sense of the word but also between the 'languages'
of disciplines, political fields, and timely spaces.

The pulse of these repetitions are different articulations of how to make
sense of 'empowerment', 'normalisation', and 'deconstruction' in a specific
field (and language). In these multiple series, the three knots tie all of the
fields together in their *joint desire* to end discrimination. For that reason, the
theory of trilemmatic inclusion can be understood as an attempt to form a
joint map of resistance in which different social movements are connected in
a mode that dissolutes the borders of identity categories by doing something
else than appealing to cross-categorial/intersectional solidarity: instead of
repeating this moralising claim, the trilemmatic map focusses on the problems we share by *analytically* drawing out the dead ends of our movements
in which we accidentally or involuntarily meet each other. Hence, this form

of fusion does not need to be wanted. In fact, it is unwanted as it arises by dilemmas. In different words: the mapped trilemmatic structure that traces the contradictory lines of flight between empowerment-approaches, politics of normalisation and deconstructive activism only ties us together by the mess we make and the dead ends we run into. It then becomes a brute fact that we are in this mess together. Of course, it is a beautiful experience to find solidarity when facing the same struggles. But to follow the logic of the trilemma, this is not a necessary condition as we naturally stumble upon our joint desires in seeing them unfullfilled.

There are two ways of introducing this theory: (1) The first one focusses on the logical core. It is void of examples and relatively easy to translate. It can even be reduced to a mathematical form with three letters and logical operators. (2) The second one is more narrative and works with translations of the particular problems of one field or axis of discrimination into the language of another particular field... and another one... and another one... until they don't feel that particular anymore. One could also call the first path the deductive way of introduction, whereas the second path develops the theory inductively – from the grass roots upwards to an abstract logical form. Readers are invited to choose where they want to start their path and to jump back and fro between these two chapters as they please.

1 The three lemmata and the logical core of the trilemma

1.1 Definitions and basic sentences/lemmata

There are three basic forms of the desire not to be discriminated: the desire for empowerment, for normalisation and for deconstruction.

Empowerment (E) is defined as the political process in which an oppressed or discriminated group forms a collective to gain power and raises the *other* voice that has been silenced and not listened to.

Normalisation (N) is defined as the process of opening privileged positions and institutions to enable full participation.

Deconstruction (D), in this context, can be defined. It is defined as the process aiming at the dissolution of dichotomous orders of difference (as, for example 'men vs. women', 'disabled vs. abled-bodied', 'white vs. black/of colour') in which the normalised is represented as desirable and as the centred position from which the others are constructed as *the others* and thereby decentred. These three vectors can be triangulated to the graph in figure 2 of contradictory desires.

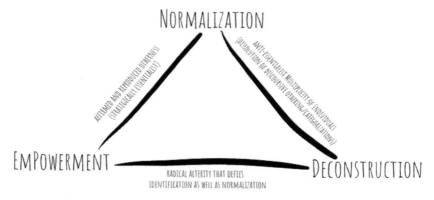

Figure 2:   Triangulation of the mapped contradictory desires

1.2   Reconstruction of the logical exclusion of the third lemma

E + N → non-D

Why is the desire for deconstruction logically excluded (/dismissed) when the desires for empowerment and normalisation are aligned?

Desiring empowerment as well as normalisation implies to wish and to fight for the right to participate in normalised structures as a part of the oppressed group that is constructed as 'not normal' and to raise the *other* voice in these normalised structures. Hence, the political ontology of '*us, the others*' is (for that moment) affirmed and reproduced, instead of deconstructed (a.k.a. "strategic essentialism" or "affirmative action"). Also, the representation of normality as desirable is affirmed and not deconstructed.

N + D → non-E

Why is the desire for empowerment logically excluded (/dismissed) when the desires for normalisation and deconstruction are aligned?

Desiring normalisation as well as a deconstruction of dichotomous constructions of difference (othering)[1] implies to wish and to fight for the right to participate in normalised structures as a an individual who is not subjected to the processes of othering and other oppressive categorisations. In this vision wherein everyone is either equally 'normal' or equally 'different' (what some people call 'radical diversity'), the two terms lose their power. Hence, in this political ontology of *inter-individual differences (in infinite plurality) that*

---

1   Said (1978).

refuse to be grouped or categorised, there is no one left to raise the *other* voice out of a collective. Empowerment is impossible without naming and forming a *collective of others* that is relatively oppressed in comparison to a normalised/privileged group (in other words: no identity politics without identity categories).[2]

D + E → non-N

Why is the desire for normalisation logically excluded (/dismissed) when the desires for empowerment and deconstruction are aligned?

Desiring empowerment as well as a deconstruction of dichotomous constructions of difference (othering) implies to wish and to fight for the right to create third spaces in which new and empowering imaginations of what it means to be 'different' can arise. Hence, in this political ontology of *resisting/radical alterity* normalisation is logically excluded, as this composition of desires aims at the exact opposite: proactively resisting normalisations and the normalised gaze (e.g., the white gaze, the ableist gaze ...).

Why do you write "logically excluded (/dismissed)"?

The logical exclusion of the third lemma would not be one if it wasn't necessarily the case. But it is not necessarily true that someone subjected to this logically contradictive structure always dismisses the third aspect. People don't behave logically. Empirically, people can go mad over the fact that they can't have it all – in the best (Foucauldian) and in the worst sense of the word. They can deny this logical impossibility, narcissistically believe themselves to be superior to the ones who lost a point, or phantasise themselves to be subversive by not letting 'Western'[3]/Aristotelian logic win.

---

2   In the language of Lacanian Analysis: this alignment of desires aims at a transformation of the symbolic order by imagining a world wherein there is no need to empower an oppressed group (anymore). In this *délir-désir* the subject tries to subvert the symbolic order by *acting as if* it wasn't in place. As this leads to the crucial question of whether the imaginary is a dismissive and/or a creative force, the theory of trilemmatic inclusion engages in a comparison between the Lacanian and the rhizomatic/schizo analytic concept of the imaginary (Boger 2019b; 2019d).

3   The author of this paper considers the term 'Western logic' to be an insult to the one true and universal logic ;-) Seriously: As a psychoanalytical researcher, I obviously love the fact that human beings do not submit to logical reasoning, as my job would either be boring or inexistent if they did. But calling logic 'Western' appears to be a form of internalised oppression. If anything, a specific combination of submission/subjectivation and dismissal of logic can be characterised as 'typically Western' but not logical reasoning itself.

Table 1:   Overview of the political ontologies mapped in the trilemma

	E+N	N+D	D+E
political ontology of otherness/ difference/ alterity	affirmation and representation of otherness (strategic essentialism)	inter-individual differences in infinite plurality (anti-essentialist deconstruction of the ascribed otherness)	radical alterity that cannot be repre- sented within the symbolic order and its normalised (and normalising) gaze
corresponding ontological status of 'normality'	normality is affirmed and (re)presented as the object of desire	normality as a con- tingent discursive formation that needs to be decon- structed to dissolu- te processes of othering	normality as a (im- perial form of) hege- mony from which one desires to be eman- cipated/freed
associated with the right ...	... to partici- pate in norma- lity as the other	... not to be othered (as every- body's different)	... to refuse to be normalised

As we are talking about desires, everything is possible. But logically it is not. That's the beauty of **desiring the impossible**.[4]

2   Inductively exploring the trilemma

The question "Where are you (originally) from?" is a good example for the importance of looking at the specific context one moves and speaks in when working with theories of inclusion and anti-discrimination. In Germany, where the author of this paper currently lives, there is this theory from the intranslatable field of what would be called 'Critical Race Theory' in the United States (and various other countries). It claims that the question "Where are you from?" – when asked by a white German to a person of colour – rearticulates racialising structures of belonging in a predominantly white society, as it suggests that a person with a darker complexion or other bodily features which are constructed as 'non-German' cannot be part of this

---

4   The underlying psycho-logic of this logical structure was conceptualised on the basis of a comparison of 'desire and the imaginary' via Lacan and Schizoanalysis (Boger 2019a-d).

nation – a nation that oftentimes seems to be still not used to being a diverse society. Many people of colour in Germany therefore perceive this question as inquisitive, inappropriate, and as a part of the discursive order of othering that presents them as strangers in their own country. The US-American version of this question – "What is your heritage?" – sounds funny or awkward in German(y). It just does not exist as a discursive fragment. In this sense, it is intranslatable: I once experimented with asking Germans what their heritage is (literally translated: "Was ist dein (kulturelles) Erbe?"). Most looked at me as if I was crazy and didn't know what to answer. Some answered what their parents do (or did) for a living – which means: they associated the question with class instead of race/ethnicity. Others answered what music and which books they like. As this example shows, the 'unexpected' answers are really interesting: what does it say about a society whether it (primarily) connects the question of '(cultural) heritage' with class or with race/ethnicity? Obviously, the US-American question is neither a satisfactory translation nor an equivalent to the German "Where are you from?/Where do you come from originally?" Both questions refer back to the people asking them by questioning their respective society. Every good theory on inclusion and discrimination keeps that in mind: it is rooted in a specific context and works with this situated knowledge.

In the field of activism, one regularly encounters the paradox of one activist pointing out that another one's means of fighting discrimination are discriminatory. In this case, it started with an encounter with a colleague from Australia whom we met at an international conference. Although – or maybe because? – it was a conference on racism and whiteness, one of the German activists found him 'absurdly racist for an anti-racist activist' as he would always ask "Where are you from?" as the first question when meeting someone new. Fortunately, it was possible to resolve the conflict: he explained to us that for him – as an Aboriginal man – this question is highly important as he is subjected to a form of racism that aims at erasing his heritage and making it invisible. By paying attention to the context wherein both anti-racist activists came to their seemingly unshakeable opinions on why the other's behaviour is counterproductive, they found a path of making sense of another's actions.

This short example shows three things: first, it shows that both persons responded to the everyday racism they encounter in the countries they live in (and in this case they also both had an elaborated theory filled with situated knowledge on why (not) asking this question is (not) racist).

Second, it shows that discrimination can unfold in opposite vectors. In some contexts, the predominant form of articulation of racism works with making heritage hyper-visible (accompanied by exotism, the curiosity of a conqueror, and inquisitive behaviours). In other contexts, racism unfolds with the opposite means: invisibilisation (instead of forced transparency), silencing (instead of questioning), and a pressure to assimilate and blend in. It would be another illegitimate shortcut to think that the first is always the case in Germany and the latter in Australia. Most people subjected to racism probably know both of the opposing vectors of racism – no matter where they live. What counts in a given situation is not only the nation one lives in and its history. Various factors, intersectional crossings included, can shift the weights in a context. In any case, the more basic hypothesis stands: discrimination unfolds in opposing, self-contradictory vectors. It can work with forced integration/assimilation as well as with forced segregation. It can work with invisibilisations as well as the opposite, and so on.

Third, this story shows that consequently the responses to discriminatory structures are as contradictory as the vectors of discrimination. Both activists answer to the problems they confront, *thereby inheriting the contradictions of the structure they are opposing.* In a nutshell: discrimination is not logically consistent, it changes its direction and form again and again – and so do the anti-discriminatory and inclusive practices and theories that are answering to this chaotic mess.

The theory of trilemmatic inclusion maps this contradicting structure by following the vectors in which discrimination unfolds and reading the desires of people driven by the respective lack that a discriminatory vector leaves. In the terminology of the trilemmatic theory, this first example shows a typical conflict between the line of 'deconstructing normality' (ND in the triangular figure above) and the opposing point 'empowerment' (E facing the ND-line). Whereas one person speaks about the desire to be seen as an individual person (ND, instead of permanently being categorised as a member of a group who has to declare their belongings), the other person focusses on his belonging to a group, articulating the desire to be visible and heard *as a member of this group*, thereby resisting against an individualist mainstream (E).

As one can see, both desires are equally valid and traceable. The lack of the object of desire is what keeps us driven. We would not need to wish and hope for it if we already had it. Although every trilemmatic point and line is theoretically desirable, the actual desire of a discriminated subject is therefore linked to the discriminatory vector that dominates the specific context said subject is living in.

Another example: in the German school system, children with disabilities have been subjected to forced segregation in a separate form of school for decades. The predominant concept of inclusion born out of this situation focused on the right to integration/desegregation. It aims at full participation in the *normal* school track and hence can be read as a desire for normalisation (N). Coming from this situation, the first time I went to an international Disability Studies conference I was astonished how many *voluntarily* segregated empowerment groups for disabled people there are in other

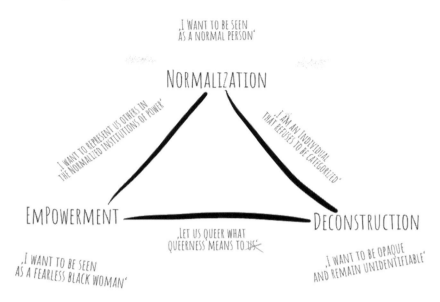

Figure 3: Map of desires with example sentences

countries. In this example, it is not a word that is intranslatable. It is a feeling: after decades of forced segregation, it takes a long historical process to find something desirable in being exclusively amongst disabled people – *again*. From this perspective, it is not surprising that some disability activists have no idea why *Crip Culture* could be subversive – or rather: they have no corresponding feeling, no access to this vision that could be embodied after they were trapped in this culture that other disability activists celebrate.

This second conflict is equally well known in other discriminated groups. It is the conflict between the desire to participate in normalised institutions (e.g. breaking the glass ceiling, not being excluded from privileged schools, universities etc., having a chance to get into powerful positions) and the desire to happily live in a *different* world, a (ethnic) subculture or even counter-culture without being forced to assimilate (e.g. by speaking the dominant language, wearing a white mask/'acting white', imitating a masculine bourgeoise habitus). Without discrimination, this conflict would not exist: people would not have to choose between assimilation and embracing their otherness. But in a world with structural forces of discrimination, desires against forced normalisation and desegregration (opposing line: DE) *or* against forced denormalisation and segregation (opposing point: N) are articulated, depending on the situation one lives in. And again, it shows that discrimination unfolds in opposing contradictory vectors – and so does the desire to end it.

A third example: as promised, this trilemmatic theory is about logical contradictions. These can be seen from every standpoint. The empirical part of the process of generating the theory started with desires of discriminated people, but logic still is what serves and tortures us all. One of the shortest ways to phrase the three dilemmatic lines of flight *from the standpoint of members of the privileged group* is in the language of anti-racist activism. The three imperatives on how to be a good ally can be summarised like this: "Be the advocate against advocacy. Be the emperor against imperialism. Appreciate otherness without othering" (Boger 2016: 85).

The logical core of the trilemma has nothing to do with singular subjective standpoints, but as the following example shows, the addressed dilemmas are articulated and embodied differently depending on one's own position. A discriminated subject might experience these contradictions as an inner conflict, or they might feel safe on their chosen line of flight enjoying a stable repression, or they might struggle with an instable disavowal of the lost point, or keep it foreclosed. In homology with these options of a singular subject, also activist groups might have open discussions and conflicts within their group on which way to go, or they might be determined to stay on one of the three paths while repressing critiques arising from the missing third point, disavowing or foreclosing its existence. The same can be found in allied subjects. An example drawn from the third of the mapped conflicts (EN vs. D): most of the people who want to join the fight against discrimination from a privileged position start with the trilemmatic line that combines empowerment and normalisation (EN) as it seems to be the most intuitive one in many contexts. It works with the concept of sharing one's privilege by helping to amplify the voices of the oppressed group, supporting them and making them visible in the powerful places of normalised institutions. There was this professor who tried to go down this path by supporting students who are the first ones in their family to go to college. In his lecture, he told his students that he wanted to help to empower first generation students and that they could always come to his office if they had any questions. Unfortunately, this form of representation provoked lots of uncertainties: "Why does he think, I need help?" The conflict escalated when a colleague called him out on his 'classism' for assuming that first generation students couldn't follow his lecture without needing extra-time in one-on-one-sessions in his office. If it wasn't that tragic, one might laugh at these thousand variations of critiquing anti-discriminatory actions as discriminatory. But as a matter of fact, claims that are based on strategic essentialism that aim at making the problems of a specific group visible – such as "First generation students need more support" – represent this group as homogenous (in their inferiority ...). Some might read it as an empowering sentence. To others, it is an insult.

Independent of which professor one might agree with – the one working with strategic essentialism or the one deconstructively working against it –, this last example makes it obvious that also privileged subjects cannot escape the ambivalences und contradictory lines of anti-discriminatory and inclusive practices.

3   Triangulating circles

One last translational bridge will help to come to a conclusion: in the German language, we 'vomit in circles' and 'jump in triangles'. What do these idioms refer to? The first one depicts the circular movement one feels after having discussed something *ad nauseam* while at the same time being unable to evade this reoccuring pattern (close to what is described as 'my head is spinning' in English). Activist work against discrimination sometimes comes with this frustrating feeling of moving in circles without seeing anything change: again and again, we are forced to repeat the same slogans, theories, practices. In this sense, the theory of trilemmatic inclusion maps repetitive re-petitions. It moves in circles as it reads unfulfilled desires and their inter-locking ontologies of otherness/difference/alterity. At the beginning, the question was asked, what is left of a map that has been transposed by translating it? What remains are the three contradicting desires which form the base of the logical architecture of the trilemma. They reoccur in different languages, spaces, settings; they circulate through political and academic fields and keep us moving – hopefully not always in circles. Void of examples, the trilemmatic map focusses on relations between desires – within ourselves as well as between subjects. The emptied map can therefore be 're-filled' and fueled by singular rearticulations of desires again and again. It remains open for inscriptions of new theories, new names – who knows which signifier will come after 'inclusion' and 'diversity'? – and new languages. Accepting the fact of the unhappy marriage of difference and repetition, a question of hope opens up a horizon: how can we circle back to the wisdom of generations of resisting oppression and learn from it without accepting that we are trapped in the relentless repetition of said oppressive structures?

The second idiom – jumping in triangles – is an image of madness and/or anger, sometimes even rage. It is used to depict a person who is agitated but has no place to go, as if one was looking for a refuge, a potential line of flight, without being able to find one. Energy is spent on agitations of a body that finds itself trapped no matter where it moves. In the image of this idiom, a painful mode of dealing with the triangular structure is made tangible: a disorientation that arises from wanting to escape without knowing how and whereto. Maps are a means of orientation. To use them, we need to locate ourselves on them first: where do I stand at the moment? And how do I trans_pose myself into a different position?

By following our desires, we probably won't find an answer – but we will find a path.

References

Auma, Maisha M./Kinder, Katja/Piesche, Peggy (2019): Diversitätsorientierte institutionelle Restrukturierungen – Differenz, Dominanz und Diversität in der Organisationsweiterentwicklung. Impulse zu Vielfalt 2019/3. Edited by DeutschPlus e.V. – Initiative für eine plurale Republik.

Boger, Mai-Anh (2016): The Trilemma of Anti-Racism. In: Dada, Anum/Kushal, Shweta (eds.): Whiteness Interrogated. Oxford.

Boger, Mai-Anh (2017): Theorien der Inklusion – eine Übersicht. Ausgabe 01/2017: Zeitschrift für inklusion-online.net. https://www.inklusion-online.net/index.php/inklusion-online/article/view/413

Boger, Mai-Anh (2019a): Die Methode der sozialwissenschaftlichen Kartographierung – Eine Einladung zum Mitfühlen – Mitdiskutieren – Mitdenken (open access ebook). Münster: edition assemblage.

Boger, Mai-Anh (2019b): Subjekte der Inklusion – Die Theorie der trilemmatischen Inklusion zum Mitfühlen. Münster: edition assemblage.

Boger, Mai-Anh (2019c): Politiken der Inklusion – Die Theorie der trilemmatischen Inklusion zum Mitdiskutieren. Münster: edition assemblage.

Boger, Mai-Anh (2019d): Theorien der Inklusion – Die Theorie der trilemmatischen Inklusion zum Mitdenken. Münster: edition assemblage.

Czollek, Leah Carola/Perko, Gudrun/Kaszner, Corinne/Czollek, Max (2019): Praxishandbuch Social Justice und Diversity. Theorien – Training- Methoden – Übungen. Weinheim/Basel: Beltz/Juventa.

Deleuze, Gilles/Guattari, Felix (1977): Rhizom. Berlin.

Deleuze, Gilles/Guattari, Félix (1992): Anti-Ödipus. Frankfurt am Main: Suhrkamp.

Haraway, Donna (1995): Ein Manifest für Cyborgs. In: Haraway, Donna/Hammer, Carmen (eds.): Die Neuerfindung der Natur. Primaten, Cyborgs und Frauen. Frankfurt/Main: Campus-Verl., pp. 33–72.

Harding, Sandra G. (1986/1991): Feministische Wissenschaftstheorie. Zum Verhältnis von Wissenschaft und sozialem Geschlecht. Hamburg: Argument-Verl.

Said, Edward W. (1978): Orientalism. London.

The Social Category of 'Disability' as a Desideratum of Intersectional Childhood Studies

Anja Tervooren

Although critical debate about the normalisation of childhood is one of the most productive strands of German-language childhood studies, the category of 'disability', which can be construed in potential opposition to a conception of normality, plays a subordinate role there. 'Disability' as a category and its interdependence with other social categories offer an indispensable analytical perspective when it comes to the adequate descripttion of children's growing up. Even more importantly, the understanding of 'disabled' childhoods is crucial in order for childhood studies – a field that has established itself largely through a critique of the developmental paradigm – to reflect on its own presumable theoretical foundations.

Since the 1990s, educational and social science research on childhood in German-speaking countries has been significantly differentiated through references to social categories. These included the categories of gender and, to some extent, sexuality, followed by those of social milieu and migration, each invoked with the aim of understanding processes of inter- and intra-generational production of differences – especially in educational institutions of childhood. Only the category of 'disability' has been slow to enter the debate. In Germanophone regions, there has been an increase in publications on methodological considerations regarding the participation of 'disabled' children in research. In childhood studies, however, only a few studies have focused on the life-worlds of children considered 'disabled', their lives in educational institutions, their leisure time, their friendship groups, and so on. Hardly any have considered 'disability' in childhood from an intersectional perspective in connection with one or two additional social categories. Even more concerning is the fact that comprehensive reflection upon one's own theoretical presuppositions within the concept of childhood is not possible without reference to theories of the interrelation of dependency and independence as they have been developed in debates about disability and about gender.

This is remarkable given that an expansive research field has been developed since the turn of the century in the context of British and Scandinavian childhood research, in which the children's growing up has been examined by means of the theoretical and methodological approaches of childhood and of disability studies. It is even more astonishing because the new social childhood studies build upon a critique of the developmental paradigm which in German-speaking countries is connected with a critical debate about the normalisation of childhoods. Normalisation is explored at the intersection of historical and social science research on childhood (Kelle/Tervooren 2008), especially with reference to Michel Foucault's productive concept of power (Kelle/Mierendorff 2013), as a form of modern subjectification and discipline often occurring in educational institutions of childhood.

Another possible side of this theoretical perspective is missing in such debates of childhood studies: the life-worlds of those children who deviate from the normal, who evade normalisation, or who were or are excluded in or through educational institutions. Thus, children whose growing up is hindered are still only rarely taken into consideration.[1] Moreover, the constitutive dependence of the human being and the vulnerability of the body are only hesitantly taken up in the theoretical debate about the question of what childhoods are and how they are constituted differently in the generational order.

In the following, therefore, the first step is to draw upon childhood studies' critique of the developmental paradigm and to ask why this theoretical starting point depends not only on the analysis of the normalisation of childhoods but also on the analysis of what is left out of the process. Second, the essay shows how 'disability' as a social category is taken up – occasionally explicitly and, more often, implicitly – in the debates of German-language research on childhood. It is precisely this thematisation that has the potential to address the permeability and fragility of social categories in general, which is one of the theoretical prerequisites of intersectional cultural studies. Third, there is a brief elaboration of the analytical contribution of the international debate on 'disabled children's childhood studies', in its double critique of the care paradigm and its relation to disability studies. The essay concludes with a sketch of a childhood studies perspective that understands the analysis of 'disabled' childhoods as an indispensable point of reference, not only but also in connection with other lines of difference.[2]

---

1   And this, despite the fact that disability studies have been proposed from the very beginning as a research approach that makes it possible to focus on the constitutional conditions of the distinction between 'normal' and 'non-normal' or "developmentally delayed", and thus to examine the normativity of a developmental logic itself. (Kelle/Tervooren 2008: 11).

2   A version of this essay first appeared in a volume edited by Raphael Bak and Claudia Machold (2022).

1 Childhood studies as critique of the developmental paradigm and of the (re)production of presupposed normality

Childhood studies has long been focused on the critique of paradigms that identify children as vulnerable, first and foremost, and often as a passive group; it also challenges paradigms that view childhood from the perspective of an adulthood to be achieved and that subordinate children's current experiences and lives, accordingly. From the sociology of childhood perspective, what is criticised above all is the developmental paradigm, which is oriented towards the individual and was expanded in the psychology of the early twentieth-century and elsewhere (Honig 1999). However, this paradigm has been in place since the middle of the eighteenth century, when the anthropological premise of the need for education was identified as a central characteristic of being human, and when a reflection on childhood as a specific phase of life was developed.

At the same time, a scientific pedagogy was established in which observations of many children were compared and gradually systematised. Beginning in the early twentieth century, these observations were also used to make statements about children's futures; that is, they were read as prescriptive (Tervooren 2008: 56). These developments emerged internationally and were profoundly shaped by the newly established field of population sciences, the development of statistics, and the introduction of intelligence tests (Turmel 2008). In German-speaking countries in particular at this time, a field of research on children was becoming established which brought with it a paradigm shift in the view of childhood. It "established a new form of temporalization in the approach to children: The future of children was now determined by a natural and constant process of development in which knowledge of the laws and rules according to which development took place made it possible to predict in the here and now what would become of children tomorrow" (Eßer 2014: 134). The associated perspective of childhood as a phase from which one's future as an adult person could be read renders childhood as particularly susceptible to dangers, and as a phase of life to be constantly worked on. This also makes it necessary to regulate childhood, given its importance for the reproduction of the population (Grosvenor et al. 2009: 13).[3]

---

3   The structurally functionalist socialisation paradigm, which, in contrast to the psychological developmental paradigm, does not focus on the individual and his or her development but rather on social structures, nevertheless shares with the latter the teleological orientation under which childhood is ultimately described as a transitional stage.

As a critique of the teleology embedded in this perspective, childhood studies has expanded and developed its theoretical and methodological repertoire internationally since the 1980s. It understands childhood as a social category and analyses the constitution of the generational order at particular points in time and in different societies. It addresses children as experts on their own lives and takes their expertise into consideration in the development of research methods and research ethics (e.g., Qvortrup et al. 2009).

The investigation of the normalisation of childhood that builds upon this developmental paradigm and its critique has long been one of the central, internationally connectable topics of German-language childhood studies. It takes note of an increase in developmental diagnostics and asks how "the distinction between 'normal' and 'non-normal' development is discursively determined and practically processed in preschools, schools, and out-of-school diagnostic practice" (Kelle/Tervooren 2008: 8) and examines how "discourses of risk and, deviation and optimization" (Kelle/Mierendorff 2013: 13) are understood. Among other things, it is argued that 'normal' child development is a cultural project that is worked on, for example, at the level of international organisations (Kelle 2008) and pediatrics (Kelle 2010; Ott 2010) as well as within families (Bollig 2013). In this context, childhood studies empirically examines developmental diagnostics and their expansion, especially in early childhood, and primarily focuses on the educational institutions of early childhood (Cloos/Schulz 2011; Diehm et al. 2013; Kuhn/Diehm 2015; Kelle 2018).

If the normalisation of children in various educational institutions and stages of life is analysed, this also implies that a dividing line is drawn in the process, albeit one that remains fragile and permeable: children who do not undergo individual developments, or who do so differently, and who are not included in what is considered 'normal' despite the fluid boundaries of normality, are often identified as a separate group that could be described within the social category of 'disability'. In contrast to international childhood studies, the German-speaking work in the field largely leaves out 'disability' as an explicitly named category. Thus, representatives of German-language childhood studies cannot be accused of hastily reifying the social category of 'disability'. In the end, however, these childhood studies debates lack the suitable terms necessary to 'see' this group of children and the conditions in which they are growing up, and to understand their life circumstances.

2   German-language childhood studies and its restraint regarding the social category of 'disability'

Even if the term 'disability' is ultimately to be understood as an umbrella category[4], and its contours must be worked out anew in every analysis, without it, childhood studies runs the risk of taking too little account of a large proportion of all children and of not being able to systematically analyse childhood in general as well as 'disabled' childhoods in particular.[5] German-language historical and qualitative research on childhood sporadically encompasses those children who are not included in the group of those considered 'normal'. This opens up the possibility of exploring the specificity of individual phenomena and to investigate the constitution of the category itself. Analyses include, for example, scientific discourses on the treatment of so-called Thalidomide children and their bodies (Freitag 2003), strategies of the normalisation of infants born prematurely who weighed much more than the average child (Peter 2013), the activity of so-called overweight children (Eßer 2017), and the growing up of children with hearing impairment (Chilla/ Fuhs 2013). The figure of the inattentive child has also been analysed in historical perspective (Reh 2008, 2015) and in the form of AD(H)D as a contemporary phenomenon (Liebsch et al. 2013).

In particular, historical and international studies look at the constitution of normality, on the one hand, and of deviations from normality, on the other hand, reconstructing how boundaries are established. Beddies, Fuchs and Rose (2015) demonstrate how a 'breadth of normality' was taken as a basis in dealing with so-called 'psychopathic' children and adolescents in Berlin and Brandenburg during the Weimar Republic. However, it is precisely the type of school that organised relatively age-homogeneous groups and established group-related systems of reporting on children and adolescents that increasingly produced opportunities for or the necessity of the development of norms of childhood – and their editing – throughout the twentieth century.

---

4   The term 'disability', which only became established in the 1960s, still encompasses heterogeneous phenomena that were historically described using different terms: in medieval literature, for example, the term 'fool' (Bernuth 2006, 2012); later and into the twentieth century, the term 'feeble-minded' (Grossberg 2011; Hofmann 2019), or at the end of the nineteenth century the term 'cripple' (Fuchs 2012).

5   At the same time, it remains necessary above all, as Vera Moser (2019) argues from a historical perspective, "to reconstruct expectations of normality with regard to childhood, specifying them as historically shifting expectations of a specific *ability* in conjunction with moral integrity and autonomy ('*morality*'), the *capacity for learning* and the opportunity to participate" (Moser 2019: 76, emphasis in original).

These, in turn, depended upon the respective national context and school system (on the Finnish educational system, for instance, see Koskela and Vehkalahti 2017). Josefina Granja Castro (2009) uses the analysis of school records and teachers' reports on student performance to show how the Mexican school system established the concept of "school retardation" (145) as a deviation of children's learning levels from the average in their respective school year. Studies by Patrick Bühler (2017, 2019) use the example of the Swiss observation classes in the period between 1930 and 1950 to reconstruct the establishment of the therapeutic function of school. Nelleke Bakker (2017) shows a strong expansion in diagnostics in the second half of the twentieth century, with a focus on Dutch children exhibiting problems in learning or behaviour.

While recent qualitative research on childhood exhibits a dearth of studies on 'disabled' childhoods, and historical research on childhood includes only a few, there has been more continuous work on this topic at the nexus of science and politics, especially using quantitative childhood research methods. These studies are more successful in bringing 'disabled' children into the discourse precisely because their approaches offer less problematisation of the mutually constituting relationship between normality and its opposite, regardless of whether they focus on the reduction of complexity with respect to diagnoses, the degree of 'disability' according to the latest German social security legislation, or the school-based determination of the need for special education support.[6] In the German-speaking countries, expert reports on 'disabled' children have been available since the beginning of the 2000s, for example, as part of the preparation of the Children and Youth Reports (Beck 2002), or the National Education Report (Lingenauber 2012) which took "People with Disabilities in Education" as its subject.[7] The Program for International Student Assessment, commonly known as PISA, initially excluded the school performance of students with special needs but now tests them as well (Kuhl et al. 2015). Following on from some of these primarily quantitative studies, several projects are underway to further develop and modify research methods – especially those of quantitative youth research in particular – so that research can be conducted without excluding individual

---

6   There is an increasing number of publications on the peer groups of children with disabilities and which take an identified need for special educational support as their starting point (Müller 2019; Brehme et al. 2020). However, they are not able to critically reflect on the constitution of the social category itself (for a critique, see also Pfaff/Tervooren, 2022).

7   The expert report by Sabine Lingenauber (2012) does not focus so much on children themselves, but rather on the use of childcare facilities by families and their children. Only in the group she calls "children with severe disabilities" (ebd.: 5) does she focus on children themselves.

groups of children (Böhm/Schütz 2016; Schütz et al. 2017; Brodersen et al. 2018; Gaupp et al. 2018).[8]

Thus, it is still early days for German-language research on 'disabled' children that takes up the current complexity of debates about childhood and about 'disability' and constantly questions the boundaries of 'disability' as a social category. German-speaking countries have not seen the establishment of a research direction that works with insights from childhood studies and from disability studies, a field that experienced a boom internationally in the 1990s and in Germanophone countries since the turn of the millennium. The reluctance of German-language researchers to work with a fixed category of 'disability' and their intensive preoccupation with the 'normalisation of childhood' make a research stance possible from which the limits of the category, its fragility, and its interdependencies with other categories can be questioned again and again. Against this background, this newly begun debate about 'disabled' childhoods becomes particularly connectable to intersectional childhood studies.

3   A double critique: 'disability' as a central social category of international childhood studies

Research on childhood and 'disability' has been going on in the United Kingdom since the late 1990s, and it was especially there and in Scandinavian contexts that the research paradigm of disabled children's childhood studies developed in the 2010s.[9] Building upon the theoretical foundations of disability studies, it works in the first instance with the social model of 'disability' (Oliver 1990; Morris 1991), which primarily identifies the material nature of a social environment as disabling and adopts an individual model of 'disability'. The starting point of the double critique is the paradigm of care that shapes the lives of children and of 'disabled people' and constructs 'disabled' children in a potentiated way as a passive group. Beginning with

---

8   In the context of the German Youth Institute, a productive discussion of the participation of 'disabled' children and adolescents in research has recently developed.

9   From the beginning, publications appeared in the existing infrastructure of peer-reviewed journals for both research approaches (such as *Childhood and Society*, *Childhood*, or *Children's Geographies* for cultural studies, and *Disability Studies Quarterly* and *Disability and Society* for disability studies) as well as in handbooks for both research approaches (e.g., Davies 2014). Curran, Liddiard and Runswick-Cole (2018) also point out that since 2008, children, youth, parents, activists, and researchers have come together annually to form a Disabled Children's Research Network at the Child, Youth, Family and Disability conference.

the social construction of 'disability' as a category, it examines 'disabled' children's living conditions, perceptions, and actions – as well as the circumstances and actions in confrontation with local conditions and structured by them – from the children's own perspective.

An early example of this is Mark Priestley's (1998) research agenda, entitled "Childhood Disability and Disabled Childhoods", which points out central challenges, presents the results of childhood studies in connection with disability studies, and pleads for an intersectional approach: "Preoccupations with impairment have pathologized childhood disability within an individual model. The construction of disabled children as 'vulnerable' and passive has desensitized us from their agency as social actors [....] [a]bove all, disabled children continued to be constructed within a unitary identity that is largely degendered, asexual, culturally unspecific and classless" (219f.). Seeing children's identities solely in terms of 'disability' risks denying them the expression of other parts of their identity. On the other hand, failure to take this sign into account means ignoring central, often definitive factors of their identity. Therefore, it is necessary to examine how membership in different social categories reinforces or mitigates disabling barriers.

E. Kay Tisdall (2012) also shows the parallels between the research approaches of childhood studies and disability studies, which emerged almost simultaneously in the 1990s. In her view, both build upon a social constructivist approach to oppose to dominant paradigms of care that deny members of the represented groups their full civil rights. In the process, both refer to human rights debates, engage in intensive discussions about how to successfully enable participation in research, and put common issues on the agenda. As she explains: "Thus, both childhood and disability studies suggest theoretical and practical reconsiderations of 'normality', competency, independence and dependency" (Tisdall 2012: 183). Hence, Tisdall shows very clearly how much a research agenda of childhood studies systematically depends on the contribution of the debates around the category of 'disability', and especially on reflections upon the relationship between autonomy and independence.

Since the turn of the millennium, a large body of international empirical research (see, for example, Hodge/Runswick-Cole 2013; Holt 2003, 2004; McLaughlin et al. 2018) has explored the in-school and out-of-school lifeworlds of 'disabled' children, how they grow up, and their everyday interests, hopes, and aspirations. This has included a radical orientation toward children's participation and a clear emphasis on the reconstitution of the generational order as a constant challenge in terms of research ethics, as questions of power and domination have been raised in intensified ways and increasingly sensitive means of co-producing knowledge with 'disabled' children and young people have been developed (see, for example, Goodley/ Runswick-Cole 2012; Stockall 2013; Liddiard et al. 2018). In the emerging field of disabled children's childhood studies, 'disability" has therefore invariably been framed as a process of negotiation with the symbolic environment as well as with the material[10] one. McLaughlin, Coleman-Fountain and Clavering (2018) therefore describe children "whose minds-bodies interact with the world in a different way; a difference that places them in recognised categories, established in medicine, validated by state institutions, and maintained by how others in society, known and unknown, engage with them" (ibid.: 4).

Childhood studies research in German-speaking countries has not yet addressed the complex theories offered by international disability studies, nor has Germanophone disability studies taken childhood as an analytical focus as a way of understanding the category of 'disability' and its changes throughout the life course. This outlines an extensive research programme that will benefit greatly from the reception of international debates in the field.

4   Challenges of intersectional childhood studies related to the complexity of the social category of 'disability'

Research on childhood in German-speaking countries has systematically integrated social categories into its analyses of children's growing up; it should also address the category of 'disability' and its specific manifestation in childhood and analyse it in its complexity in order to develop childhood studies further. 'Disability' should not serve merely as the next social category upon which to focus as part of future intersectional childhood studies; it is not enough to examine it and its interconnectedness with other social categories, or to analyse how differences structure children's lives and often produce social inequalities in the process. For, as has been argued here, the social category of 'disability' is indispensable to the whole project of childhood studies per se, because – provided the category's complexity, fragility and historical mutability are taken into account – the analysis of the category

---

10 In general, many representatives of British disabled children's childhood studies are linked to materialist rather than poststructuralist approaches to disability studies. The latter emerged more in the US context, also as a contribution of the humanities to the interdisciplinary debates (see, e.g., Snyder et al. 2002). According to Michel Foucault (see e.g., Tremain 2005), these work out the complexity of the category and are therefore extremely compatible with intersectional perspectives. However, this can only be hinted at here.

once again puts to the test the central theoretical foundations of childhood studies.

Although childhood studies is based on the critique of presumably teleological notions of development in childhood oriented towards an increasingly autonomous human being, approaches to the field thus far have been only partially successful in understanding more precisely the relationship between independence and dependency, and, ultimately, between vulnerability and corporeality in the context of the generational order. Fundamental anthropological questions such as those about the constitutive dependency of human beings in their changing positionings within the generational order can only be made the subject of theoretical and empirical studies of childhood if they encompass the social category of 'disability' in its entire scope. For childhood studies, then, it is necessary to ask, for example, how a reciprocal interrelationship of 'disabled' children's vulnerability and agency might be conceptualised. Or: how do children who are dependent on the care of their primary caregivers and likely to remain so as adults understand themselves as agents of their own actions? How can vulnerability and asymmetric (care) relationships in families and in educational institutions be analysed and how are they shaped? And how can the generational order be understood as an interdependent constellation between dependency and independence?

In the context of the increasingly differentiated debates about intersectionality in general, childhood studies now has the opportunity to analyse the category in its interconnectedness with other social categories from the beginning. However, this can only succeed if the complexity within the category of 'disability' is first taken into account and as long as there is no premature move toward an examination of different categories and their mutual influence. In this way, an understanding of the interdependent relationship between autonomy and dependency – one of the central topics of childhood studies and disability studies – could receive crucial new impetus in the interweaving of the two research approaches.

References

Bak, Raphael/Machold, Claudia (2022): Kindheit und Kindheitsforschung intersektional denken. Theoretische, empirische und praktische Zugänge im Kontext von Bildung und Erziehung. Reihe Kinder, Kindheiten, Kindheitsforschung. Wiesbaden: Springer VS (2022).

Bakker, Nelleke (2017): A culture of knowledge production: testing and observation of Dutch children with learning and behavioural problems (1949-1985). In: Paedagogica Historica 53, 1-2, pp. 7-23.

Beck, Iris (2002): Die Lebenslagen von Kindern und Jugendlichen mit Behinderung und ihre Familien in Deutschland: soziale und strukturelle Dimensionen. In: Sachverständigenkommission 11. Kinder- und Jugendbericht: Gesundheit und Behinderung im Leben von Kindern und Jugendlichen. München: Verlag Deutsches Jugendinstitut, pp. 175-315.

Beddies, Thomas/Fuchs, Petra/Rose, Wolfgang (2015): „Die Breite des Normalen" – Zum Umgang mit Kindern im Schwellenraum zwischen „gesund" und „geisteskrank" in Berlin und Brandenburg 1918-1933. Berlin: be.bra Verlag.

Bernuth, Ruth (2006): Fool. In: Albrecht, Gary L. (ed.): Encyclopedia of Disability, vol. 2. Thousand Oaks: SAGE Publications, pp. 738-740.

Bernuth, Ruth (2012): Bettler, Monster und Zeichen Gottes: Behinderung in der Frühen Neuzeit. In: Tervooren, Anja/Weber, Jürgen (eds.): Wege zur Kultur: Barrieren und Barrierefreiheit in Kultur- und Bildungseinrichtungen. Köln: Böhlau Verlag, pp. 116-132.

Boggis, Allison (2018): Dis/abled Childhoods? A Transdisciplinary Approach. London: Palgrave Macmillan.

Böhm, Eva T./Schütz, Sandra (2016): Alle Steinchen zusammen ergeben erst ein Bild! Der Mosaic Approach als methodischer Zugang in der Inklusionsforschung mit Kindern und Jugendlichen. In: Sturm, Tanja/Köpfer, Andreas/Wagener, Benjamin (eds.): Perspektiven sonderpädagogischer Forschung. Bildungs- und Erziehungsorganisationen im Spannungsfeld von Inklusion und Ökonomisierung. Bad Heilbrunn: Verlag Julius Klinkhardt, pp. 127-136.

Bollig, Sabine (2013): ‚Individuelle Entwicklung' als familiales Projekt. Zur Normativität von Normalisierungspraktiken in kindermedizinischen Vorsorgeuntersuchungen. In: Kelle, Helga (ed.): Normierung und Normalisierung der Kindheit. Weinheim/Basel: Beltz Juventa, pp. 99-118.

Brehme, David/Gerullis, Anita/Huber, Christian (2020): Fachbeitrag: Normalität und Behinderung aus Kindersicht. Ergebnisse einer qualitativen Interviewstudie an inklusiven Grundschulen. In: Vierteljahresschrift für Heilpädagogik und ihre Nachbargebiete 89, 1, pp. 50-63.

Brodersen, Folke/Ebner, Sandra/Schütz, Sandra/Gaupp, Nora (2018): Perspektive: Inklusive Jugendforschung. Multi-Modalität als Strategie zur Befragung von Jugendlichen mit Behinderungen. In: Feyerer, Ewald/Prammer, Wilfried/Prammer-Semmler, Eva/Kladnik, Christine/Leibetseder, Margit/Wimberger, Richard (eds.): System. Wandel. Entwicklung. Akteurinnen und Akteure inklusiver Prozesse im Spannungsfeld von Institution, Profession und Person. Bad Heilbrunn: Verlag Julius Klinkhardt, pp. 349-354.

Bühler, Patrick (2017): „Diagnostik" und „praktische Behandlung". Die Entstehung der therapeutischen Funktion der Schule. In: Reichenbach, Roland/Bühler, Patrick (eds.): Fragmente zu einer pädagogischen Theorie der Schule. Erziehungswissenschaftliche Perspektiven auf eine Leerstelle. Weinheim/Basel: Beltz Juventa, pp. 176-195.

Bühler, Patrick (2019): Beobachten in Basel. Pädagogische und psychologische Praxis in den Basler Beobachtungsklassen 1930-1950. In: Berdelmann, Kathrin/Fritzsche, Bettina/Rabenstein, Kerstin/Scholz, Joachim (eds.): Transformation von Schule, Unterricht und Profession. Wiesbaden: VS Verlag für Sozialwissenschaften, pp. 213-227.

Castro, Javier G. (2009): Thinking childhood: Categories of Schooling in Mexico, 1850-1930. In: Grosvenor, Ian/Lohmann, Ingrid/Mayer, Christine (eds.): Children and Youth at Risk. Historical and International Perspectives. Frankfurt am Main: Peter Lang, pp. 137-166.

Chilla, Solveig/Fuhs, Burkhard (2013): Kindheiten zwischen Inklusion, Normalisierung und Autonomie. Das Beispiel Hörbeeinträchtigungen. In: Kelle, Helga/Mierendorff, Johanna (eds.): Normierung und Normalisierung der Kindheit. Weinheim/Basel: Beltz Juventa, pp. 142-156.

Cloos, Peter/Schulz, Marc (2011): Kindliches Tun beobachten und dokumentieren: Perspektiven auf die Bildungsbegleitung in Kindertageseinrichtungen. Kindheitspädagogische Beiträge. Weinheim: Beltz Juventa.

Corker, Marian/Priestley, Mark/Watson, Nick (1999): Unfinished business: disabled children and disability identity. In: Disability Studies Quarterly 19, 2, pp. 90-98.

Curran, Tillie/Liddiard, Kirsty/Runswick-Cole, Katherine (2018): The everyday worlds of disabled children. In: Thomas, Gareth M./Sakellariou, Dikaios (eds.): Disability, Normalcy and the Everyday. London: Routledge, pp. 41-60.

Curran, Tillie/Runswick-Cole, Katherine (2013): Disabled Children's Childhood Studies. Critical Approaches in a Global Context. Basingstoke: Palgrave Macmillan.

Davies, John (2014): Conceptual issues in childhood and disability: integrating theories from childhood and disability studies. In: Watson, Nick/Roulstone, Alan/ Thomas, Carol (eds.): Routledge handbook of disability studies. London/New York: Routledge Handbooks, pp. 414-425.

Diehm, Isabell/Kuhn, Melanie/Machold, Claudia/Mai, Miriam (2013): Ethnische Differenz und Ungleichheit. Eine ethnographische Studie in Bildungseinrichtungen der frühen Kindheit. In: Zeitschrift für Pädagogik 59, 5, pp. 644-656.

Eßer, Florian (2014): Die verwissenschaftlichte Kindheit. In: Baader, Meike/Eßer, Florian/Schröer, Wolfgang (eds.): Kindheiten in der Moderne. Eine Geschichte de Sorge. Frankfurt am Main/New York: Campus Verlag, pp. 124-153.

Eßer, Florian (2017): Enacting the overweight body. Children's agency beyond the nature-culture divide. In: Childhood 24, 3, pp. 286-299.

Freitag, Walburga (2003): Bodycheck – wieviel Körper braucht das Kind? Über wissenschaftliche Diskurse der Habilitation so genannter Contergan-Kinder. In:

Hengst, Heinz/Kelle, Helga (eds.): Kinder, Körper, Identitäten. Weinheim/München: Beltz Juventa, pp. 161-180.

Fuchs, Petra (2012): „Behinderung" in Deutschland. Aspekte der Kultur und Geschichte des Umgangs mit physischer, psychischer und mentaler Differenz. In: Tervooren, Anja/Weber, Jürgen (eds.): Wege zur Kultur: Barrieren und Barrierefreiheit in Kultur- und Bildungseinrichtungen. Köln: Böhlau Verlag, pp. 133-151.

Gaupp, Nora/Ebner, Sandra/Schütz, Sandra/Brodersen, Folke (2018): Quantitative Forschung mit Jugendlichen mit Behinderungen – Stand der Forschung, Entwicklungsbedarfe, Möglichkeiten und Grenzen einer inklusiven Jugendforschung. In: Inklusion-Online 13, 2. https://www.inklusion-online.net/index.php/inklusion-online/article/view/437 [accessed 10 December 2021].

Goodley, Dan/Runswick-Cole, Katherine (2012): Decolonizing methodologies: disabled children as research managers and participant ethnographers. In: Grech, Shaun/Azzopardi, Andrew (eds.): Inclusive Communities. A Critical Reader. Rotterdam: Sense Publishers, pp. 215-225.

Grossberg, Michael (2011): From feeble-minded to mentally retarded: child protecttion and the changing place of disabled children in the mid-twentieth century United States. In: Paedagogica Historica 47, 6, pp. 729-747.

Grosvenor, Ian/Lohmann, Ingrid/Mayer, Christine (2009): Children and Youth at Risk. Historical and International Perspectives. An introduction. In: Grosvenor, Ian/Lohmann, Ingrid/Mayer, Christine (eds.): Children and Youth at Risk. Historical and International Perspectives. Frankfurt am Main: Peter Lang, pp. 9-21.

Hodge, Nick/Runswick-Cole, Katherine (2013): "They never pass me the ball": exposing ableism through the leisure experiences of disabled children, young people and their families. In: Children's Geographies 11, 3, pp. 311-325.

Hofmann, Michèle (2019): A weak mind in a weak body? Categorising intellectually disabled children in the nineteenth and early twentieth centuries in Switzerland. In: History of Education 48, 4, pp. 452-465.

Holt, Louise (2003): (Dis)abling children in primary school micro-spaces: geographies of inclusion and exclusion. In: Health & Place 9, 2, pp. 119-128.

Holt, Louise (2004): Children with mind–body differences: performing disability in primary school classrooms. In: Children's Geographies 2, 2, pp. 219-236.

Honig, Michael-Sebastian (1999): Entwurf einer Theorie der Kindheit. Frankfurt am Main: Suhrkamp.

Kelle, Helga (2008): „Normale" kindliche Entwicklung als kulturelles und gesundheitspolitisches Projekt. In: Kelle, Helga/Tervooren, Anja (eds.): Ganz normale Kinder. Heterogenität und Standardisierung kindlicher Entwicklung. Weinheim/München: Beltz Juventa, pp. 187-205.

Kelle, Helga (2010): Kinder unter Beobachtung. Kulturanalytische Studien zur pädiatrischen Entwicklungsdiagnostik. Opladen/Farmington Hills: Verlag Barbara Budrich.

Kelle, Helga (2018): Entgrenzung der vorschulischen Diagnostik. In: Zeitschrift für Grundschulforschung 11, 1, pp. 85-100.

Kelle, Helga/Mierendorff, Johanna (2013): Normierung und Normalisierung der Kindheit. Weinheim/Basel: Beltz Juventa.

Kelle, Helga/Tervooren, Anja (2008): Ganz normale Kinder. Heterogenität und Standardisierung kindlicher Entwicklung. Weinheim/München: Beltz Juventa.

Koskela, Anne/Vehkalahti, Kaisa (2017): Child in a form: the definition of normality and production of expertise in teacher statement forms – the case of northern Finland, 1951-1990. In: Paedagogica Historica 53, 4, pp. 460-476.

Kuhl, Poldi/Stanat, Petra/Lütje-Klose, Birgit/Gresch, Cornelia/Pant, Hans A./Prenzel, Manfred (2015): Inklusion von Schülerinnen und Schülern mit sonderpädagogischem Förderbedarf in Schulleistungserhebungen. Wiesbaden: VS Verlag für Sozialwissenschaften.

Kuhn, Melanie/Diehm, Isabell (2015): Sprechen über das Sprechen der Kinder. Thematisierungsweise „ungesprochener" Mehrsprachigkeit im elementarpädagogischen Feld. In: Schnitzer, Anna/Mörgen, Rebecca (eds.): Mehrsprachigkeit und (Un-)Gesagtes. Sprache als soziale Praxis in der Migrationsgesellschaft. Weinheim/Basel: Beltz Juventa, pp. 109-130.

Liddiard, Kirsty/Runswick-Cole, Katherine/Goodley, Dan/Whitney, Sally/Vogelmann, Emma/Watts, Lucy (2018): "I was Excited by the Idea of a Project that Focuses on those Unasked Questions". Co-Producing Disability Research with Disabled Young People. In: Children & Society 33, 2, pp. 154-167.

Liebsch, Katharina/Haubl, Rolf/Brade, Josephin/Jentsch, Sebastian (2013): Normalität und Normalisierung von AD(H)S. Prozesse und Mechanismen der Entgrenzung von Erziehung und Medizin. In: Kelle, Helga/Mierendorff, Johanna (eds.): Normierung und Normalisierung der Kindheit. Weinheim/Basel: Beltz Juventa, pp. 158-175.

Lingenauber, Sabine (2012): Kinder mit Behinderungen in Kindertageseinrichtungen. Expertise zum Nationalen Bildungsbericht 2014 „Menschen mit Behinderungen".

McLaughlin, Janice/Coleman-Fountain, Edmund/Clavering, Emma (2018): Disabled Childhoods. Monitoring differences and emerging identities. London: Routledge.

Morris, Jenny (1991): Pride against Prejudice. Transforming Attitudes to Disability. London: Women's Press.

Moser, Vera (2019): ‚Behinderte' Kindheit. In: Drerup, Johannes D./Schweiger, Gottfried (eds.): Handbuch Philosophie der Kindheit. Stuttgart: Metzler, pp. 76-82.

Müller, Christoph M. (2019): Trend: Kinder und Jugendliche mit einer Behinderung und ihre Klassenkamerad/innen. Perspektiven für die zukünftige Forschung. In: Vierteljahresschrift für Heilpädagogik und ihre Nachbargebiete 88, 3, pp. 240-245.

Oliver, Michael (1990): The Politics of Disablement. London: Macmillan.

Ott, Marion (2010): ‚Messen' und ‚sich messen' – zur diagnostischen Überprüfung motorischer Leistungen. In: Kelle, Helga: Kinder unter Beobachtung. Kulturanalytische Studien zur pädiatrischen Entwicklungsdiagnostik. Opladen: Verlag Barbara Budrich, pp. 179-205.

Peter, Claudia (2013): Normalisierungsstrategien zu dicken und frühgeborenen Kindern. Medizinische und gesundheitspolitische Diskurse. In: Kelle, H./Mierendorff, J. (eds.): Normierung und Normalisierung der Kindheit. Weinheim/Basel: Beltz Juventa, pp. 120-141.

Pfaff, Nicolle/Tervooren, Anja (2022): Differenztheoretische Ansätze. In: Krüger, Heinz H./Grunert, Cathleen/Ludwig, Katja (eds.): Handbuch Kindheits- und Jugendforschung, vol. 3, revised and expanded. Wiesbaden: VS Verlag für Sozialwissenschaften, pp. 217-248.

Priestley, Mark (1998): Childhood Disabilities and Disabled Childhoods. Agendas for Research. In: Childhood 5, 2, pp. 207-223.

Qvortrup, Jens/Corsaro, William A./Honig, Michael-Sebastian (2009): The Palgrave Handbook of Childhood Studies. Basingstoke: Palgrave Macmillan.

Reh, Sabine (2008): Vom „deficit of moral control" zum „attention deficit". Zur Geschichte der Konstruktion des unaufmerksamen Kindes. In: Kelle, Helga/Tervooren, Anja (eds.): Ganz normale Kinder. Heterogenität und Standardisierung kindlicher Entwicklung. Weinheim/München: Beltz Juventa, pp. 109-125.

Reh, Sabine (2015): Der „Kinderfehler" Unaufmerksamkeit. Deutungsmuster zwischen Kulturkritik und professionellen Handlungsproblemen im Schulsystem in Deutschland um 1900. In: Reh, Sabine/Berdelmann, Kathrin/Dinkelaker, Jörg (eds.): Aufmerksamkeit: Zur Geschichte, Theorie und Empirie eines pädagogischen Phänomens. Wiesbaden: VS Verlag für Sozialwissenschaften, pp. 71-93.

Runswick-Cole, Katherine/Curran, Tillie/Liddiard, Kirsty (2018): The Palgrave Handbook of Disabled Children's Childhood Studies. London: Palgrave Macmillan.

Schütz, Sandra/Brodersen, Folke/Ebner, Sandra/Gaupp, Nora (2017): Wie inklusiv ist die empirische Jugendforschung? Aktuelle deutsche Jugendstudien und die Dimension Behinderung. In: Laubenstein, Désirée/Scheer, David: Sonderpädagogik zwischen Wirksamkeitsforschung und Gesellschaftskritik. Bad Heilbrunn: Verlag Julius Klinkhardt, pp. 85-93.

Snyder, Sharon L./Brueggemann, Brenda J./Garland-Thomson, Rosemarie (2002): Disability Studies: Enabling the Humanities. New York: The Modern Language Association of America.

Stockall, Nancy (2013): Photo-elicitation and visual semiotics. A unique methodology for studying inclusion for children with disabilities. In: International Journal of Inclusive Education 17, 3, pp. 310-328.

Tervooren, Anja (2008): „Auswickeln", entwickeln und vergleichen. Kinder unter Beobachtung. In: Kelle, Helga/Tervooren, Anja (eds.): Ganz normale Kinder. Heterogenität und Standardisierung der kindlichen Entwicklung. Weinheim/München: Beltz Juventa, pp. 41-58.

Tisdall, E. Kay M. (2012): The Challenge and Challenging of Childhood Studies? Learning from Disability Studies and Research with Disabled Children. In: Children & Society 26, 3, pp. 181-191.

Traustadóttir, Rannveig/Ytterhus, Borgunn/Egilson, Snæfríður T./Berg, Berit (2015): Childhood and Disability in the Nordic Countries. London: Palgrave Macmillan.

Tremain, Shelley (2005): Foucault and the government of disability. Ann Arbor: University of Michigan Press.

Turmel, André (2008): A Historical Sociology of Childhood. Developmental Thinking, Categorization and Graphic Visualization. Cambridge: Cambridge University Press.

Positioning of Children in Research on Assessment Practices in Primary School

Alessandra Imperio, Simone Seitz[1]

1   Introduction

The issue of assessment in the first cycle of education has been a much-debated topic since decades, and one of the features of the early years of this century was the overdevelopment of assessment (Murillo/Hidalgo 2017: 15). Strengthened in particular by large-scale assessment studies, measurable achievement in the sense of competencies and output orientation has gained importance in international discourse (e.g., Pereyra et al. 2011).

Linked to this discourse, the role of schools in replicating and reinforcing educational inequities has been the subject of many debates, and an inequity-critical perspective regarding non-discriminatory access to primary education (Bartnitzky 2019) has been amplified. Discourses regarding this culminate in analyses of primary and secondary effects of social backgrounds of children and their families in relation to school and the habitus concept (Bourdieu/Passeron 1971; Montt 2011), which come into focus above all in assessment practices around transition and tracking. In this regard, possible differences between segregated education systems and those with an inclusive structure, like e.g., the Italian one (INDIRE 2013), are of particular interest because social practices of feedback and assessment take place in non-segregated classrooms with children from different backgrounds.

Regarding this, some current studies revealed that primary school teachers react to differences in the socio-economic status of children by "downgrading" those from families with a low status through lower demands and a lower levelling of the subject matter in classrooms (Kabel 2019).

This puts the focus on the children, who are an active part of assessment as social practice in the role of students but – as we will show in this contri-bution – are still rarely asked about what this means for them. In this contribution we focus on the role of children within assessment research practices discussed in the framework of educational justice. In detail, we

---

1   Alessandra Imperio wrote paragraphs 3, 4 and 5. Simone Seitz wrote paragraph 1, 2 and 6.

present a review of the international literature that illustrates how children's voices within primary school research still have a marginal function.

2   Assessment and educational justice

Assessment takes place within social interactions in the classroom and goes hand in hand with the production and negotiation of social difference (Boaler et al. 2005). Thereby, reference is often made to habitual assignment problems and hegemonies (Kramer 2017; Gomolla 2012). Children are thus constantly confronted with hegemonic expectations of adjusted behaviour and achievement in school (Breidenstein/Thompson 2014; Flashman 2012).

The relation thus implied between social background and educational success, concretised via assessment, is discussed differently in different countries (Allemann-Ghionda 2013; OECD 2019). Referring to stratified systems, assessment is often understood as an instrument to regulate individual educational pathways, recurring to a structural-functionalist perspective (Pfeffer 2008; Brügelmann 2014). It is strongly criticised that this attributes educational inequity (Breidenstein 2018; Berkemeyer 2018), while the social status of children is co-evaluated behind the scenes (Baeriswyl et al. 2011; see also Streckeisen/Hungerbühler/Hänzi 2007). This is specifically meaningful on the primary school level where assessment as social practice takes place within a power-related unequal generational dynamic between adults and children (Heinzel 2011; 2022). With a view on inclusively structured school systems, such as the Italian one, the main function of assessment in primary schooling is often seen as a formative one of assessment *for* learning, polarised from assessment *of* learning and aimed at understanding how learning takes place in each child (Nigris/Agrusti 2021). This is seen as reliant on a dialogue between teacher and child on learning. Various strategies and tools are available for this purpose which also take into account the children's right to information and participation, for example, portfolios (Brendel/Noesen 2014; Grittner 2009; Winter 2018). Thus, a central assumption of these approaches is that the responsibility for learning does not lie solely with the child. Indeed, educational success in schools depends on complex relationships among children and how education is offered, diversity is dealt with, and differences are created in schools.

It becomes clear that assessment is a crucial aspect of teachers' professionality which is particularly linked with power and responsibility (Strauss et al. 2017) and at the same time interwoven in institutionally given rules. This implies that it is not possible to simply transfer concepts and research results on assessment from different countries and education systems to one another.

Taking this up brings into focus the varying meaning of assessment within different educational systems, on the one hand, and the importance of a more detailed knowledge of children's perception of assessment, on the other. Therefore, there are two aspects to consider here: firstly, children's participation in social practices of feedback and assessment at the classroom level and secondly, the theoretical conception of the child in scientific educational research, which is reflected in-depth first of all in the context of childhood studies (Heinzel 2022).

This contribution takes up the need for more detailed knowledge on children's voices regarding assessment, presenting a literature review where primary school children were given a voice on assessment and framing it with a reflection on assessment and educational justice.

3   Childhood Studies and students' voices on assessment

Views of children generated by research are of particular relevance to debates on educational policies and practices (Cook-Sather 2018; Dutro/Selland 2012; Melton/Gross-Manos/Ben-Arieh/Yazykova 2014), as well as to school improvement (Tuten 2007; Ainscow/Messiou 2018).

According to the paradigm of Social Childhood Studies, children are seen as competent actors, experts, and main informants of their lives and should be considered as such and not as people "who have still to grow up" (Hunner-Kreisel/Kuhn 2011: 115; see also Clark/Eisenhuth 2011; Jover/Thoilliez 2011; Kampmann 2014; Melton et al. 2014). Similarly, the Student Voice Movement claims that students' perspectives should be included in the dialogue with teachers and researchers (Grion/Cook-Sather 2013), including the views perceived as difficult or inappropriate (Pearce/Wood 2019), as students are seen as capable to contribute actively and intentionally to processes happening in their school life (Grion 2014: 11). This shift in perspective recognises children as holders of rights (Reisenauer 2020), and it is relevant to equity-related reflections, as this leads to a closer look at the realisation of children's rights in research on assessment. Indeed, school assessment is a valuable dimension to be considered since assessment is known to exert power over students' behaviours and how they feel perceived as individuals (Carless/Lam 2014: 315). It has been shown that, if the assessment intention is perceived as formative, students are more likely to develop an active role as learners, unlikely when students' perception of assessment is accrediting (Remesal 2009: 49).

These assumptions lead us to consider how children are positioned in research on assessment. In the following, to structure our reflections on children's voices in research on assessment, we refer to a four-dimensional model based on different levels of student involvement in schools and classrooms, suggested by Fielding (2013). In short, children can be simple data sources or, with increasing involvement, active respondents, co-researchers, and researchers. Depending on the role of the children, many aspects change: the engagement of each agent, the reasons, the kind of knowledge used, how engagement takes place, and how meaning is made (see Fielding 2013: 77).

In the following section, we assigned similar roles to children according to different situations in the context of scientific research. However, it was not always easy to position the studies due to a lack of explicit declaration of the role of children or a lack of specific information. Generally, we considered children that usually produce a large-scale set of information without the possibility of adding personal reflections and opinions as *data sources* (e.g., by answering a closed-answer questionnaire developed only by adults). According to us, they take on the role of *active respondents* when they can answer open-structured questions with the possibility of adding their views, either in written or oral form (e.g., by drawing with caption, or semi-structured interviews), especially when data analysis follows an inductive approach. We perceive children as *co-researchers* not only when they are engaged in the processes of data collection and interpretation of results alongside researchers but also when the level of awareness of their role and room for freedom increase or when the child is left free to experience their context without any demand from the adult (e.g., by ethnographic observations and spontaneous interactions, photo-voice method or interviews with few questions in which the children can express themselves by wandering off and choosing themselves where to focus their discourse). The child's position as a *researcher* emerges when they are fully aware of their role or/and when they are initiators and leaders of a project, planning and listening to peers, adults, and experts to make them contribute to a deeper understanding of learning.

At this point, two premises have been gained: the assumption of childhood as "a culture in its own right with its own institutions, norms, customs, dialects and styles" (Melton et al. 2014: 16) and the need to concretely put into practice the legal recognition of children's rights (Levesque 2014).

Based on these assumptions, the following section aims to describe what has already been done worldwide in this direction on the topic of assessment in primary schools. The review shows which methods have been used, and what role children have had in those studies.

4   A brief literature review on primary-school children's conceptions of performance and assessment

A look at the state of research on assessment as a social practice reveals that "much of the classroom assessment literature is about what teachers do, or what they should do" (Brookhart/Bronowicz 2003: 221), while there are a few studies on student conceptions of assessment (Brown/Harris 2012; DeLuca et al. 2018; Köller 2005) and feedback (Hargreaves 2013; Harris/Brown/Harnett 2014), even less when referring to primary school students (Beutel/Vollstädt 2002; Carless/Lam 2014; Dutro/Selland 2012; Harris/Harnett/Brown 2009; Monteiro/Mata/Santos 2021; Kolb 2007; Murphy/Lundy/Emerson/Kerr 2013). Similarly, little is known about the relationship between their conceptions of feedback and self-regulated learning, self-efficacy beliefs, and school performances (Brown/Peterson/Yao 2016: 606; Grittner 2009). Particularly, the specific question of inclusion-oriented practices of assessment and conceptions of achievement in inclusive class-rooms has hardly been explored empirically (Moon et al. 2020; Peacock 2016; Beutel/Pant 2020; Noesen 2022; Kaiser/Seitz *in this book*).

We considered 47 studies that emerged from the web search and reference lists of publications relevant to the topic, as long as they were linguistically accessible. The expressions used in the web search were 'student conceptions' or 'student perceptions' along with the words 'assessment', 'performance' or 'achievement', and 'elementary school' or 'primary school'.

The studies are summarised in Tables 1 to 5, according to the continents in which they were conducted: 1 in Africa (Table 1), 7 in Asia (Table 2), 19 in North America and 1 in South America (Table 3), 13 in Europe (Table 4), and 6 in Oceania (Table 5).

Studies in which children attend primary schools but the sample consists of students aged over 11 years old were not considered in this review, in line with the focus on primary school level pursued here (e.g., Williams 2010). We did the same when: the study focuses on teacher outcomes and the sample of students is one unit (e.g., Servan 2011); the focus of the research is more related to students' conceptions and approaches to knowledge construction and learning (e.g., Klatter/Lodewijks/Aarnoutse 2001; Tsai/Chai/Hong/Koh 2017); the research is about students' perceptions of student-teachers performance (e.g., Cortis/Grayson 1978); the topic is about students' views on differences in characteristics, peer treatment and teacher treatment of high- and low-achieving students (e.g., Marshall/Weinstein/Sharp/Brattesani 1982). Studies that describe different aspects or insights of the same research already considered in another paper are not mentioned (e.g., Stipek 1981; Wheelock/Bebell/Haney 2000b).

Apart from the number of studies in each continent and their specific topic, the main difference among these studies lies in the choice of qualitative or quantitative methods and the role given to children in the research.

The only *African* study (Malmberg/Wanner/Sumra/Little 2001) uses quantitative methods and the children have the role of data sources.

In *Asia*, some studies use quantitative methods (i.e., Chan 2002; Guo/Yan 2019; Hue/Leung/Kennedy 2015; Wong 2017), while others use mixed-methods approaches (i.e., Wong 2016; Xiang 2002). We only found one qualitative study (Carless/Lam 2014). In all purely quantitative studies examined, children take on the role of data sources due to the data collection and analysis tools used and a large number of participants (i.e., Chan 2002; Guo/Yan 2019; Hue/Leung/Kennedy 2015; Wong 2017). Even in the two studies by Wong (2016) and Xiang (2002), children took on the position of data sources due to the nature of the qualitative or mixed data collection tools used, which are highly structured or with little room for argumentation for the interviewees, as well as the predominantly quantitative approaches of data analysis.

In Carless and Lam's (2014) qualitative study, which uses focus groups and caption drawings as data collection tools, students are not fully positioned as active respondents since the coding process appears to have taken place mainly with a deductive approach, and results are organised into the three main themes of investigation. Indeed, in spite of the openness of questions and the room for freedom children have, the main themes for the analysis were predetermined, and only subcategories emerged from the evidence of the polarisation of students' opinions along a positive-negative continuum.

In the *Americas*, both quantitative (i.e., Evans/Engelberg 1988; Hughes/Zhang 2006; Mac Iver 1988; Paris/Roth/Turner 2000; Peña-Garcia 2010; Stipek/Gralinski 1996) and qualitative approaches (i.e., Brookhart/Bronowicz

2003; Dutro/Selland 2012; Freeman/Mathison n.d.; Triplett/Barksdale 2005; Wheelock/Bebell/Haney 2000a) are represented in the studies. Mixed methods studies are available as well (i.e., Blumenfeld/Pintrich/Hamilton 1986; DeLuca et al. 2018; Filby/Barnett 1982; Henk/Melnick 1998; Newman/Spitzer 1998; Nicholls/Miller 1984; Stipek/Tannatt 1984; Thorkildsen 1999; Xiang/Solmon/McBride 2006).

In the purely quantitative studies examined, since the data are collected through standardised or highly structured questionnaires with close-ended questions, and/or the sample is broad, children have the role of data sources (e.g., Evans/Engelberg 1988; Hughes/Zhang 2006; Mac Iver 1988; Paris/Roth/Turner 2000; Peña-Garcia 2010; Stipek/Gralinski 1996), whereas in almost all the qualitative studies explored, children can be seen at least as active respondents (e.g., Brookhart/Bronowicz 2003; Dutro/Selland 2012; Freeman/Mathison n.d.). More specifically, in the qualitative study by Dutro and Selland (2012), the focus on children's perspective that positions them not as mere data sources but as constructive and analytical respondents is stated in a finalised section of the article. Both the choices of ethnographic methods for gathering information (i.e., low-structured interviews, focus groups, participatory observations) and the approach in which the analysis of the information was conducted (i.e., through analysis of the sociocultural aspects of language use to discern power issues) position children on a continuum between active respondents and co-researchers. Similarly, in the study by Freeman and Mathison (n.d.), the variety of qualitative tools for data collection, which offer a great deal of room for expression, shifts the children's role as active respondents to that of co-researchers. In the last two studies, the participants' level of awareness, their possible involvement in the research stages, and in the interpretation of data could be significant elements in shifting the children's role more into one direction than the other.

In contrast, Triplett and Barksdale (2005) and Wheelock, Bebell, and Haney (2000a) use children's drawings with possible captioning as a data collection tool in their research and both proceed, albeit differently, with an inductive approach in the elaboration of categories. Furthermore, the results are presented in descriptive form with the possible use of frequencies. Despite these characteristics suggesting that children are positioned as active respondents, the choice of how this qualitative data was collected, i.e., emailed by the respective teachers, leads to some reflections on the ambivalence of their role.

The scenario changes with mixed methods studies, where peculiar situations can be found. Despite the differences among their research designs, in several mixed-methods studies (Filby/Barnett 1982; Henk/Melnick 1998; Newman/Spitzer 1998; Nicholls/Miller 1984; Stipek/Tannatt 1984), the positioning of children is hard to define due to the use of structured or standardised interviews, sometimes with short answers and little room for argumentation, or the employment of a deductive approach for coding, or the choice to derive trends through quantitative evidence rather than reconstruct the profile of individual cases. In these studies, the positioning of children seems to lie somewhere between that of the data source and active respondents, with different degrees of convergence. In other mixed-methods studies, students can be data sources and active respondents in the same research according to the tool utilised (e.g., DeLuca et al. 2018; Xiang/Solmon/ McBride 2006). Actually, the interest in knowing students' perspectives seems to be greater than interest in their positioning. Otherwise, in the study by Blumenfeld/Pintrich/Hamilton (1986) for the specific within-subject research design using initially open-ended questions to construct the categories inductively and then closed-ended items in a 5-point Likert scale, children still appear to be positioned as active respondents.

Finally, in her chapter, Thorkildsen (1999) describes highly structured interviews that she used to derive children's theories on how much testing is fair in schools through different methods of analysis: a structural analysis conducted in the tradition of Piaget's clinical method (1951, as cited by the author), the search for lines of thought (p. 65), and a content and psychometric analysis. The author positions herself on the role of children as competent critics of their educational experiences and highlights how educational practices reveal the existence of power hierarchies in the classroom, where children assume a passive role. Despite her positioning, it is complex to define what role children take in this study. On the one hand, they seem to assume the role of active respondents, especially in the way children's different rationalities are derived. On the other hand, the high degree of structuring of the interviews may cast doubt on this positioning.

As a final point, it is worth highlighting that about half of the studies from the Americas were conducted in the previous century, while those from Africa and Asia were undertaken in the current century.

In *Europe*, there seem to be more qualitative studies both with respect to the choice of tools for data collection and the methods used for their analysis (i.e., Beutel/Vollstädt 2002; Eriksson/Björklund Boistrup/Thornberg 2020; Gipps/Tunstall 1998; Hargreaves 2013; Monteiro/Mata/Santos 2021; Murillo/ Hidalgo 2017; Remesal 2009; Tunstall/Gipps 1996). There are also quantitative studies (i.e., Chapman/Skinner 1989; Meroño/Calderón/Arias-Estero/ Méndez-Giménez 2017; Murphy/Lundy/Emerson/Kerr 2013; Weidinger/ Steinmayr/Spinath 2019) as well as mixed methods ones (i.e., Atkinson 2003). Most European studies were conducted in the present century.

In almost all studies using quantitative or mixed methods, the position of children is that of data source (e.g., Atkinson 2003; Chapman/Skinner 1989; Meroño/Calderón/Arias-Estero/Méndez-Giménez 2017; Weidinger/Steinmayr/Spinath 2019). However, in the quantitative research by Murphy and colleagues (2013), a group of 32 sixth- (primary school) and seventh-grade (secondary school) students, as explicitly stated by the authors themselves, took on the role of co-researchers. This included for example, assisting with the design of the survey questionnaire, interpretation of results, or suggesting solutions to issues raised by the research (p. 590). In the same project, children who filled out the questionnaire with mainly closed questions took on the role of data sources.

Finally, in studies using qualitative approaches, children appear to play the role of active respondents (Beutel/Vollstädt 2002; Eriksson/Björklund Boistrup/Thornberg 2020; Gipps/Tunstall 1998; Hargreaves 2013; Monteiro/ Mata/Santos 2021; Murillo/Hidalgo 2017; Remesal 2009; Tunstall/Gipps 1996). In some of these (Eriksson/Björklund Boistrup/Thornberg 2020; Hargreaves 2013; Murillo/Hidalgo 2017), children might hold an intermediate position between active respondents and co-researchers, with a different degree of convergence and freedom of response and argumentation (e.g., through leaving the child free to experience their context employing videotapes, or a completely inductive approach to analysis).

In *Oceania*, quantitative (i.e., Brown/Harris 2012), qualitative (i.e., Burnett/Mandel 2010; Harris/Harnett/Brown 2009), and mixed methods studies (i.e., Harris/Brown/Harnett 2014; 2015; Wurf/Povey 2020) are represented. However, the qualitative study by Harris, Harnett, and Brown (2009), as an example, is part of a larger study using mixed methods.

In the quantitative research of Brown and Harris (2012) it is easier to recognise the role children play as data sources. Although the study by Burnett and Mandel (2010) uses qualitative approaches for both data collection and analysis, the use of very structured interview questions with rather short answers seems to leave little room for argumentation by the interviewee and thus, positions children not entirely as active respondents. In contrast, in the qualitative study section described by Harris, Harnett, and Brown (2009), children take on the role of active respondents due to the choice of drawings with a caption as a data collection tool and an inductive approach to data analysis.

In mixed methods studies children assume different positions depending on the research design and data-collection methods employed. For instance, in the studies of Harris and colleagues (2014) and Wurf and Povey (2020), children take on both the roles of the data source or active respondent according to the method of data collection used. In contrast, in the 2015 study by Harris and colleagues (2014), despite the use of qualitative methods for data collection, the children appear to be data sources, as their peer and self-assessment productions are collected by their teachers without any involvement of children themselves.

5   Discussion

In the studies reviewed in the previous section, children play the role of data sources or active respondents, except for the study by Murphy and colleagues (2013). However, in this study, the children as co-researchers were already in the sixth or seventh grade. Nevertheless, we have seen that there is no shortage of attempts to empower children in projects where the questions are less structured and more open to listening, that is, where the degree of freedom to express one's point of view is greater.

In the literature, there appear to be a few studies with primary school children (first to fifth grade) as co-researchers or researchers, but none in the area of assessment. For instance, Lundy, McEvoy, and Byrne (2011) describe a research project with first-year primary school children (aged 4–5 years) as co-researchers. The research team established Children's Research Advisory Groups, which were consulted for the development of the research sub-questions and data-collection methods, and engaged in data interpretation and dissemination. Also, a second study of Lundy and McEvoy (2009), which focused on the promotion of academic achievement and positive engagement, involved eight primary school children from Year 7 (aged 10–11 years) as co-researchers. The children had the opportunity to advise on the research process, the interpretation of the survey results and findings of the literature review and the identification of practical implications (p. 48).

As with the study by Murphy and colleagues (2013), in the latter two studies (Lundy/McEvoy 2009; Lundy/McEvoy/Byrne 2011), one group of children assumes the role of co-researcher and another group, to whom the survey is addressed, takes the role of the data source. In the research by Kumpulainen, Lipponen, Hilppö, and Mikkola (2013), all 29 primary school children from two third-grade classes (aged 9–10 years) participated in the role of co-researchers. The study aimed to discover how children's sense of agency is socially constructed, and how it manifests as children reflect on self-produced digital photos documenting positive events in their lives. The photos were then discussed collectively in the social context of the classroom with the opportunity to give meaning to what is depicted in their lives (p. 214).

Along with these studies, but back to the topic of school assessment, we were able to find only one project where primary school children are engaged in formative assessment processes with different degrees of involvement. Nevertheless, it is not included in the review because the involvement of students takes place in the classroom context and not in the research concept, albeit the consequences are reflected in the latter. Indeed, in Allal's research (2021), primary school children from grades 5–6 were involved in formative assessment. Children participated actively in classroom discussions of assessment criteria and co-constructed assessment tools. The author studied the implementation of these activities in three classrooms through qualitative observations, analysing statistically the frequency and types of revisions of texts made thanks to guidelines jointly developed and their self- and peer-assessments. She found that in the classroom where children's active participation was higher and the guidelines were more elaborated, the process of co-regulation in formative assessment contributed to a relevant improvement of the student's final products.

In summary, our review shows that the positioning of children in research on assessment varies in different countries and parts of the world, which in itself is not surprising and points to differently conducted discourses in relation to the respective education systems. Moreover, it is striking that only one study could be found (Allal 2021) in which children play an active role and are involved in assessment practice, though not in the research concept.

This leads us to the impression that in the field of research on assessment, where the power imbalance between teachers and their students, interwoven with the ambivalence between participation and control (Breidenstein/Rademacher 2017), is particularly prominent, a positioning of primary school children as actors capable of providing information is strikingly rare. This seems to be especially the case when assessment has the function of accountability on a national level. It is therefore necessary to ask what this means in concrete terms for further research on assessment in more or less structured educational systems.

6   Conclusion

Based on our analyses, it could be concluded first of all that a focus on children's voices within the research field of assessment practices in primary education would be a promising new perspective for gaining a deeper understanding of these contradictory relationships. In view of the broad state of research, however, it should be noted that this was already theoretically and methodologically established at the end of the last millennium in the work of the "new childhood research", and that primary school has been described from a child's perspective in many respects (Petillon 1993; Zeiher 1996; Honig 1999), at the international level primarily via the children's World Surveys (e.g., Rees/Main 2015). Nevertheless, and this is instead the central finding for the question pursued here, there are very few studies to date that shed light on children's perspectives on aspects of achievement and assessment (Bonanati 2018; Noesen 2022). Above all, there is a lack of international comparative studies on primary education (Heinzel 2022) as a whole and specifically on this issue. However, this is accompanied by the call to also reflect on limitations of this claim. It is therefore significant to also reflect on research as a social practice involving adults and children. As our review shows, studies on children's perspectives are also those in which mainly adult researchers decide which aspects are given relevance in the construction of the research design and particularly in evaluation processes. Children's perspectives gained in data collection are usually interpreted one-sidedly by adults and prepared for a knowledge discourse led by adults (Honig 1999).

Wherever an attempt is made to break this up and allow children's perspectives to flow into analytical processes, for example, opportunities arise to critically question generational power relations between adults and children, as it must be borne in mind that children in research arrangements on school topics are not free from the socialisation and role requirements of being a student. If research designs that focus on children's voices are not to reproduce established power relations through research, then asymmetries between researchers, who are dependent on the creation and discursive negotiation of knowledge and positioning in the academic world, and children, who have no direct access to this, must be reflected in quantitative as well as qualitative research processes.

Taking this further, this finding could also indicate that the dual task of primary schools to meet the needs of the child and their obligation to society seems to be particularly difficult to deal with in the context of feedback. If we consider this relationship as relational, following Heinzel (2022), then practices of assessment can be understood as intergenerational social practices in primary schools at the level of negotiation – related to the performativity of learning. This opens up further possibilities for theory development on the "performativity" of achievement in classrooms and implies links to new lines of childhood studies. Such interweaving of primary school education research and childhood studies could altogether be a promising strategy on the way to further knowledge development, conceiving children as participating human beings in society.

All in all, it can be assumed that the topic of assessment is particularly meaningful for a better understanding of power relations between (adult) teachers and (school)children at the primary school level so that further findings on children's conceptions on assessment in different countries could shed new light on this.

References

Ainscow, Mel/Messiou, Kyriaki (2018): Engaging with the views of students to promote inclusion in education. In: Journal of Educational Change 19, 1, pp. 1-17.

Allal, Linda (2021): Involving primary school students in the co-construction of formative assessment in support of writing. In: Assessment in Education: Principles, Policy & Practice 28, 5-6, pp. 584-601.

Allemann-Ghionda, Cristina (2013): Bildung für alle, Diversität und Inklusion: Internationale Perspektiven. Schöningh.

Atkinson, Patricia (2003): Assessment 5-14: What do pupils and parents think? (Spotlight No. 87). Edinburgh, UK: The SCRE Centre, University of Glasgow.

Baeriswyl, Franz/Maaz, Kai/Trautwein, Ulrich (2011): Herkunft zensiert? Leistungs-diagnostik und soziale Ungleichheiten in der Schule. Eine Studie im Auftrag der vodafone Stiftung Deutschland. Düsseldorf: Vodafone Stiftung.

Bartnitzky, Horst (ed.). (2019): Auf dem Weg zur kindgerechten Grundschule. Frankfurt am Main: Grundschulverband.

Berkemeyer, Nils (2018): Über die Schwierigkeit, das Leistungsprinzip im Schulsystem gerechtigkeitstheoretisch zu begründen. Replik auf Christian Nerowski. In: Zeitschrift für Erziehungswissenschaft 21, pp. 447-464.

Beutel, Silvia Iris/Pant, Hans-Anand (2020): Lernen ohne Noten. Alternative Konzepte der Leistungsbewertung. Stuttgart: Kohlhammer.

Beutel, Silvia-Iris/Vollstädt, Witlof (2002): Kinder als Experten für Leistungsbewertung. In: Zeitschrift für Pädagogik 48, 4, pp. 591-613.

Blumenfeld, Phyllis C./Pintrich, Paul R./Hamilton, V. Lee (1986): Children's Concepts of Ability, Effort, and Conduct. In: American Educational Research Journal 23, 1, pp. 95–104.

Boaler, Jo/Wiliam, Dylan/Brown, Margaret (2005): Students' experiences of ability grouping – disaffection, polarisation and the construction of failure. In: Nind, Melanie/Rix, Jonathan/Sheehy, Kieron/Simmons, Katy (eds.): Curriculum and pedagogy in inclusive education: Values into practice. London, New York: Routledge, pp. 41-55.

Bonanati, Marina (2018): Lernentwicklungsgespräche und Partizipation. Rekonstruktionen zur Gesprächspraxis zwischen Lehrpersonen, Grundschülern und Eltern. Wiesbaden: Springer VS.

Bourdieu, Pierre/Passeron, Jean-Claude (1971): Die Illusion der Chancengleichheit: Untersuchungen zur Soziologie des Bildungswesens am Beispiel Frankreichs. Stuttgart: Klett.

Breidenstein, Georg (2018): Das Theorem der ‚Selektionsfunktion der Schule' und die Praxis der Leistungsbewertung. In: Reh, Sabine/Ricken, Norbert (eds.): Leistung als Paradigma: Zur Entstehung und Transformation eines pädagogischen Konzepts. Springer VS, pp. 307-327.

Breidenstein, Georg/Thompson, Christiane (2014): Schulische Leistungsbewertung als Praxis der Subjektivierung. In: Thompson, Christiane/Jergus, Kerstin/Breidenstein, Georg (eds.): Interferenzen: Perspektiven kulturwissenschaftlicher Bildungsforschung. Weilerswist: Velbrück, pp. 89-109.

Breidenstein, Georg/Rademacher, Sandra (2017): Individualisierung und Kontrolle. Empirische Studien zum geöffneten Unterricht in der Grundschule. Wiesbaden: Springer VS.

Brendel, Michelle/Noesen, Melanie (2014): Portfolioarbeit und Entwicklung inklusiven Unterrichts. In: Schuppener, Saskia/Bernhardt, Nora/Hauser, Mandy/Poppe, Frederik (eds.): Inklusion und Chancengleichheit. Diversity im Spiegel von Bildung und Didaktik. Bad Heilbrunn: Verlag Julius Klinkhardt, pp. 244–251.

Brookhart, Susan M./Bronowicz, Diane L. (2003): 'I don't like writing. It makes my fingers hurt': Students talk about their classroom assessments. In: Assessment in Education 10, 2, pp. 221-242.

Brown, Gavin/Harris, Lois (2012): Student conceptions of assessment by level of schooling: Further evidence for ecological rationality in belief systems. In: Australian Journal of Educational & Developmental Psychology 12, pp. 46-59.

Brown, Gavin T. L./Peterson, Elizabeth R./Yao, Esther S. (2016): Student conceptions of feedback: Impact on self-regulation, self-efficacy, and academic achievement. In: British Journal of Educational Psychology 86, pp. 606–629.

Brügelmann, Hans (2014): Sind Noten nützlich und nötig? Ziffernzensuren und ihre Alternativen im empirischen Vergleich. Eine wissenschaftliche Expertise des Grundschulverbandes (3rd ed.). Frankfurt: Grundschulverband.

Burnett, Paul C./Mandel, Valerie (2010): Praise and Feedback in the Primary Classroom: Teachers' and Students' Perspectives. In: Australian Journal of Educational & Developmental Psychology 10, pp. 145-154.

Carless, David/Lam, Ricky (2014): The examined life: perspectives of lower primary school students in Hong Kong. In: Education 3-13: International Journal of Primary, Elementary and Early Years Education 42, 3, pp. 313-329.

Chan, David W. (2002): Perceived Domain-Specific Competence and Global Self-Worth of Primary Students in Hong Kong. In: School Psychology International 23, 3, pp. 355-368.

Chapman, Michael/Skinner, Ellen A. (1989): Children's Agency Beliefs, Cognitive Performance, and Conceptions of Effort and Ability: Individual and Developmental Differences. In: Child Development 60, 5, pp. 1229–1238.

Clark, Zoé/Eisenhuth, Franziska (2011): The Capability Approach and Research on Children. In: Andresen, Sabine/Diehm, Isabell/Sander, Uwe/Ziegler, Holger (eds.): Children and the Good Life: New Challenges for Research on Children. Children's Well-Being: Indicators and Research Series: Vol. 4. London: Springer, pp. 69-74.

Cook-Sather, Alison (2018): Tracing the evolution of student voice in educational research. In: Bourke, Roseanna/Loveridge, Judith (eds.): Radical collegiality through student voice. Educational experience, policy and practice. Singapore: Springer, pp. 17-38.

Cortis, Gerald/Grayson, Anne (1978): Primary school pupils' perceptions of student teachers' performance. In: Educational Review 30, 2, pp. 93-101.

DeLuca, Christopher/Chapman-Chin, Allison E.A./LaPointe-McEwan, Danielle/Klinger, Don A. (2018): Student perspectives on assessment for learning. In: The Curriculum Journal 29, 1, pp. 77-94. DOI: 10.1080/09585176.2017.1401550.

Dutro, Elizabeth/Selland, Makenzie (2012): "I Like to Read, but I Know I'm Not Good at It": Children's Perspectives on High-Stakes Testing in a High-Poverty School. In: Curriculum Inquiry 42, 3, pp. 340-367.

Eriksson, Elisabeth/Björklund Boistrup, Lisa/Thornberg, Robert (2020): "You must learn something during a lesson": how primary students construct meaning from teacher feedback. In: Educational Studies, pp. 1-18.

Evans, Ellis D./Engelberg, Ruth A. (1988): Student perceptions of school grading. In: Journal of Research & Development in Education 21, 2, pp. 45–54.

Fielding, Michael (2013): Gli studenti: agenti radicali di cambiamento. In: Grion, Valentina/Cook-Sather, Alison (eds.): Student Voice: Prospettive Internazionali e Pratiche Emergenti in Italia. Milano, Italy: Edizioni Angelo Guerini e Associati Srl, pp. 62-82.

Filby, Nicola N./Barnett, Bruce G. (1982): Student perceptions of "Better Readers" in elementary classrooms. In: The Elementary School Journal 82, 5, pp. 435–449.

Flashman, Jennifer (2012): Academic Achievement and Its Impact on Friend Dynamics. In: Sociology of Education 85, 1, pp. 61-80.

Freeman, Melissa/Mathison, Sandra (n.d.). The impact of state-mandated testing on urban and suburban fourth graders. http://blogs.ubc.ca/evaluation/files/2012/06/Kids-and-Testing.pdf

Gipps, Caroline/Tunstall, Pat (1998): Effort, ability and the teacher: Young children's explanations for success and failure. In: Oxford Review of Education 24, 2, pp. 149-165.

Gomolla, Mechtild (2012): Leistungsbeurteilung in der Schule: Zwischen Selektion und Förderung, Gerechtigkeitsanspruch und Diskriminierung. In: Fürstenau, Sara/Gomolla, Mechtild (eds.): Migration und schulischer Wandel: Leistungsbeurteilung. Wiesbaden: Springer VS, pp. 25-50.

Grion, Valentina (2014): Meanings of 'student voice' In Italy: Emerging experiences and practices. In: Connect supporting student participation, 207, pp. 19-22. https://research.acer.edu.au/cgi/viewcontent.cgi?referer=https://www.google.com/&httpsredir=1&article=1216&context=connect.

Grion, Valentina/Cook-Sather, Alison (2013): Introduzione. In: Grion, Valentina/Cook-Sather, Alison (eds.): Student Voice: Prospettive Internazionali e Pratiche Emergenti in Italia. Milano, Italy: Edizioni Angelo Guerini e Associati Srl, pp. 15-23.

Grittner, Frauke (2009): Leistungsbewertung mit Portfolio in der Grundschule. Eine mehrperspektivische Fallstudie aus einer notenfreien sechsjährigen Grundschule. Bad Heilbrunn: Klinkhardt.

Guo, Wu Y./Yan, Zi (2019): Formative and summative assessment in Hong Kong primary schools: students' attitudes matter. In: Assessment in Education: Principles, Policy & Practice 26, 6, pp. 675-699.

Hargreaves, Eleanore (2013): Inquiring into children's experiences of teacher feedback: reconceptualising Assessment for Learning. In: Oxford Review of Education 39, 2, pp. 229-246.

Harris, Lois R./Brown, Gavin T.L./Harnett, Jennifer A. (2014): Understanding classroom feedback practices: A study of New Zealand student experiences, perceptions, and emotional responses. In: Educational Assessment, Evaluation and Accountability 26, pp. 107–133.

Harris, Lois R./Brown, Gavin T.L./Harnett, Jennifer A. (2015): Analysis of New Zealand primary and secondary student peer- and self-assessment comments: applying Hattie and Timperley's feedback model. In: Assessment in Education: Principles, Policy & Practice 22, 2, pp. 265-281.

Harris, Lois R./Harnett, Jennifer A./Brown, Gavin T. L. (2009): "Drawing" Out Student Conceptions: Using Pupils' Pictures to Examine Their Conceptions of Assessment. In: McInerney, Dennis M./Brown, Gavin T.L./Liem, Gregory A.D. (eds.): Student perspectives on assessment: What students can tell us about assessment for learning. Charlotte, NC: Information Age Pub, pp. 53-83.

Heinzel, Friederike (2011) (ed.): Generationenvermittlung in der Grundschule. Ende der Kindgemäßheit. Bad Heilbrunn: Klinkhardt, pp. 40-68.

Heinzel, Friederike (2022): Kindheit und Grundschule. In: Krüger, Heinz-Hermann/ Grunert, Cathleen/Ludwig, Katja (Eds.), Handbuch Kindheits- und Jugend- forschung (3rd revised edition). Wiesbaden: Springer VS, pp. 751-780.

Henk, William A./Melnick, Steven A. (1998): Upper elementary-aged children's re- ported perceptions about good readers: A self-efficacy influenced update in tran- sitional literacy contexts. In: Reading Research and Instruction 38, 1, pp. 57-80.

Hirschfeld, Gerrit H. F./Brown, Gavin T.L. (2009): Students' Conceptions of Assess- ment: Factorial and Structural Invariance of the SCoA Across Sex, Age, and Ethnicity. In: European Journal of Psychological Assessment 25, 1, pp. 30–38.

Honig, Michael-Sebastian (1999): Entwurf einer Theorie der Kindheit. Frankfurt am Main: Suhrkamp.

Hue, Ming-Tak/Leung, Chi-Hung/Kennedy, Kerry J. (2015): Student perception of assessment practices: towards 'no loser' classrooms for all students in the ethnic minority schools in Hong Kong. In: Educational Assessment, Evaluation and Accountability 27, 3, pp. 253-273.

Hughes, Jan N./Zhang, Duan (2007): Effects of the structure of classmates' percep- tions of peers' academic abilities on children's perceived cognitive competence, peer acceptance, and engagement. In: Contemporary Educational Psychology 32, 3, pp. 400-419.

Hunner-Kreisel, Christine/Kuhn, Melanie (2011): Children's Perspectives: Methodo- logical Critiques and Empirical Studies. In: Andresen, Sabine/Diehm, Isabell/ Sander, Uwe/Ziegler, Holger (eds.): Children and the Good Life: New Challenges for Research on Children. Children's Well-Being: Indicators and Research Series: Vol. 4. London: Springer, pp. 115-118.

INDIRE (Istituto nazionale di documentazione innovazione e ricerca educative). (2013): Il sistema educativo italiano. https://www.indire.it/lucabas/lkmw_file/ eurydice/QUADERNO_per_WEB.pdf.

Jover, Gonzalo/Thoilliez, Bianca (2011): Exploring Children's Voices from a Peda- gogical Perspective. In: Andresen, Sabine/Diehm, Isabell/Sander, Uwe/Ziegler, Holger (eds.): Children and the Good Life: New Challenges for Research on Children. Children's Well-Being: Indicators and Research Series: Vol. 4. Lon- don: Springer, pp. 119-130.

Kabel, Sascha (2019): Soziale Herkunft im Unterricht. Rekonstruktionen pädagogischer Umgangsmuster mit Herkunftsdifferenz im Grundschulunterricht. Wiesbaden: Springer VS.

Kampmann, Jan (2014): Young children as learners. In: Melton, Gary B./Ben-Arieh, Asher/Cashmore, Judith/Goodman, Gail S./Worley, Natalie K. (eds.): The SAGE Handbook of Child Research. SAGE Publications Ltd, pp. 136-152.

Klatter, Ellen B./Lodewijks, Hans G.L.C./Aarnoutse, Cor A.J. (2001): Learning conceptions of young students in the final year of primary education. In: Learning and Instruction 11, pp. 485-516.

Kolb, Annika (2007): Portfolioarbeit. Wie Grundschulkinder ihr Sprachenlernen reflektieren. Tübingen: Narr.

Köller, Olaf (2005): Formative Assessment in Classrooms: A Review of the Empirical German Literature. Formative Assessment. Improving Learning in Secondary Classrooms. Paris: OECD, Publishing and Centre for Educational Research and Innovation, pp. 265–279.

Kramer, Rolf-Torsten (2017): „Habitus" und „kulturelle Passung". In: Rieger-Ladich, Markus/Grabau, Christian (eds.): Pierre Bourdieu: Pädagogische Lektüren. Springer VS, pp. 183-205.

Kumpulainen, Kristiina/Lipponen, Lasse/Hilppö, Jaakko/Mikkola, Anna (2013): Building on the positive in children's lives: a co-participatory study on the social construction of children's sense of agency. In: Early Child Development and Care 184, 2, pp. 211-229.

Levesque, Roger J.R. (2014): Childhood as a legal status. In: Melton, Gary B./Ben-Arieh, Asher/Cashmore, Judith/Goodman, Gail S./Worley, Natalie K. (eds.): The SAGE Handbook of Child Research. SAGE Publications Ltd, pp. 38-53.

Levin, Ben (2013): Porre gli studenti al centro della riforma educativa. In: Grion, Valentina/Cook-Sather, Alison (eds.): Student Voice: Prospettive Internazionali e Pratiche Emergenti in Italia. Milano, Italy: Edizioni Angelo Guerini e Associati Srl, pp. 83-99.

Lundy, Laura/McEvoy, Lesley (2009): Developing outcomes for educational services: a children's rights-based approach. In: Effective Education 1, 1, pp. 43-60.

Lundy, Laura/McEvoy, Lesley/Byrne, Bronagh (2011): Working With Young Children as Co-Researchers: An Approach Informed by the United Nations Convention on the Rights of the Child. In: Early Education & Development 22, 5, pp. 714-736.

Mac Iver, Douglas (1988): Classroom environments and the stratification of pupils' ability perceptions. In: Journal of Educational Psychology 80, 4, pp. 495–505.

Malmberg, Lars-Erik/Wanner, Brigitte/Sumra, Suleman/Little, Todd D. (2001): Action-control beliefs and school experiences of Tanzanian primary school students. In: Journal of Cross-Cultural Psychology 32, 5, pp. 577-596.

Marshall, Hermine H./Weinstein, Rhona S./Sharp, Lee/Brattesani, Karen A. (1982): Students' descriptions of the ecology of the school environment for high and low achievers. Paper presented at the annual meeting of the American Educational Research Association, New York, March 19-23, 1982 (ED219447). ERIC. https://files.eric.ed.gov/fulltext/ED219447.pdf.

Melton, Gary B./Gross-Manos, Daphna/Ben-Arieh, Asher/Yazykova, Ekaterina (2014): The nature and scope of child research: learning about children's lives. In: Melton, Gary B./Ben-Arieh, Asher/Cashmore, Judith/Goodman, Gail S./Worley, Natalie K. (eds.): The SAGE Handbook of Child Research. SAGE Publications Ltd, pp. 3-28.

Meroño, Lourdes/Calderón, Antonio/Arias-Estero, José-Luis/Méndez-Giménez, Antonio (2017): Questionnaire on Perceived Competency-based Learning for primary school students (#ICOMpri1). In: Cultura y Educación 29, 2, pp. 279-323.

Monteiro, Vera/Mata, Lourdes/Santos, Natalie N. (2021): Assessment Conceptions and Practices: Perspectives of Primary School Teachers and Students. In: Frontiers in Education 6, Article 631185, pp. 1-15.

Montt, Guillermo (2011): Cross-national Differences in Educational Achievement Inequality. In: Sociology of Education 84, 1, pp. 49-68.

Moon, Tonya R./Brighton, Catherine M./Tomlinson, Carol A. (2020): Using Differentiated Classroom Assessment to Enhance Student Learning. Routledge.

Murillo, F. Javier/Hidalgo, Nina (2017): Students' conceptions about a fair assessment of their learning. In: Studies in Educational Evaluation 53, pp. 10-16.

Murphy, Colette/Lundy, Laura/Emerson, Lesley/Kerr, Karen (2013): Children's perceptions of primary science assessment in England and Wales. In: British Educational Research Journal 39, 3, pp. 585–606.

Newman, Richard S./Spitzer, Sue (1998): How children reason about ability from report card grades: A developmental study. In: The Journal of Genetic Psychology: Research and Theory on Human Development 159, 2, pp. 133-146.

Nicholls, John G./Miller, Arden T. (1984): Reasoning about the Ability of Self and Others: A Developmental Study. In: Child Development 55, 6, pp. 1990–1999.

Nigris, Elisabetta/Agrusti, Gabriella (eds.) (2021): Valutare per apprendere. La nuova valutazione descrittiva nella scuola. Milano, Italy: Pearson Italia.

Noesen, (2022): Portfolioarbeit und Lernen – eine qualitative Studie in einer inklusionsorientierten Grundschule im Kontext der luxemburgischen Bildungsreform. Dissertation: University of Luxemburg.

Organisation for Economic Co-Operation and Development (OECD) (2019): PISA 2018 Results (Volume II): Where All Students Can Succeed. Paris: PISA, OECD Publishing.

Paris, Scott G./Roth, Jodie L./Turner, Julianne C. (2000): Developing disillusionment: Students' Perceptions of Academic Achievement Tests. In: Issues in Education 6, 1/2, pp. 17-46.

Peacock, Alison (2016): Assessment for Learning without Limits. London: Open University Press.

Pearce, Thomas C./Wood, Bronwyn E. (2019): Education for transformation: an evaluative framework to guide student voice work in schools. In: Critical Studies in Education 60, 1, pp. 113-130.

Peña-Garcia, Sibele N. (2020): The concepts of learning and evaluation in primary education students. In: Panorama 14, 27.

Pereyra, Miguel A./Kotthoff, Hans-Georg/Cowen, Robert (eds.) (2011): PISA Under Examination: Changing Knowledge, Changing Tests, and Changing Schools. SensePublishers.

Petillon, Hanns (1993): Das Sozialleben des Schulanfängers. Die Schule aus der Sicht des Kindes. Weinheim: Beltz.

Pfeffer, Fabian T. (2008): Persistent Inequality in Educational Attainment and Its Institutional Context. In: European Sociological Review 24, 5, pp. 543-565.

Rees, Gwyther/Main, Gill (eds.). (2015): Children's views on their lives and well-being in 15 countries: An initial report on the Children's Worlds survey, 2013–14. York: Children's Worlds Project (ISCWeB).

Reisenauer, Cathrin (2020): Kinder- und Jugendpartizipation im schulischen Feld – 7 Facetten eines vielversprechenden Begriffs. In: Gerhartz-Reiter, Sabine/Reisenauer, Cathrin (eds.): Partizipation und Schule. Perspektiven auf Teilhabe und Mitbestimmung von Kindern und Jugendlichen. Wiesbaden: Springer, pp. 3–22.

Remesal, Ana (2009): Accessing Primary Pupils' Conceptions of Daily Classroom Assessment Practices. In: McInerney, Dennis M./Brown, Gavin T.L./Liem, Gregory A.D. (eds.): Students Perspectives on Assessment. What students can tell us about assessment for learning. Charlotte, NC: Information Age Pub, pp. 25-51.

Servan, M. José (2011): Percepciones e interpretaciones de las comunidades educativas en torno a la evaluación externa de los aprendizajes escolares. Estudios de caso sobre la evaluación de diagnóstico en Andalucía. In: Cultura y Educación 23, 2, pp. 221-234.

Stipek, Deborah J. (1981): Children's perceptions of their own and their classmates' ability. In: Journal of Educational Psychology 73, 3, pp. 404-410.

Stipek, Deborah/Gralinski, J. Heidi (1996): Children's beliefs about intelligence and school performance. In: Journal of Educational Psychology 88, 3, pp. 397-407.

Stipek, Deborah J./Tannatt, Lupita M. (1984): Children's judgments of their own and their peers' academic competence. In: Journal of Educational Psychology 76, 1, pp. 75-84.

Strauss, Nina-Cathrin/Zala-Mezö, Enikö/Herzig, Pascale/Häbig, Julia/Müller-Kuhn, Daniela (2017): Partizipation von Schülerinnen und Schülern ermöglichen: Perspektiven von Lehrpersonen. In: Journal für Schulentwicklung 21, 4, pp. 13-21.

Streckeisen, Ursula/Hungerbühler, Andrea/Hänzi, Denis (2007): Fördern und Auslesen: Deutungsmuster von Lehrpersonen zu einem beruflichen Dilemma. Wiesbaden: VS.

Thorkildsen, Theresa A. (1999): The way tests teach: Children's theories of how much testing is fair in school. In: Leicester, Mal/Modgil, Celia/Modgil, Sohan (eds.): Values, culture, and education. London: Falmer, pp. 61-79.

Triplett, Cheri F./Barksdale, Mary A. (2005): Third through sixth graders' perceptions of high-stakes testing. In: Journal of Literacy Research 37, 2, pp. 237-260.

Tsai, Pei-Shan/Chai, Ching S./Hong, Huang-Yao/Koh, Joyce H.L. (2017): Students' conceptions of and approaches to knowledge building and its relationship to learning outcomes. In: Interactive Learning Environments 25, 6, pp. 749-761.

Tunstall, Pat/Gipps, Caroline (1996): 'How does your teacher help you to make your work better?' Children's understanding of formative assessment. In: Curriculum Journal 7, 2, pp. 185-203.

Tuten, Jennifer (2007): "There's Two Sides to Every Story". How Parents Negotiate Report Card Discourse. In: Language Arts 84, 4, pp. 314-324.

Weidinger, Anne F./Steinmayr, Ricarda/Spinath, Birgit (2019): Ability Self-Concept Formation in Elementary School: No Dimensional Comparison Effects Across Time. In: Developmental Psychology, 2019, February 7, Advance online publication.

Wheelock, Anne/Bebell, Damian J./Haney, Walt (2000a): What Can Student Drawings Tell Us About High-Stakes Testing in Massachusetts? In: Teachers College Record, 2000, November 2. http://www.tcrecord.org/PrintContent.asp?ContentID=10634.

Wheelock, Anne/Bebell, Damian J./Haney, Walt (2000b): Student self-portraits as test-takers: Variations, contextual differences and assumptions about motivation. In: Teachers College Record, 2000, November 2. http://www.tcrecord.org/PrintContent.asp?ContentID=10635.

Williams, Judy A. (2010): 'You know what you've done right and what you've done wrong and what you need to improve on': New Zealand students' perspectives on feedback. In: Assessment in Education: Principles, Policy & Practice 17, 3, pp. 301-314.

Winter, Felix (2018): Lerndialog statt Noten. Neue Formen der Leistungsbeurteilung. Weinheim: Beltz.

Wong, Hwei M. (2016): I can assess myself: Singaporean primary students' and teachers' perceptions of students' self-assessment ability. In: Education 3-13: International Journal of Primary, Elementary and Early Years Education 44, 4, pp. 442-457.

Wong, Hwei M. (2017): Implementing self-assessment in Singapore primary schools: effects on students' perceptions of self-assessment. In: Pedagogies: An International Journal 12, 4, pp. 391-409.

Wurf, Gerald/Povey, Rachel (2020): "They show how smart you are": A mixed methods study of primary students' perceptions of assessment tasks. In: Issues in Educational Research 30, 3, pp. 1162-1182.

Xiang, Ping (2002): Chinese children's self-perceptions of ability in physical education. In: Journal of Research in Childhood Education 17, 1, pp. 97-105.

Xiang, Ping/Solmon, Melinda A./McBride, Ron E. (2006): Teachers' and Students' Conceptions of Ability in Elementary Physical Education. In: Research Quarterly for Exercise and Sport 77, 2, pp. 185-194.

Zeiher, Helga (1996). Kinder in der Gesellschaft und Kindheit in der Soziologie. Zeitschrift für Sozialisationsforschung und Erziehungssoziologie 16, 1, 26–46.

Giftedness and Achievement within Discourses

Michaela Kaiser, Simone Seitz

1   Giftedness and achievement

Debates on giftedness and the promotion of achievement have raised broad public awareness in national and international discourses. A closer look at these debates reveals inconsistencies in the relationship between giftedness, achievement and diversity. Based on this presumption, in the following it will be analysed according to which mechanisms knowledge concerning the promotion of giftedness and achievement at school is produced in the scientific discourses.

The starting point is the observation that socially shared or dominant ideas of giftedness and achievement are developed discursively. They are consolidated in scientific publications, in political debates and in educational interactions. What is understood by giftedness and what is recognised as academic achievement and what is not, is negotiated at various levels. Regarding this, public debates and professional discourses overlap and influence each other, for example, through media representations which are impulses both for the science discourse in professional journals as well as for knowledge discourses in schools. Due to changed and accelerated communication practices, impulses and developments at the international level are increasingly interwoven with debates at the national level. In these dynamics, certain ways of understanding prevail, while others penetrate less.

Dominant understandings that influence the development of knowledge and the actions of individuals can be understood as knowledge regimes. These institutionalise a knowledge order for certain fields of practice (Foucault 1977; Berger/Luckmann 1977; Grek 2009) and in this form are influential for educational practice. In concrete terms, this can be seen, for example, in the question of whether an educational institution recognises the practised multilingualism of a child from a family with a migration history as an achievement or evaluates it as a deficit in relation to monolingualism (Gomolla 2009). The corresponding norms and ideas of achievement and giftedness are therefore bound to perspective and interwoven with ideas of normality. Thus, they are also historically changeable and can differ culturally (Baird 2009; Ricken 2018).

This already indicates that the concept of giftedness is the subject of many controversial debates. The term came particularly under criticism in the context of the reception of critical sociological writings on education (Bourdieu 1982). Various operationalisations were presented in the following years, which attempted to describe the relationship between disposition, development and education as well as educational institutions in this regard in more detail (e.g., Sternberg 2003; Renzulli/Reis 2014). In the context of stronger debates and research activities on output of schools, the term was again increasingly included and discussed in-depth in connection with the concept of achievement (International Panel of Experts for Gifted Education [iPEGE] 2009; Müller-Oppliger/Weigand 2021).

Overall, output-orientation and the notion of effective competence acquisition in schools have been discernibly determining the international discourse in recent years, especially in connection with large-scale assessments (Popkewitz 2011; Pereyra/Kotthoff/Cowen 2011). In this context, the concept of achievement and the idea of measurability and comparability of academic performance moved more clearly into the discourse of educational science (Schäfer 2018). In particular, research on giftedness and achievement is itself entangled in the discourse on the meaning and understanding of these terms because it uses them to determine its subject matter and its self-positioning as a line of research. These discursive developments coincide with the internationally agreed agendas of sustainability and inclusion in education (United Nations 2006, 2015), which act as normative impulses in the political, scientific, and practice-related debates of the individual countries. In this context, achievement orientation and inclusion orientation of education systems are often interpreted as conflicting requirements (e.g., Sturm/Wagner-Willi 2016; Speck-Hamdan 2016; Wagener 2020). In other places, however, it is emphasised that inclusive education systems are achievement-oriented education systems (Prengel 2017; Seitz et al. 2016; Seitz/Kaiser 2020) and that achievement is a central dimension of schools to which inclusion and exclusion are systematically linked (Ainscow et al. 2006; Peacock 2016).

Starting from this, we ask about the discourse on giftedness, achievement, and inclusion in the context of the international agendas on output and achievement enhancement as well as inclusion and sustainability, focusing on the level of discourse that has hardly been considered so far (Seitz/Kaiser 2020). We thus do not focus directly on the educational practical level and its description, but on supra-situational and supra-individual figures of knowledge and meaning to the relation between giftedness, achievement, and inclusion. Based on this, we raise the question of how the discourse of promoting giftedness and achievement is formed, which patterns of interpretation of inclusion are produced and reproduced here, and which narrative structures are behind the patterns of interpretation.

2 Methodological Design

In our study, we analysed the mechanisms of structuring knowledge orders in the school-based promotion of giftedness and achievement with a specific focus on diversity. With Keller (2004) we assume that the analysed discourse names the topics of diversity, giftedness and achievement in different ways and combines them into a specific shape of narrative structure (cf. Keller 2004: 99). The analysis therefore aims to open up the individual dimensions of the discourse on giftedness and achievement as well as connections and relations between patterns that configure narrative strands on giftedness, achievement, and inclusion (cf. Keller 2004: 106–110). The focus here is on academic discourse, which is conducted primarily via academic journals but also via book publications.

With the discourse on the German education system, we focus specifically on a field that is characterised by a strong connection between socio-economic status and educational success in an international comparison and is therefore considered to be particularly shaped by injustice (e.g., Ditton 2013). It can therefore be asked which understanding of justice is being followed here and whether inequities – understood in this way – come to a head in a particular way in the field of giftedness support. For the formation and maintenance of elites via giftedness promotion contributes to the reproduction of educational inequities and injustices (Hartmann 2006), and support for giftedness in this context has long had to defend itself against accusations of elitism (Ullrich/Strunck 2008; Schregel 2020) even though there is no specific law that would ensure specific support for children seen as gifted like in other countries.

On the other hand, education policy has long proclaimed the strengthening of educational equity (e.g., Hopf/Edelstein 2018) and continued to push for this through education policy agendas, especially the inclusion agenda. It can be assumed that this causes specific tensions between the discourses on the promotion of giftedness and the discourses on inclusion. Therefore, our analysis of the discourse starts after the entry into force of the UN Convention on the Rights of Persons with Disabilities (United Nations 2006) in Germany in 2009. The ratification was an important impulse regarding the thematisation of diversity and inequity for educational research (Emmerich/Hormel 2013) and also for the research on giftedness and achievement in particular. The influence is evident over a decade, as can also be observed in the most recent data from 2022. The selection of documents analysed here thus refers to key contributions to the scientific discourse of the last decade 2008–2019.

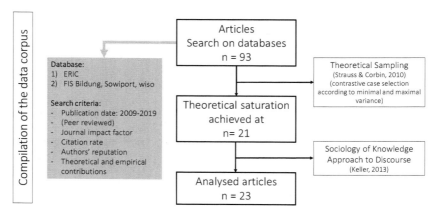

Figure 1:   Compilation of the data corpus

To compile the data corpus, a database search (ERIC) with the search terms 'giftedness' AND 'inclusion' OR 'diversity' was initially used to retrieve key texts according to the criteria 'peer review' and reputation of the authors. During the database search, however, it became apparent that no German-language journals with the claim of peer review were listed in the Eric database or in the Social Sciences Citation Index (SSCI). Following the research question, the search was therefore extended in a further step to include the databases FIS Bildung, Sowiport and wiso, which are established in German-speaking countries. The restriction to formally listed peer-reviewed journal articles had to be dispensed with in favour of a broader selection of articles, as only two journals in German language are considered to have peer-review procedures. Thus, in addition to the journal articles, thematically relevant anthology articles were also included in the sample, and attention was paid here to the reputation of the authors in the field of gifted education because it can be reasonably assumed that this also influences the perception of the publications in the scientific field of giftedness promotion. The scientific discourse can be seen as significantly controlled by this and thus discourse power of the contributions found in this way can be presumed. However, the category of thematic focus in the field of gifted education and the number of publications by authors with a focus in the thematic field were the primary criteria. Advice literature was excluded from the data collection due to the lack of comparability of text structure and addressees.

As a result, a total of 93 articles published between 2008 and 2019 in journals and edited volumes met the general search criteria. In the further course of theoretical sampling (Glaser/Strauss 1998) within the analysis process and along the more precise selection criteria, a corpus of 23 reference texts emerged according to maximum and minimum variance, which formed the subject of the in-depth analysis of the discourse on giftedness, achievement, and inclusion (summarised in anonymised form in Table 1).

Following Keller's (2013) Sociology of Knowledge Approach to Discourse (SKAD), we first examined the situatedness and material nature of the data corpus within the framework of the interpretative analysis and then took a look at the formal and rhetorical-linguistic structure. This is where the interpretative-analytical reconstruction of the textual material began. Following the procedure of Grounded Theory (Glaser/Strauss 1998; Strauss/Corbin 1996), it was examined in terms of its phenomenal structure and the interpretative and narrative patterns (cf. Keller 2013: 28). Our approach is thus based on sociologically founded research procedures of discourse analysis but is here concretised in the context of an educational research question in a meaningful and subject-related way.

Theoretical sampling and analysis

The aim of theoretical sampling is to dovetail case or data selection and data evaluation. In this process, the iterative selection and analysis of the material enables a procedural process of knowledge (Glaser/Strauss 1998). In doing so, deliberately contrasting and mutually irritating or validating texts are selected. This enables a successive specification in that, on the one hand, the range of the discourse on giftedness, achievement, and inclusion is reflected and, on the other hand, the analysis of the discourse is differentiated through variations by drawing on similar comparative texts (cf. Glaser/Strauss 1998: 55; Kelle/Kluge 2010; Strübing 2008). Within the framework of open, axial, and selective coding, the analytical process aims at the formation of central categories characterising the relationship between giftedness, achievement, and inclusion. These are not to be understood as describing and reducing but as categories that are condensed in terms of their theoretical content (Strauss/Corbin 1996), which elaborate the phenomenal structure underlying the texts and reveal interpretative patterns through the sequential procedure. The contrastive comparison of the texts contributes to the condensation by sharpening, developing and, where necessary, revising categories (cf. Keller 2013). Through this, the connection between giftedness, achievement, and inclusion is illuminated and increasingly abstracted in terms of the narrative structure, based on the textual material studied (cf. Przyborksi/Wohlrab-Sahr 2014: 209; Keller 2013: 28).

3   Key Findings of the Discourse Analysis

The analysis of the discourse on giftedness, achievement, and inclusion points across texts to a narrative structure that aims to first (1) clarify and locate the concept of giftedness from a disciplinary perspective. In a second step (2), with reference to educational policy agendas, the figure of dichotomisation is used to construct two opposing risk groups that (3) require specific pedagogical approaches, which are finally (4) justified with the underlying *dispositif* of giftedness and achievement (see Fig. 2).

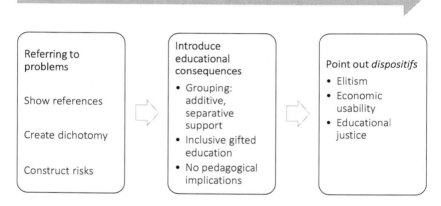

Figure 2:   Narrative structure of the scientific discourse

3.1   Conceptual formations

The text corpus initially shows a line of texts that explicitly position themselves as education of the gifted (*Begabtenförderung*) and focus on a small group that can be identified on the basis of psychometric characteristics (e.g., E./T./T. 2017; G. 2008[1]). According to the argumentation, performance shown at school and/or psychometric variables are indicators for the attribution of giftedness, so that a specific target group is constructed on this basis. In contrast, this is explicitly criticised in another line (T./Q. 2013) where the authors present giftedness-/ or talent-oriented education (*Begabungsförde-*

---

1   The references analysed have been anonymised.

rung) as more open to prerequisites and emphasise that it should be oriented towards the different potentials and interests of students in a broader understanding or explicitly demand this (N.-P. 2011; X 2011c; T./Q./T. 2012).

The argument here is that the hitherto selective provision of support for the gifted needs to be opened to a broader group. This is particularly evident in an argumentation that refers to current developments in education policy and interprets them as a call to address questions of inclusion and exclusion in research on giftedness education. In this way, an understanding of (high) giftedness that is reserved for an exclusive, criterially definable group of people is contrasted with the (potential) giftedness of many or even all students.

Overall, the majority of the texts analysed refer to the educational policy agenda of inclusion. In a small number of texts, there is a critical reflection on the definition of intelligence and giftedness as being essentially naturalising. Where this is done, it is compared with the construct of minor giftedness or special educational needs, which is criticised at the same time (e.g., T./Q. 2013). There are a striking number of reflections, clarifications and justifications on the semantic field of giftedness – mostly apparently in the function of a self-assurance of the subject matter. In this context, numerous synonymous equivalents for giftedness have also found their way into the professional discourse. These range from "talent" (e.g., E. et al. 2017), "intelligence" (e.g., E. et al. 2017; W./H./Q. 2017; W./Q./L. 2014) "abilities" (e.g., Q./L. 2016) and "expertise" (e.g., Q./C. 2013; A./T. 2011) to "potential" (e.g., B./W./G. 2014; Ce. 2013; G. 2008; I. 2012; Lu./I. 2019; Ta. 2010, 2014) and to "interest" (N.-P. 2011; T. et al. 2012), with "potential" as the most common equivalent.

It is clarified historically which semantic relationships exist between the concept of "talent" and that of "potential" or "interest". A key element in this regard is noted in the shift from the statistical to the dynamic concept of giftedness and the associated systemic accentuation of the discussion (X. 2011b).

In a psychologically arguing line of text, a cognitively determined concept of giftedness is elaborated (E. et al. 2017). According to this, giftedness is a cognitive ability to think, which is expressed in the intelligence of students and is reflected in academic performance. Without high intelligence, then, high achievement is impossible. It is therefore also argued that outstanding academic performance is a reliable expression of intelligence. Therefore, the intelligence quotient is used as an indicator of achievement. From here, the potential for giftedness is inferred (E. et al. 2017; Teid./T./Q. 2014). These contributions also reveal a hierarchisation of cognitive and non-cognitive aspects of giftedness, as cognitive aspects are identified as operationalisable and therefore more significant. The understanding of giftedness and achievement elaborated in these contributions can thus be described as mechanistic and deterministic because without cognitive potential, according to this approach, there is no (positive) development of performance. In this context, high intelligence is seen as the lowest common denominator from which performance in a wide range of areas is conceivable (cf. Q./L. 2016).

Elsewhere, a multidimensional perspective on giftedness and achievement is adopted (Ie. et al. 2010; Qe. 2008; Ce. 2013; G. 2008; I. 2012; Lu./I. 2019; Teid. et al. 2014; To. 2019; A./I./U. 2011). Here, it is assumed that intelligence alone cannot explain high performance. Therefore, systemic influences are considered relevant. From this perspective, giftedness encompasses more than an operationalisable (cognitive) performance potential of a person and should therefore not be viewed in isolation from the social context (e.g., I. 2012; Qe. 2008). In some cases, reference is made to Gardner's theory of multiple intelligences, although the scientific quality is criticised at the same time (e.g., I. 2012). In both perspectives, school is often described as a place of performing and measuring achievement and there are only few references to school as a place of developing achievement. Overall, we describe this discourse family as psychological. Generalised, giftedness is here interpreted as an individual (Ce. 2013; E. et al. 2017; G. 2008; I. 2012; Teid. et al. 2014; To. 2019; A. et al. 2011) and latent genetic (Lu./I. 2019; Xei. 2012) potential, the transformation of which into demonstrated performance takes place within the framework of cognitive or cognitive-emotional regulation processes (Lu./I. 2019; Cu. et al. 2019), which are moderated by social influences.

In contrast, in another discourse family, giftedness is not described as a specific personal characteristic. Instead, following an understanding of potential for education, it is assumed that every person is endowed with diverse and individual talents (X. 2011b). Following on from this, giftedness is interpreted as a potential that cannot be thought of in isolation from individual life situations and the socio-cultural milieu. In this context, unequal opportunities for the development of giftedness are also addressed (X. 2011b). Overall, the potential capacity of an individual is thus referred to as giftedness (Teid. 2014), whereby the socio-cultural context is attributed a moderating influence because here giftedness is recognised and promoted differently (I. 2012; N.-P. 2011; Teid. 2014; X. 2011b; Xei 2012).

Elsewhere, it is also argued that structural and institutional conditions determine the likelihood of "showing" and "recognising" giftedness and achievement. Therefore, following this argumentation, giftedness and achievement cannot be exclusively linked to the individual but are also and above all a systemic issue (A. et al. 2011; A./T. 2011). In addition, giftedness is also understood as a socio-cultural negotiation process, which, on the one hand, is milieu- and context-bound (e.g., Ta. 2010, 2014), and, on the other hand, is discursively shaped (e.g., N.-P. 2011). This is accompanied by criticism of the debate on giftedness and performance in psychological terms from some quarters (L. 2014; T. et al. 2012). In this context, a dynamic concept of giftedness is strengthened, which broadens the target group of giftedness support or calls for a dissolution of target group orientation (cf. T. et al. 2012; L. 2014). In summary, this family of discourses reveals a social constructivist model of giftedness (T./Q. 2013; T./Q./M./S./T. 2016).

Finally, arguing from a functionalist perspective, a third discourse family interprets giftedness predominantly as a socially relevant potential that becomes a social gain for society through the transformation of giftedness into performance (N.-P. 2011; W./I. 2007; A./T. 2011; A. et al. 2011). In this context, the economic dependence on the excellent performance of individual members of society is brought to the fore and the need to identify and promote socially relevant talent potential is derived from this (I. 2008; W./I. 2007; A. et al. 2011). Thus, from this perspective, giftedness and achievement have a specific and significant function within the social system. According to this view, the provision of performance on the basis of individual talents is the foundation for a stable society (N.-P. 2011) and economy (W./I. 2007; A. et al. 2011). This justifies the promotion of giftedness as a social investment, places the maximisation of human capital at the centre and giftedness, in short, is understood as what proves to be socially useful potential.

The texts that can be assigned to a pedagogical argumentation between the models of giftedness and achievement described above attempt to mediate between their milieu-bound nature and the view that both are expressed individually (N.-P. 2011; X. 2011b). This argumentation is based on both the individual motive of developing potential and the motive of social responsibility, which is linked to the transformation of giftedness into achievement. In doing so, it is shown that neither the one exclusive support of the gifted nor a systemic approach, which refers solely to the individual, lead further (X. 2011b). This interactive pedagogical understanding of giftedness and achievement thus can be seen as having a hinge function between the models.

3.2   Problematisation

Numerous statements in the data corpus aim to legitimise specific educational interventions on the basis of models of giftedness and achievement. The argumentation is either PISA-related or refers to the UN-CRPD; only occasionally is there recourse to both frames of reference.

Legitimisation: a dominant form of legitimisation of specifically gifted educational interventions for a small group of students is grouped around the international large-scale-assessment studies (PISA). In part of the underlying texts, the national findings of the PISA studies are used to point out that the competence levels of the top performers are not high enough in international comparison and the positively connoted goal of homogenising achievement at a high level has not been achieved (Teid. et al. 2014). Furthermore, a general need for the German education system to catch up in dealing with differences in achievement is stated (B. et al. 2014), and it is emphasised as an alarming finding that in the comparative studies, improvements had been shown for children at the lower levels of competence, but not for children at the higher levels of competence (B. et al. 2014). Following the authors, this justifies specific attention to students with special talents and corresponding programmes as these do not yet sufficiently benefit from the greater willingness to orientate teaching to the heterogeneity of the learners and differentiation (see also To. 2019). In this way, the PISA studies are referred to as a central point of reference and the goal of re-concentrating on high-achieving and (highly) gifted pupils is empirically justified and objectified.

The internationally agreed development of an inclusive education system in the UN CRPD can be highlighted as a further legitimising figure. This is introduced into the argumentation as a reason for education policy to reflect on the promotion of giftedness and talent on the basis of requirements and principles founded on inclusive education. In doing so, a social-constructivist concept of giftedness and achievement is called for, thus constructing a parallel figure to the understanding of disability in the UN CRPD (United Nations 2006). In this way, a normative legitimation is created discursively – in contrast to the reference to PISA, which is made as an empirical legiti-mation.

Overall, it is often stated that the promotion of giftedness is faced with the challenge of reflecting on its own object of research in relation to inclusion-related requirements (cf. Q./L. 2016). From this perspective, an inner connection between gifted education and inclusion is also identified, which is reflected in both theoretical and didactic concepts (L. 2014; T./Q. 2013; T. et al. 2012). On the other hand, a relativisation is introduced with reference to the inclusion-related developments. In a second step, the national results of the international large-scale assessment studies are referred to and a positive discrimination of the lower and a negative discrimination of the upper performance peaks are established. This is then described as a field of tension between competing tasks because – following the argumentation – teachers have to decide between the promotion of the "weak" and the "strong" and would distribute their resources more strongly to the weak students under normative pressure (To. 2019). Based on this, a structural disadvantage of (highly) gifted and high-achieving students is pointed out: according to this discourse, their existing gifts are too often not recognised as such and there-fore do not come into play (B. et al. 2014), which at the same time declares clearly distinguishable groups of students to be an entity.

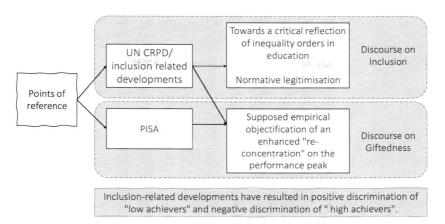

Figure 3:   Lines of discourse

With the comparison of supposedly high-achieving and low-achieving students, a negative counter-horizon is thus raised. It is suggested that inclusion-related developments shift the focus one-sidedly to low-performing students and that this is at the expense of high-performing and (highly) gifted students. This introduces a competitive mindset that comes to a head in the critical assessment that special needs education receives more attention than giftedness education (B. et al. 2014).

There are isolated signs of a shift in the discourse on giftedness towards an overarching concept of giftedness that addresses all students and is not in competition with inclusive school practice. However, this is obscured by a dominant recognition of the concentration on the group of (highly) gifted and high-achieving students. This way the groups of high-achieving and low-achieving students are dichotomised.

Dichotomisation: Through explicit and implicit references to the PISA data, the dichotomisation of high-achieving and low-achieving students, as already indicated, is built up and stabilised in the discourse – there is just a singular critical perspective on the constructive character and consequences of this approach. In doing so, the spread of student performance shown by the PISA results is taken up and the changes in education policy associated with the UN CRPD are used as empirical evidence that this temporal marker would place special emphasis on the group of so-called low-achieving learners. In individual texts, the extent to which this group is responsible for the performance development of the high-achieving students is explicitly elaborated. This is because, according to the argumentation, a shift towards the low-performing students goes hand in hand with a deterioration of the competence levels of (highly) gifted and high-performing students (B. et al.

2014; Teid. et al. 2014), and the goal of improving the weak learners is achieved by the (relative) deterioration of the good learners (Teid. et al. 2014). This argument is further exacerbated when school practice is said to provide intellectually capable students with less demanding lessons because weaker students are kept happy by lowered performance expectations and a reduced learning pace (Teid. et al. 2014). In this way, heterogeneity in the classroom, which is a basic condition of an inclusive education system, is interpreted and defined as a disadvantageous structure for strong learners.

The concept of intelligence is used as another dividing line between (highly) gifted and (less) gifted (e.g., G. 2008; Q./L. 2016; W./H./Q. 2017). More often, however, it is the demonstrated performance strength that is named, which is considered more appropriate with reference to a systemic concept of giftedness (I. 2012). Nevertheless, intelligence measurement is highlighted as a central interest of giftedness research in order to be able to describe difference with reference to intelligence distribution and to delimit the object of the research line (Q./L. 2016). This position is characterised by a hierarchical language that both explicitly and implicitly upgrades and downgrades students on the basis of their performance (attributed to intelligence) in the school context. Throughout the data corpus, high-performing and (highly) gifted students are primarily associated with positive characteristics, while low-performing students are associated with negative characteristics, for example, with regard to their self-concept and their interests (Ce. 2013; N. 2015; Toe./T. 2009) or with regard to their economic relevance (A. et al. 2011).

In this respect, individual contributions state in a polarising manner that the promotion of low achievers has increased the quantity of the "lower" achievers and improved their performance (Teid. et al. 2014; To. 2019). This is contrasted with a declining trend in the promotion of the "top" achievers, which leads to stagnating performance of the particularly high achievers. It is indicated that the top performers have not been able to maintain their lead over the "lower performers" (to the desirable extent) and that their positioning seems to be at risk. This dynamic has noticeably intensified since the ratification of the UN CRPD and the resulting school developments (Teid. et al. 2014; To. 2019). This form of creating difference thus contributes decisively to the construction and stabilisation of performance-related entities to then juxtapose them in a hierarchical manner.

Dichotomisations are also introduced at the level of discipline, and gifted education is contrasted with special education from an observational position (T./Q. 2013; T. et al. 2012). The disciplines are compared to identify parallel mechanisms of discrimination in both fields (T./Q. 2013). Separating promotion based on the assumption of stable characteristics is then criticised in relation to both fields. In this way, the dichotomisation of gifted education and special needs education is taken up on a meta-level by pointing to the disciplinary entanglement in diagnostic practices, which produce the object of the discipline, as a commonality.

Risk constructions: In many places, the necessity is mentioned to critically observe school-related developments in terms of whether they threaten the status and learning conditions of the top achievers. In some of the texts analysed, this goes hand in hand with the tendency, already indicated, to hold the group of low-performing students responsible for a supposedly threatening loss of performance and status of the high-performers. The figure of dichotomisation thus produces a specific risk group, namely that of the disadvantaged high achievers.

In the process, the group of gifted and highly gifted students is singled out as a psychometrically ascertainable group that requires corresponding support concepts. The argument goes that if (highly) gifted and high-achieving children are not addressed appropriately, this can lead to underachievement among these students (To. 2019; G. 2008). The resulting group of highly gifted underachievers (G. 2008) are therefore highlighted as a specific risk group for broad-based gifted education. Many of the authors therefore agree that the joint teaching of high-achieving and low-achieving students poses a risk for the performance development of students who are assessed as gifted (Teid. et al. 2014; A. et al. 2011). Referring to the findings of PISA studies, it is emphasised that this results in a disadvantageous picture for higher-achieving students (Q./L. 2016). In this argumentation, upward mobility of the lower achievers opens up the risk of relegation of the upper achievers, which is connoted with concern. The scenario that is drawn tends to be that of an educated elite whose achievements lose value if they do not substantially stand out from the normal field.

It should also be noted that individual contributions highlight the socio-cultural construction of the concept of giftedness and achievement. Here, giftedness is seen as dependent on the context of observation and as a discursively negotiated construct (e.g., L. 2014; N.-P. 2011; T./Q. 2013; T. 2010). The authors question the logical connections in the relationship between subject, giftedness and performance and describe how the attribution of performance expectations in school constructs and positions supposedly gifted students (L. 2014; T. et al. 2012, 2016; T./Q. 2013). The social constructivist character of high achievement in school is, according to the critique, disguised or naturalised under the guise of "natural" giftedness (T./Q. 2013). Consequently, giftedness and performance are the result of framing socio-cultural norms that are reified in the performance shown. Based on this, the line of argumentation of the risk group described above is questioned and criticised in this line of discourse.

3.3   Consequences for educational practice

The pedagogical and didactical implications that arise from the problematisa-tion of the situation of students who are considered gifted relate first and foremost to the distinction between exclusive and inclusive offers of gifted education.

Additive and separative support for giftedness: The (re-)produced uncertainty about the development and support of the top achievers, which is often mentioned in the discourse, is associated with concerns about displace-ment: support programmes for high-achieving students are said to no longer be able to adequately address (highly) gifted learners due to the inclusion-related support efforts. This connection is then cited as an indication that gifted education and its concepts are being visibly neglected in parallel with inclusion-related developments (e.g., Ce. 2013; Q./L. 2016; Teid. et al. 2014). The expertise of gifted education should therefore be brought back into the discourse and practical concepts implemented more intensively, for that genetically determined interindividual differences in the form of achievement potentials are perpetuated intraindividually in the educational process (Xei. 2012).

In order to realise target group-specific support in the sense of additive didactic offers for the correspondingly diagnosed children, diagnostics that start early in the educational biography are called for (G. 2008). This approach with precisely fitting interventions for a diagnostically determined target group can thus also be understood as a categorical special education (B./W./G. 2014) in which diagnosis and programme coincide. This is often followed in the analysed data corpus by the demand for external differen-tiation in order to be able to take interindividual differences in performance into account (Ce. 2013; Q./C. 2013; Teid. et al. 2014; A. et al. 2011). In this context, it is criticised in various places that such additive measures are difficult to implement, while separate schooling for children with special needs would hardly be questioned and would be justified with the intelli-gence quotient, which would, however, deviate "downwards" from the average in the same way as that of a highly gifted child (Ce. 2013).

Other authors see the development of personal competencies as an essential factor for the transformation of giftedness into achievement (Cu. et al. 2019; Lu./I. 2019; T./T. 2013). A latently genetically determined potential for aptitude is assumed. This can be developed by also taking into account the emotional moderation of learning processes and achievement (Cu. et al. 2019; cf. Lu./I. 2019; T./T. 2013), which is why the pedagogical relationship is seen as crucial for the development of these competencies (Cu. et al. 2019). Inclusive support for giftedness: Finally, individual contributions propose pedagogical concepts of support for giftedness that open up educational opportunities for all students and oppose distinctions based on personal characteristics or diagnostic procedures. This line of discourse accordingly turns away from target group-specific interventions and advocates a support for giftedness that focuses on the recognition and development of the individual potential of all students (X. 2011). The construction of a specific target group is considered obsolete. The assumption that the development of performance is independent of categorisation legitimises inclusive pedagogical concepts in this line of discourse (L. 2014; N.-P. 2011; T. et al. 2012, 2016; T./Q. 2013). However, concrete proposals for an inclusive promotion of giftedness are rarely found (L. 2014; T. et al. 2012, 2016; U. 2012).

3.4   Dispositifs of achievement

Educational equity: Overall, there are only a few reflections on aspects of educational equity in the data corpus. Where this does occur, the selectivity in the programmes for the promotion of giftedness and achievement is observed critically. In particular, the condition of access to programmes of talent-promotion via school-based achievements that have already been achieved rather than those that can be expected in the future is the subject of criticism, as this leads to systematically unequally distributed access and thus to the stabilisation of inequity (Ta. 2014; T./X. 2019). Habitual conditions of families are discussed in relation to habitual expectations of schools (Ta. 2014), effects of socio-economic status and environmental factors are addressed and the school as an institution is critically questioned. The social responsibility of promoting giftedness and achievement within a society increasingly characterised by diversity is frequently emphasised (N.-P. 2011). Following these approaches, it is important to do justice to the individual as well as to the concern for the social community and its further development (N.-P. 2011; I. 2012; X. 2011b). This means explicitly turning away from an economic exploitation perspective and emphasising the goal of taking responsibility for one's own life plan and role in society (N.-P. 2011; X. 2011b). This places the responsibility for developing talents in a meaningful way on the subject, whereby the type of stimulation and recognition is essential (X. 2011b, 2012, 2018). Therefore, it implies that concepts of giftedness and achievement promotion should address all students regardless of their socio-economic- and ethno-cultural backgrounds, for example, by taking greater account of social heterogeneity when recognising achievements (T. et al. 2012).

Elitism: Taking responsibility is also demanded from other sides under the sign of optimising education and educational output, but here in the sense of mobilising the talent resources of (highly) gifted and high-performing students. Characteristic of this line of argument is a mechanistic rhetoric with which the offer of tailor-made training for the transformation of high aptitudes into high performance is taken up. An appeal is made to the institutional responsibility of the school to increase opportunities according to need by creating different, target group-specific offers for (different) performance development of individuals. According to the argumentation, specific school-based support for gifted students is seen as a contribution to equal opportunities and equity (Teid. et al. 2014).

It is stated that the relative performance situation of the so-called top achievers has empirically changed only little and that there is cause for concern (Teid. et al. 2014) because inclusion-related developments are accompanied by a differentiation of the performance hierarchies, and a downward mobility of the top achievers is to be feared.

Economic usability: From a functionalist perspective, the focus is on mobilising performance reserves for the purpose of maximising human capital. Accordingly, this line of argument focuses on the performance elite. Following these arguments, the group of high achievers should be promoted in a targeted and exclusive manner. This is linked to the call for a return of research on giftedness to its research focus, namely the description of performance excellence and innovation as well as their preconditions and development (A. et al. 2011). In this context, the promotion of academic achievement is explicitly addressed as an economic resource and linked to the prosperity to be achieved (gross national product) as a utilisation perspective (A. et al. 2011) as well as to the social and intellectual development of society. This perspective is thus primarily concerned with the usability of personal potential and abilities for the purpose of a prosperous society, which has a justified high interest in promoting the best (A. et al. 2011).

This is also the starting point for the demand to continuously adapt the promotion of giftedness to changing social developments and employment situations (I. 2008; W./I. 2007; A. et al. 2011) because the decisive factor is the output in the sense of the realisation of individual potential (E. et al. 2017) within an industrial society's understanding of education and work. The economically oriented exploitation of talent and performance thus stands for a *dispositif* that expresses itself in the socio-economic functionality of talent promotion.

Our analyses of the organisation of discourse are thus condensed into a narrative pattern with regard to the connection between giftedness, achievement and inclusion as well as its relevance for the practice of giftedness support.

4   Discussion

With our analyses, we firstly show how differences are created and hierar-chised in the discourse of giftedness and achievement promotion. These differences occur where the boundary between high-achieving and low-achieving students is seen as a clear dividing line between performance entities that decides who belongs to a group. Above the concept of achieve-ment, giftedness stands in this argumentation as a distance-creating variable between students, which results as a matter of course from the supposed fact of their difference. The performance *dispositifs* invoked indicate the realm of conceivable and legitimised performance and, as a consequence, the practices of giftedness promotion, which is to be balanced against the realm of non-conceivable performance. The legitimisation of an orientation towards the educational elite, supposedly neglected by the discourse of inclusion, is experiencing a particular boom in the discourse on giftedness, achievement, and inclusion. A special feature is that the re-concentration on the supposedly neglected top achievers is argued as just and constructed as a pedagogical problem, and the promotion of giftedness is linked to the determination and graduation of school-recognised achievement. In this context, both giftedness and achievement can be understood as constructs that are produced by means of assessment according to the code "better" or "worse" (Luhmann 2002: 66; Bräu/Fuhrmann 2015). The question of an equitable promotion of giftedness then finds an answer with recourse to the results of PISA studies.

Overall, the promotion of giftedness and achievement in the discourse analysed is linked to two central themes of the educational science discus-sion: the findings of international large-scale assessment studies and the inclusion agenda. Through this the giftedness discourse legitimises itself. The promotion of giftedness, which addresses students identified as gifted, is repeatedly criticised for contradicting the principle of educational equity (Giesinger 2008; Stojanov 2008, 2011, 2019; Schregel 2020). This is because the form of hierarchisation generated by the achievement principle assigns children to essentialistically constructed groups of differently gifted children (Stojanov 2019). The individual child is held responsible in school through the dictum of being positioned as gifted or not gifted, or high or low achiever. This way of thinking about 'fair' support for giftedness, which justifies and conceives support on the basis of (cognitive) starting conditions, quasi gifted-ness, and ultimately performance, is criticised as inappropriate from a pers-pective of equity theory (Giesinger 2008; Böker/Horvarth 2018). For in the sense of promoting giftedness towards the formation of elites and economic usability, selective promotion concentrated on the 'top performers' is only fair if it is legitimised by expected high performance. Such a 'performance-and talent-based' selection justifies the intended positive selection into corresponding programmes of gifted education or the negative selection of the 'lower achievers' from such programmes in an essentialist way. Stojanov (2019) exposes logical errors in this regard when he criticises underlying implicit meritocratic premises: central to the critique is the assumption that ability is a quasi-natural quality, whereas it would be the task of the institution of schooling to cultivate it. For this reason, children cannot be held solely responsible for their development. Therefore, according to the critique, promoting (and selecting) children in school according to their assumed talents is fundamentally incompatible with inclusive education (Stojanov 2019). This is because the assessment of performance is entangled in the self-referentiality of the school performance principle, which is falsely presented as meritocratic in its internal logic.

Our analyses also point out that although giftedness and achievement are powerfully negotiated, neither is a permanent quantity beyond their interactive negotiation (see also Reh/Ricken 2018). In order to avoid essentiallisation, giftedness can therefore be described in relation to the concept of achievement. Performance boundaries cannot be linearly related to the concept of giftedness but are understood as dynamic or contingent (Hirschauer 2014). This overcomes approaches that describe the connection between giftedness and performance differences along ontological 'facts' (Budde 2012: 528) or categories of difference, such as school-assessed achievement or IQ. Whether this critical analysis of the developmental dynamics of educational differences can be successful must, according to the results of our study, remain an open question because demarcations continue to be central mechanisms for effectively defining giftedness along performance entities (e.g., Helper/ Krüger 2015; Reh/Ricken 2018; Krüger/Helsper 2014). Along these demarcations, however, it can be discussed at which levels in the system of giftedness and achievement support (Seitz/Kaiser 2020) closure processes come into play.

In conclusion, it becomes clear that the insistence on distinctiveness not only safeguards unequal approaches and positions but also those of (special) education approaches and its programmes. The further development of multidimensional notions of diversity, as they are present in the discourse of inclusion, is thus seen as a risk for giftedness research, so that it cannot have any interest in it.

A specific epistemic value of our contribution may be seen in the clear focus on the German area, taking into account existing international literature-reviews on similar subjects (e.g., Steenbergen-Hu/Olszewski-Kubilius/ Calvert 2020; Mun/Ezzani/Lee 2020; White/Graham/Blaas 2018) which do not involve and reflect the specific features of the German educational system. At the same time, the restriction to German-language texts is a recognisable limitation of the study, and it must be considered that the German-language educational science discourse as a whole tends to be self-referential.

Therefore, in a second step, the analyses should be replicated or extended to the international discourse, which is currently being realised (Auer et al., in preparation). In view of the specifically strong selection dynamics in the German education system and the associated social closure processes, however, the findings on the discourse related to this are also of particular relevance from an international perspective. The question now arises as (to whether and) to what extent specific characteristics are evident here that are not to be found in the discourses on giftedness and achievement – which refer to less selectively structured education systems and differentiated forms of government – and whether there are substantial differences here. This is therefore a viable starting point for further international research projects.

References

Ainscow, Mel/Booth, Tony/Dyson, Alan (2006): Improving schools, developing inclusion. London: Routledge.

Auer, Petra/Bellacicco, Rosa/Kaiser, Michaela/Seitz, Simone (in prep.): Giftedness, achievement, and inclusion – A discourse analysis.

Baird, Jo-Anne (2009): Macro and micro influences on assessment practice. In: Assessment in Education. Principles, Policy & Practice 16, 2, pp. 127–129.

Berger, Peter L./Luckmann, Thomas (1977): Die gesellschaftliche Konstruktion der Wirklichkeit: Eine Theorie der Wissenssoziologie (5th ed.). Frankfurt am Main: Fischer.

Böker, Arne/Horvath, Kenneth (2018): Begabung und Gesellschaft. Sozialwissenschaftliche Perspektiven auf Begabung und Begabtenförderung. Wiesbaden: Springer VS.

Bourdieu, Pierre (1982): Die feinen Unterschiede. Kritik der gesellschaftlichen Urteilskraft. Frankfurt am Main: Suhrkamp.

Bräu, Karin/Fuhrmann, Laura (2015): Die soziale Konstruktion von Leistung und Leistungsbewertung. In: Bräu, Karin/Schlickum, Christine (eds.): Soziale Konstruktionen in Schule und Unterricht. Zu den Kategorien Leistung, Migration, Geschlecht, Behinderung, soziale Herkunft und deren Interdependenzen. Opladen: Barbara Budrich, pp. 49-64.

Budde, Jürgen (2012): Die Rede von der Heterogenität in der Schulpädagogik. Diskursanalytische Perspektiven. In: Forum qualitative Sozialforschung 13, 2, https://doi.org/10.17169/fqs-13.2.1761.

Ditton, Hartmut (2013): Kontexteffekte und Bildungsungleichheit. Mechanismen und Erklärungsmuster. In: Becker, Rolf/Schulze, Alexander (eds.): Bildungskontexte. Strukturelle Voraussetzungen und Ursachen ungleicher Bildungschancen. Wiesbaden: Springer, pp. 173–206.

Emmerich, Marcus/Hormel, Ulrike (2013): Heterogenität – Diversity – Intersektionalität. Zur Logik sozialer Unterscheidungen in pädagogischen Semantiken der Differenz. Wiesbaden: Springer VS.

Foucault, Michel (1977): Überwachen und Strafen. Die Geburt des Gefängnisses. Frankfurt am Main: Suhrkamp.

Giesinger, Johannes (2008): Begabtenförderung und Bildungsgerechtigkeit. In: Ullrich, Heiner/Strunck, Susanne (eds.): Begabtenförderung an Gymnasien. Wiesbaden: Springer VS, pp. 271–291.

Glaser, Barney G./Strauss, Anselm L. (1998): Grounded Theory: Strategien qualitativer Forschung. Bern: Huber.

Gomolla, Mechthild/Radtke, Frank-Olaf (eds.) (2009): Institutionelle Diskriminierung. Die Herstellung ethnischer Differenz in der Schule. Wiesbaden: Springer VS.

Grek, Sotiria (2009). Governing by numbers. The PISA 'effect' in Europe. In: Journal of Education Policy 24, 1, pp. 23–37.

Hartmann, Michael (2006). Leistungseliten–soziale Selektion durch Herkunft und Hochschule. In: Ecarius, Jutta/Wigger, Lothar (eds.): Elitebildung–Bildungselite. Erziehungswissenschaftliche Diskussionen und Befunde über Bildung und soziale Ungleichheit. Opladen: Barbara Budrich, pp. 206–225.

Helsper, Werner/Krüger, Heinz-Hermann. (2015): Auswahlverfahren in Bildungsinstitutionen – eine Einleitung. In: Helsper, Werner/Krüger, Heinz-Hermann (eds.): Auswahl der Bildungsklientel. Zur Herstellung von Selektivität in „exklusiven" Bildungsinstitutionen. Wiesbaden: Springer VS, pp. 9–27.

Hirschauer, Stefan (2014): Un/doing Differences. Die Kontingenz sozialer Zugehörigkeiten. In: Zeitschrift für Soziologie 43, 3, pp. 170–191.

Hopf, Wulf/Edelstein, Benjamin (2018): Chancengleichheit zwischen Anspruch und Wirklichkeit. Dossier Bildung. Bundeszentrale für politische Bildung. In: Dossier. Bildung. Bonn: Bundeszentrale für politische Bildung, pp. 91–100. https://hdl.handle.net/10419/191913.

International Panel of Experts for Gifted Education [iPEGE] (2009): Professionelle Begabtenförderung. Empfehlungen zur Qualifizierung von Fachkräften in der Begabtenförderung. http://www.ipege.net/wp-content/uploads/2018/06/iPEGE_Broschuere.pdf.

Kelle, Udo/Kluge, Susann (2010): Vom Einzelfall zum Typus. Wiesbaden: Springer VS.

Keller, Reiner (2004): Diskursforschung. Eine Einführung für SozialwissenschaftlerInnen. Wiesbaden: Springer VS.

Keller, Reiner (2013): Zur Praxis der Wissenssoziologischen Diskursanalyse. In: Keller, Reiner/Truschkat, Inga (eds.): Methodologie und Praxis der Wissenssoziologischen Diskursanalyse. Wiesbaden: Springer VS, pp. 27–68.

Krüger, Heinz-Hermann/Helsper, Werner (2014): Elite und Exzellenz im Bildungssystem – Nationale und Internationale Perspektiven. Einleitung. In: Zeitschrift für Erziehungswissenschaft 17, 3, pp. 1–10.

Luhmann, Niklas (2002): Das Erziehungssystem der Gesellschaft. Frankfurt am Main: Suhrkamp.

Müller-Oppliger, Victor/Weigand, Gabriele (eds.) (2021): Handbuch Begabung. Weinheim: Beltz.

Mun, Rachel/Ezzani, Miriam D./Lee, Lindsay Ellis (2020): Culturally relevant leadership in gifted education: A systematic literature review. In: Journal for the Education of the Gifted 43, 2, pp. 108-142.

Peacock, Alison (2016): Assessment for Learning without Limits. New York: McGraw-Hill.

Pereyra, Miguel A./Kotthoff, Hans-Georg/Cowen, Robert (eds.) (2011): PISA Under Examination: Changing Knowledge, Changing Tests, and Changing Schools. Rotterdam: SensePublishers.

Popkewitz, Thomas S. (2011): PISA. Numbers, standardizing conduct, and the alchemy of school subjects. In: Pereyra, Miguel A./Kotthoff, Hans-Georg/Cowen, Robert (eds.): PISA Under Examination. Changing Knowledge, Changing Tests, and Changing Schools. Rotterdam: SensePublishers, pp. 31–46.

Prengel, Annedore (2017): Individualisierung in der „Caring Community" – Zur inklusiven Verbesserung von Lernleistungen. In: Textor, Annette/Grüter, Sandra/Schiermeyer-Reichl, Ines/Streese, Bettina (eds.): Leistung inklusive? Inklusion in der Leistungsgesellschaft. Band II: Unterricht, Leistungsbewertung und Schulentwicklung. Bad Heilbrunn: Klinkhardt, pp. 13–27.

Przyborski, Aglaja/Wohlrab-Sahr, Monika (2014): Qualitative Sozialforschung. Ein Arbeitsbuch. Berlin: De Gruyter Oldenbourg.

Reh, Sabine/Ricken, Norbert (2018): Leistung als Paradigma. Zur Entstehung und Transformation eines pädagogischen Paradigmas. Wiesbaden: Springer VS.

Renzulli, Joseph S./Reis, Sally M. (2014): The Schoolwide Enrichment Model. A How-To Guide for Talent Development. New York: Routledge.

Ricken, Norbert (2018): Konstruktionen der ‚Leistung'. Zur (Subjektivierungs-)Logik eines Konzepts. In: Reh, Sabine/Ricken, Norbert (eds.): Leistung als Paradigma. Zur Entstehung und Transformation eines pädagogischen Paradigmas. Wiesbaden: Springer VS, pp. 43–60.

Schäfer, Alfred (2018): Das problematische Versprechen einer Leistungsgerechtigkeit. In: Sansour, Theresa/Musenberg, Oliver/Riegert, Judith (eds.): Bildung und Leistung. Differenz zwischen Selektion und Anerkennung. Bad Heilbrunn: Klinkhardt, pp. 11–58.

Schregel, Susanne (2020): „Extrawürste für die Elite?" Ungleichheit und Differenz in der bundesdeutschen Hochbegabungsdebatte. In: Geschichte und Gesellschaft 46, 2, pp. 313–338.

Seitz, Simone/Kaiser, Michaela (2020): Zur Entwicklung leistungsfördernder Schulkulturen. In: Fischer, Christian/Fischer-Ontrup, Christiane/Käpnick, Friedhelm/Neuber, Nils/Solzbacher, Claudia/Zwitserlood, Pienie (eds.): Begabungsförderung, Leistungsentwicklung, Bildungsgerechtigkeit – für alle. Beiträge aus der Begabungsforschung. Münster: Waxmann, pp. 207–222.

Seitz, Simone/Pfahl, Lisa/Lassek, Maresi/Rastede, Michaela/Steinhaus, Friederike (2016): Hochbegabung inclusive. Inklusion als Impuls für Begabungsförderung an Schulen. Auf dem Weg zu mehr Bildungsgerechtigkeit. Weinheim: Beltz.

Speck-Hamdan, Angelika (2016): Inklusion. Der Anspruch an die Grundschule. In: Blömer, Daniel/Lichtblau, Michael/Jüttner, Ann-Kathrin/Koch, Katja/Krüger, Michaela/Werning, Rolf (eds.): Perspektiven auf inklusive Bildung. Gemeinsam anders lehren und lernen. Wiesbaden: Springer VS, pp. 13–22.

Stamm, Margit (2010): Begabung, Kultur und Schule. Gedanken zu den Grundlagen der Begabtenförderung. In: ZEP 3, 1, pp. 25–33.

Steenbergen-Hu, Saiying/Olszewski-Kubilius, Paula/Calvert, Eric (2020): The effectiveness of current interventions to reverse the underachievement of gifted students: Findings of a meta-analysis and systematic review. In: Gifted Child Quarterly 64, 2, pp. 132-165.

Sternberg, Robert J. (2003): A Broad View of Intelligence. The Theory of Successful Intelligence. In: Consulting Psychology Journal Practice and Research 55, 3, pp. 139–154.

Stojanov, Krassimir (2008): Bildungsgerechtigkeit als Freiheitseinschränkung. In: Zeitschrift für Pädagogik 54, 4, pp. 516–531.

Stojanov, Krassimir (2011): Bildungsgerechtigkeit. Rekonstruktionen eines umkämpften Begriffs. Wiesbaden: Springer VS.

Stojanov, Krassimir (2019): Inklusion als Imperativ von (Bildungs-)Gerechtigkeit. In: Zeitschrift für Inklusion 10, 2. Retrieved from: https://www.inklusion-online. net/index.php/inklusion-online/article/view/527.

Strauss, Anselm L./Corbin, Juliet (1996): Grounded Theory. Grundlagen qualitativer Sozialforschung. Weinheim: Beltz.

Strübing, Jörg (2008): Grounded Theory. Zur sozialtheoretischen und epistemologischen Fundierung eines pragmatistischen Forschungsstils. Wiesbaden: Springer VS.

Sturm, Tanja/Wagner-Willi, Monika (2016): Herstellung und Bearbeitung von Leistungsdifferenzen im kooperativ gestalteten inklusiven Fachunterricht. In: Zeitschrift für Pädagogik. Beiheft, 62, pp. 75–89.

Ullrich, Heiner/Strunck, Susanne (2008): Begabtenförderung und Elitenbildung an Gymnasien: Einführung in den Themenbereich. In: Ullrich, Heiner/Strunck, Susanne (eds.): Begabtenförderung an Gymnasien. Entwicklungen, Befunde, Perspektiven. Wiesbaden: VS, pp. 9–35.

United Nations (2006): Convention on the Rights of Persons with Disabilities. https:// www.un.org/disabilities/documents/convention/convention_accessible_pdf.pdf.

United Nations (2015): 17 Goals to Transform Our World. https://www.un.org/ sustainabledevelopment/.

Wagener, Benjamin (2020): Leistung, Differenz und Inklusion. Eine rekonstruktive Analyse professionalisierter Unterrichtspraxis. Wiesbaden: Springer VS.

White, Sonia/Graham, Linda/Blaas, Sabine (2018): Why do we know so little about the factors associated with gifted underachievement? A systematic literature review. In: Educational Research Review 24, pp. 55-66.

Part II:
Educational Justice within Different Education Systems — Some Empirical Evidence

Throughout the Day on the Way to More Educational Justice? Children's Voices on All Day-primary Schooling

Simone Seitz, Francesca Berti, Catalina Hamacher[1]

1   Introduction

All-day schooling is often seen as an instrument to strengthen educational justice and to mitigate the correlation of children's socio-economic status and educational success (Züchner/Fischer 2014). In these discourses, children are mainly thematised as learners and thus as students. Based on this, in this contribution we ask about the institutionally defined roles of children in all-day primary schools and reflect on this aspect in the context of educational justice. We start from the idea that in primary schools, children fulfil the roles of children, peers, and students at the same time (Petillon 2002, 2017; de Boer/Deckert-Peaceman 2009). As children, they are dependent on friend-ships, social belonging and recognition from adults and from other children. Moreover, they have the right to play and to participate (United Nations 1989). Still, they can neither step out of the social role of being also students, dedicated by the school, nor can they dissolve the institutionally given generational children-adults relationships (Alanen 1992; Honig/Lange/Leu 1999; Heinzel 2011). Institutional and societal boundaries, in fact, pretty much define the space within which children can act in primary schools (Hunner-Kreisel/Kuhn 2011: 116).

Based on such considerations, developments from half day primary schools with additional and facultative types of afternoon-care to all-day schools are highly significant for the understanding of the social role of children at school, as their roles change situationally (Dalhaus 2011): while in half-day primary schools, the latter are differently fulfilled whether in the lessons or during breaks. In an all-day school, children seem to have a broader range of situational roles to fulfil, which is linked to an offering of

---

1   Simone Seitz wrote chapters 1 and 5, Francesca Berti wrote chapters 2 and 4.2, Cata-lina Hamacher wrote chapter 3 and 4.1. The empirical analyses were conducted to-gether in the research group.

pedagogical relationships between children and teachers as well as children and social educators (De Boer 2006; Friebertshäuser 2008; Sauerwein 2019).

If we look from here at the political concerns and the impulses at the regulative level (Scott 2014) towards the promotion of all-day schools, as we do further below, it can be observed that such aspects are barely considered, whereas aspects of educational participation in terms of educational equity, achievement and compensation for children seen as disadvantaged dominate here (Bellin/Tamke 2010; Rabenstein/Nerowski/Rahm 2015; Capperucci/Piccioli 2015). This implies that in the discourse children are primarily addressed as students and learners who, through all-day schooling, receive better conditions for the educational success they (are supposed to) strive for or are dependent on. Such environments are intended to offer more time to efficiently support children throughout the morning *and* the afternoon, particularly those with life-conditions which are seen as disadvantaged (Edelstein 2007; Sauerwein 2019).

In the present contribution, instead, we investigate the view of children on their social role as children, peers and students and in this way combine approaches of primary school research and childhood studies (Fölling-Albers 2003; De Boer/Deckert-Peaceman 2009). We draw on empirical findings on children's voices from a completed study (Kricke/Remy/Seitz/Hamacher 2022; Seitz/Hamacher 2022) and ask how children describe their experience in all-day primary schools and which elements are assumed as relevant for them. Focusing on concrete actions where "the organic connection between education and personal experience" (Dewey 1938) comes into practice, we shed light on the relation between formal and non-formal education and the associated social roles of children, which are significant for the aim of educational justice in the implementation of all-day primary schools.

2   All-Day-Primary-School

The development of all-day primary schools varies greatly internationally. In Italy as well as in Germany, compulsory all-day school models exist in parallel to part-time models with facultative afternoon care (Allemann-Ghionda 2009; Coelen/Stecher 2014). Therefore, also conceptions of educational justice, within different countries as well as political and educational systems, are discussed in different ways (Allemann-Ghionda 2013; OECD 2019). In the following we give a brief overview of the situation in Italy and Germany.

2.1 All-Day-Primary-School in Italy

In Italy, all-day school (*tempo pieno*) was already established in the course of the educational reform of 1971. This implementation of an inclusively structured compulsory school system – a five-year primary school plus a three-year middle school (Law 820/1971) – aimed at more educational justice, thus linked at the outset with the concern for greater participation of children in education, regardless of social backgrounds (Allemann-Gionda 2009: 197; Cerini 2004). The underlying understanding of the all-day school as a "house of learning" expressly addressed the personality development of children, put participation at the centre and sought to fulfil democratic education (Damiano 2003: 244; Baur 2005: 74). Its promotion was inspired by the democratic waves of 1968 which supported the idea of an active school, the exploration of the territory and the opening of the school to the local community (Cambi 2003). In the background, the critical and political "Letter to a teacher" (*Lettera ad una professoressa*), a collective writing of the students of the Barbiana School animated by Don Lorenzo Milani and published for the first time in 1967 (ibid.), had a strong impact on the discourse. The philosophical pillars were inspired by democratic and active schools – from Dewey to Freinet – while the didactic approach was nourished by a growing movement (*Movimento di Cooperazione Educativa*) that promoted explorative learning, collaboration, and participation. However, the attention paid to such principles soon clashed with the structural difficulties and conditions which the compulsory imposition of all-day schools throughout the country would entail in view of the large economic gap between the northern and southern parts of Italy. Compulsory all-day schooling had been seen as a contribution to more educational justice with a focus on the weak social and economic situation of the southern regions, but this objective could not be realised. The legislature, in fact, called upon to establish the principles governing the establishment of full-time care, did not guarantee an equal distribution of supply across the territory. Instead, it left it up to the initiative responding to a need clearly expressed by families, and the minimum number of 15 children became the criterion to constitute a full-time class. This new opportunity was taken up mainly in the northern regions because in post-war Italy many families had emigrated from the southern to the northern regions due to economic reasons: the increasing number of both parents employed in the north was matched here with the lack of grandparents and relatives who could look after the children in the afternoons (Berti 2013). The municipalities in large cities such as Turin and Milan tried to meet this need by setting up "after-school" activities run by educators. It is obvious that this social need to all-day care did not necessarily go hand in hand with a pedagogical renewal of the school in general, which was pursued with the institution of all-day schools. This was a departure from important basic quality-related ideas of all-day schooling, which consisted of providing extended learning opportunities without distinguishing between morning and afternoon, and giving more space to activities outside the subject disciplines at the same time: in addition to the cognitive aspect, greater attention was to be paid to the emotional, motoric, and relational aspects of education and the diversification of teaching tools and creative activities (Capperucci/Piccioli 2015). However, the implementation of various teaching methods was largely left to the initiative of individual teachers or groups of teachers, like in the case of the "Pestalozzi school-city" (*Scuola-Città Pestalozzi*, founded in 1944) which focused on a child-centred approach, active participation, and the collaboration between teachers as in an educating community (Capperucci/Piccioli 2015: 37).

In 1990 a new reform introduced the plurality of teachers and the division of activities into so-called "modules" (Law 148). The reform represented a significant impetus towards collaboration between professionals, establishing the principle of the multi-class teacher (*insegnante multiclasse*): teachers were organised in teams, pedagogical-didactic responsibility was strengthened, thus emphasising the social and pedagogical value of all-day schools (Baur 2005). At the same time, the spread of all-day schools met with growing demand from families, indicating in this school model an answer to the working needs of parents. However, if the aim of the reform was to improve and diversify the quality of the educational offer, inevitably limited in the single teacher, the separation between morning and afternoon activities was underlined by a difference in status between "strong" teachers in the morning and "weak" ones engaged in the afternoon. Thus, the discrepancy between the ambitions of the all-day school and the legislative framework has weakened the principle of continuity between morning and afternoon activeties (Cerini 2004; Triani 2018). In 2003 a third reform abolished the concept of all-day schooling, creating a distinction between 27 hours of basic, compulsory teaching for all children and additional hours, up to a total of 40 hours (Law 53). As has been widely criticised, this reform explicitly restored the "after school" (*doposcuola*) distinguishing between morning and afternoon (Berti 2013). Finally, in 2007, a further reform – the one that defines the actual full-time model – has restored the so-called "single prevailing teacher" (*maestro unico prevalente*) while keeping the 27- or 40-hours option. This eliminated the hours shared between teachers, the possibility of working with small groups of children at the same time or dedicating time to individual learning needs, thus further undermining the collaboration among teachers, and more generally the quality of the didactic dimension of education.

Still, all-day school is currently the most popular model for families in Italy (Triani 2018: 226), but the national school landscape is mainly patchy and all-day schools coexist with half-day schools, with a prevalence of full-time provision by private educational establishments. There is, therefore, a return to after-school activities offered by private associations, either for a fee or supported by local or regional funds. Activities concern homework, sports, and arts, mostly disconnected from the morning school activities. In fact, the collaboration of teachers and externals is mainly left to the singular projects. School and extra-school remain more or less separate containers in Italy, which merely fulfil the simple organisation of care while parents are at work (Baur 2005: 78). Despite the fact that the concepts of an educating community and of "educational pacts between school and territory" (*patti educativi*) highlight the plurality of subjects that move around the school and place the child at the centre, they do not seem to solve the problem of optional participation in afternoon activities, accompanied by the risk that the originally focused compensatory mission is no longer fulfilled and especially children in weak socio-economic conditions are left out. Yet, as recently noted by Triani, there is a lack of research on all-day school, compared to the 1980s and 1990s, suggesting that the debate moved away from the pedagogical-didactic potential that inspired its institution (Triani 2018: 230).

2.2   All-Day-Primary-School in Germany

In Germany, instead, the half-day school model has dominated the discourse around primary schools up to the present, and all-day education was already advocated at the beginning of the 20th century in the context of reformist educational discourses and currents (Reh/Fritsche/Idel/Rabenstein 2015: 14). Here it was conceived, for example, by Paul Oestreich as an integrated school across all school levels (cf. Ludwig 2005; Geißler 2004). As an alternative to the cognitive one-sidedness of school reality of the 19th century, all-day-school was to be not only a place of learning but also a place of life and education for children and young people, whereby the concept of the forest school (*Waldschule*) was particularly associated with compensatory effectiveness for children living in poverty in big cities (Ludwig 2005). However, realisation tended to take place in the private school sector, while the state school remained a half-day school until childhood as a whole was strictly organised by the state under National Socialism. After the Second World War all-day schools were established only in East Germany (GDR; 1949-1989) from the 1950s/1960s onwards, although lessons were usually held in the morning. These were supplemented by educational activities in the afternoon, as well as a comprehensive range of after-school care centres (*Hort*), which had already been used by 85% of children of primary school age in the 1970s (Geißler 2004: 166) and combined state-compliant teaching and education. In West Germany (BRD), on the contrary, the half-day school model was politically favoured together with the male breadwinner model and the intention to distance oneself from GDR policies of state access to families. Consequently, both recommendations of the German Education Council for the establishment of all-day schools as early as the 1970s and the growing demand on the part of families went unconsidered for a long time. In the West German regions, the hesitant and regionally varying expansion of all-day schools only began in the 2000s.

Intensive research on all-day schooling in Germany therefore only began in the 2010s, with the StEG studies (*Studien zur Entwicklung von Ganztagsschulen*) in particular leading the way (Coelen/Stecher 2014; Rabenstein/Nerowski/Rahm 2015). The right of children to all-day schooling at primary school age has now been set for 2026 (BMFSJ 2021) and is linked with the politically motivated concern not only to make it easier for parents to reconcile work and family life, but above all to contribute to more educational justice (Staudner 2018: 67). Moreover, it is relevant to consider that the German school system is characterised by a particularly close link between social background and educational success at school in an international comparison (Ditton 2004, 2013). In this respect, the school itself contributes to a socially unequal distribution of educational opportunities – especially through the early and highly differentiated tracking system. In most of the federal states of Germany, all children are divided into different educational pathways after only four years of schooling (in two regions only after six years), with clearly diverging educational chances (Ackeren/Kühn 2017). Furthermore, a whole bundle of special schools is already provided at the primary level – despite the guaranteed human right to inclusive education, which has also been ratified in Germany (United Nations 2006). It has been shown that it is above all habitually induced divergences between normalcy-led expectations within schools, on the one hand, and varying family cultures and living conditions of children, on the other, that have a discriminatory effect in this respect (Edelstein 2006; Gomolla/Radtke 2007; Kramer/Helsper 2010; Panesar 2020).

In this context, all-day schools are expected to have a compensatory effect and to contribute to more educational justice by enabling access to education regardless of origin (Rabenstein/Nerowski/Rahm 2015; Reh/Fritzsche/Idel/Rabenstein 2015). In particular, varying affinities of families to extracurricular education and the often financially dependent access to cultural education are made relevant, as large socio-economic differences are evident here (Harring/Rohlfs/Palentien 2007; Toppe 2010; Fischer et al. 2011; Fischer/Kielbock 2021). In addition, support and qualified supervision of homework in the afternoon is often mentioned (Prüß 2008; Wiere 2011), thus remaining in the mental dichotomy of half-day school and afternoon provision. The state of research on the hoped-for effectiveness of all-day schooling in that regard is still unclear (Fischer et al. 2011; Wiere 2011). The conceptual innovation potential of the all-day structure in terms of an extended understanding of education and an educationally equitable up-bringing in the primary sector, which would go hand in hand with changed school cultures and school structures, does not (yet) seem to be realised in Germany as a whole (Staudner 2018: 84).

Thus, in the implementation of all-day education, it becomes clear that in Germany – similarly to Italy – additive structures in the pattern of "school in the morning" and "day care in the afternoon" have been established in the majority of cases. In the largest federal state, North Rhine-Westphalia, the additive structured "open all-day school" (*Offene Ganztagsschule*) with only facultative services in the afternoon is legally required; forms of compulsory all-day-schooling need the approval for each individual case by the upper school authority cases (*Schulgesetz NRW*, §9). Overall, in Germany, the framework conditions for all-day primary schooling are dramatically insufficient, which is why the lack of quality all-day school is the subject of various debates around the set right of children for 2026 (Fischer/Kielblock 2021).

2.3   Overarching challenges

Within the scientific discourse and regarding high quality all-day primary schools, there is widespread agreement on the above-mentioned aim of over-coming the separation of "lessons" in the morning and "care" in the afternoon (cf. Burow/Pauli 2006; Nordt 2017: 502; Staudner 2018) in favour of an all-day educational and living place. This is linked to an opening up of the content of the educational offer in the direction of more child-oriented forms of learning overall and the dissolution of traditional structures of time and space (Cerini 2004; Burow/Pauli 2006; Deckert-Peaceman 2006b; Derecik 2018).

A specific opportunity of integrating formal and non-formal education (Rauschenbach 2008) by dissolving the rigid distinctions between cognitive-oriented "morning education" and play-oriented "afternoon education" (Cerini 2004; Nordt 2017) seems to lie in providing impulses towards a more person-centred understanding of education that recognises children as agents and acting subjects. Such an expanded understanding of education would also strengthen the original profile of (inclusive) primary schools to be an oppor-tunity for all children to live and learn together democratically (Seitz 2014; Rabenstein/Nerowski/Rahm 2015; Reh/Fritzsche/Idel/Rabenstein 2015), following the paradoxical requirement to acquire the capacity for democracy through democracy as a social practice in educational institutions.

Due to changed family cultures and economic situations in both Germany and Italy, it can be assumed that all-day-school will become an even more essential instance of socialisation (Fölling-Albers 2003; Baader 2014) and thus the central living space of children during the next decade. In addition to the educational mandate, this requires a stronger focus on the needs of children at school. The questions of how children perceive all day school, what significance they attach to it, and how much freedom of choice they are given for shaping their lives must therefore be given greater attention in research-related contexts (cf. Deinet/Gumz/Muscutt/Thomas 2018; Deckert-Peaceman 2006a). For although children are increasingly included in school development processes and research on this subject (Müller-Kuhn et al. 2021), their perspective has so far only been rudimentarily taken up in the context of research on all-day schooling (Deckert-Peaceman 2006a; Enderlein 2015; Dzengel/Stein, 2015; Staudner 2018; Deinet/Gumz/Muscutt/ Thomas 2018; Walther/Nentwig-Gesemann/Fried 2021: 20). Available studies offer some indications of children's perceptions of high-quality all-day activities. This includes, above all, participation in terms of co-design of the all-day activities, including both lesson-oriented and leisure-time oriented activities (Sturzenhecker 2018; Sauerwein 2018). Also important are opportunities for peer activities as well as for positive pedagogical relationships, for being outside, motor activities and play, spatial retreat options and opportunities like engaging in distracting and relaxing or challenging situations (Staudner 2018: 190; Deinet/Gumz/Muscutt/Thomas 2018: 23; Walther/ Nentwig-Gesemann/Fried 2021). It is therefore to be asked how it is possible to come close to children's views and at the same time to consider the power-related difference between adult researchers and children of primary school age.

Particularly for the topic focused on here, it is, therefore, also important to reflect on one's own location in research disciplines since the question brings together school-related research and childhood studies (Kelle 2005; Heinzel 2005). Specific methodological challenges arising in this context can be seen, for example, in the different interpretations of children's views on afternoon activities by researchers. Walther and Nentwig-Gesemann (2021) highlight activities free of evaluation during the afternoon from the children's point of view and interpret this as a meaningful counterpart to school lessons, which they see as shaped by the pressure to compete and perform during the morning in general (p. 250). Regarding opportunities of participation, Deinet/ Gumz/Muscutt/Thomas (2018) as well as Sauerwein (2018) point out that children do not perceive spaces of non-formal and formal education as two separate spheres, but experience them as interconnected spheres of life (Deinet/Gumz/Muscutt/Thomas 2018: 16). Staudner shows the dependence of the children's perceptions of formal and non-formal education on the time structure of all-day schooling (Staudner 2018: 213; 217). It has also been shown that all-day schooling challenges primary-school children's capabilities to manage the different social roles as peers and as students (De Boer/ Deckert-Peaceman 2009).

Summarising and according to the state of the debate, the innovatory potential of all-day primary school unfolds mainly through the integration of formal and non-formal education in favour of an educational practice oriented towards the development of the personality as a whole. This includes a reflexive and constructive approach to inequity and diversity and conceives children as active citizens capable of taking action. Taking this up, the methodological design of a completed study conducted by us involves children's voices in the research process.

3   Methodological design

The study (2018–2021) focused on a project which pursued the aim of effectively fostering interprofessional collaboration and educational quality in five all-day primary schools in North Rhine-Westphalia. Initiated and funded by the Carl Richard Montag Foundation, collaboration between municipal steering, school administration, and Open All-day Schools (*Offene Ganztags-schulen*, hereafter OGS) was facilitated via a steering group. Furthermore, consulting, supervising, and training were offered for the personnel of the five OGS in the region over two years to promote collaboration and child-oriented educational practice. Finally, networking and exchange were specifically strengthened through learning trips to good practice examples ("OGS on Tour") as well as conferences ("OGS Academy").

The qualitative study collected the different perspectives of head teachers and all-day school coordinators as well as the views of teachers, pedagogical staff, counsellors, and children of the OGS participating in the project (for more details, see Seitz/Hamacher 2022; Kricke/Remy/Seitz/Hamacher 2022).

In this contribution we discuss in-depth the views of children with a focus on the described aspects related to educational justice in the context of all-day schooling. By focusing on the children's narrations (cf. Wagener 2012: 9; Deinet/Gumz/Muscutt/Thomas 2018: 14), we can capture their views on all-day school and discuss them with regard to the imbalances highlighted above.

In order to get closer to the perspective of children, interviews with children (n=18) were conducted, accompanied by observations, evaluated by relying on methodologies of childhood studies (Zeiher 1996; Fölling-Albers/Schwarzmeier 2005; Heinzel 2012; Joos/Betz/Bollig/Neumann 2018) and being inspired by the *Mosaic Approach* (Clark/Moss 2001; 2005). Both approaches claim to perceive children as actors in their own lives and thus as subjects capable of providing information about their point of view, as we explain in the following.

Viewing children as "actors" can be seen as a shared idea of childhood research at both the empirical and theoretical levels (cf. Betz/Eßer 2016: 303;

Baader 2014). As a "new" view of children and childhood, the agency concept was developed and unfolded its impact in diverse areas of childhood
studies during the last decades (cf. Zeiher 1996; Breidenstein/Kelle 1996;
Alanen 2005; Sgritta 2005: 63). Methodological challenges were intensively
discussed in this context (cf. Heinzel 2012; Rüsing 2006). With the self-
critical question of power relations in intergenerational relationships, previous marginalisations of children in research on childhood were uncovered,
and the commitment of researchers to children's participation in social
contexts has been strengthened (cf. Hengst/Zeiher 2005: 11).

The claim to involve children in research processes in a participatory way
is particularly and impressively evident in the United Nations Convention on
the Rights of the Child (UN CRC; United Nations 1989). With the stipulated
right to expression in Articles 12 and 13, childhood research is also called
upon to actively include children's perspectives in research processes. Along
with an emancipatory perspective, methodological questions about children's
ability to provide information were set in motion. Hereby, the purpose was to
adapt methods in childhood research to the peculiarities of children and to
involve them more in the processes (cf. Hengst/Zeiher 2005). Such a change
of paradigm moved the focus from a human-becoming to human-being
understanding and enabled children to emerge as "active members of a
society" (Honig 1999). As a result, they are to be understood as subjects
capable of providing information about their own lifeworld (cf. Clark/Moss
2001; Butschi/Hedderich, 2021: 104).

From here, a micro-sociological approach is used as a basis for a subject-
centred perspective, with which the everyday actions of children can be
recorded reconstructively via ethnographic and sociological methods (cf.
Heinzel 2012; Schütz/Böhm 2021). In doing so, "pedagogical improvisa-
tions" in the research process allow us to consider children's age and
differences regarding competence (e.g., language) (cf. Schütz/Böhm 2021).
Following the Mosaic Approach, which we also rely on (Clark/Moss 2001,
2005, 2011; Clark/Statham 2005), even very young children can be given
opportunities to express themselves, communicate and actively participate in
the research process through a variety of communication channels. The
approach – combining different types of data like photographs taken by
children, focus groups, interviews, and observation – offers a deeper
understanding of their perspectives on their own lifeworld. This way, the
approach claims to represent a multi-layered picture of children's perceptions
of the world around them. In doing so, children's heterogeneous life worlds
are considered in the research process.

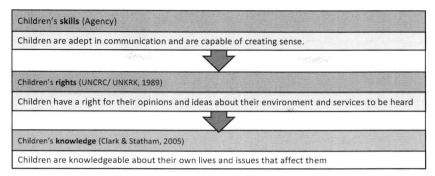

Figure 1:   Framework for Mosaic research (Adapted from Clark/Moss 2001; Rogers 2018: 3)

In such a framework, the child's perspective is not understood as a description of reality in a positivist sense. Rather, it is a matter of inferring subjective interpretations of reality that are communicated in a specific, structurally shaped social interaction between child and adult (Honig 1999: 45). A limitation associated with this is that finally corresponding research findings thus inform us first and foremost about how an adult understands the voices of children (see above). Summarising, different innovative research strategies are therefore bundled in our study to meet the multi-methodological requirement of the research topic (cf. Schütz/Böhm 2021: 174).

4   Children in all-day primary schools

Below, we draw on and reconstruct individual passages from the children's interviews to eventually relate them to the theoretical framework.

4.1   Child-orientation and autonomy in all-day primary school

In the following, two sequences from the interview with Hedda are reconstructed. She attends the fourth grade of an all-day primary school of the project. The interview excerpts are divided into two parts.

Shortly before, the interviewer had asked about the course of a day at the OGS.

Interviewer: And then what are you doing there?

Hedda: Maths, German, Religion, Science, Arts, Sports. Yes.

Interviewer: Then you've already told us a lot about your lessons. What do you like to do most?

Hedda: Maths, I like Maths a lot. German, I like / so actually I like everything, just Maths and German the most.

Interviewer: And why?

Hedda: Well, I like Maths the most because I can do arithmetics and I particularly enjoy it. I can't describe it exactly now, but well. And German I think is also fun, because (3) yes.

Interviewer: And is there also something you don't like to do at school?

Hedda: No, so only when I'm in a bad mood or had a fight or something. Then I don't feel like going to school, but otherwise I really like doing it.

Interviewer: And why are you not in OG (facultative afternoon) anymore?

Hedda: Well, I didn't like the food that much. First, I had a lot of fun. I didn't know all the equipment and so on, but now I know them all and I got bored and then I was always there and didn't have any fun anymore. And then mom didn't want to pay for it anymore and then I didn't feel like it.

Hedda responds that she likes Maths and German the most at OGS and adds that she actually likes everything but Maths the most because she can do arithmetic there and she particularly enjoys it. It is noticeable that the verb "can" in comparison to "must" rather refers to a voluntary activity. Thus, Hedda is granted or perceives a corresponding scope of autonomy in the context of learning mathematics. Also, the term "fun" is mentioned, with which free and creative activities can be implied. This can be seen as motivating as well because the activity implies fun-related challenges. Furthermore, since Hedda cannot describe it exactly, she immediately draws attention to an experience that has a strong implicit character and therefore cannot be made explicit. In this respect, it is a matter of incorporated, atheoretical knowledge (Bohnsack 2017), which she brings up here.

The statement about basically learning with fun refers to the fact that quarrels and bad moods are an exception. On the other hand, it is expressed that the mood is not detached from the lessons and the sense of fun. It can be assumed that the school atmosphere and respectful interaction among children can increase the joy of going to school and thus influence the learning culture in an OGS.

Interviewer: Then when you were still in the OG, what did you do here?

Hedda: Well, the routine of the OG is a bit like this: first, we play, then we do homework and eat. So, there's also the other way around, only on some days it's like this, then we eat, after that there's homework and then we play the whole time. Sometimes we also did experiments, but that was only very rarely. Yes.

[...]

Hedda: Well, I liked to draw, play Lego, doodle a little bit on the blackboard. Yes.

Interviewer: So, what do you like to do with your friends here at school all day?

Hedda: Well, during the break I like to play. Then I tell them something or I climb, or yeah.

Interviewer: Do you like going to school?

Hedda: Yes, very much.

[…]

Interviewer: Do you have a wish?

Hedda: Maybe that just all the kids enjoy school.

When asked what she did at the beginning of the OGS, she describes a sequence of events that could resemble a timetable. She explicitly begins with "So" which indicates a narrative and enumerates the order of activities: "First we play, then we do homework and eat". The fact that play is lined up like a task suggests that it is perceived as a normative part of school life. This leads to the hypothesis that she is positioning herself here in the role of a student in the afternoon as well. School patterns of order thus seem to continue in the afternoon and are also handed down by children in this way (Deckert-Peaceman 2009: 100). At this point, the question is how free activities are regulated in all-day school (Sauerwein 2018). Free activity finds justification in the OG and thus presupposes the expectation that Hedda can have fun there. At the same time, however, very similar aspects of joy and fun are also attributed to the subject-oriented learning activities (see above).

The second part expresses a criticism of free activity being hindered by standardised procedures. Autonomy, freedom of design in learning processes, and voluntariness in situations of learning are also reflected here, this time in relation to OG (the afternoon) but in a different way. When the interviewer asks why Hedda is no longer in the OG, she first answers that she did not like the food. Yet later she explains that at the beginning she had a lot of fun there – "first" could indicate a time reference like 'in the beginning'. Afterwards she refers to the beginning and explains that she didn't know all the "see above and such", but now (present tense) they have become boring and therefore she didn't have fun there anymore. As above, fun thus seems to be mainly in contrast to boredom and is fulfilled by varied activities that are not characterised by repetition nor by successive procedures that are predictable.

This description of Hedda refers to a critique of the all-day school from the perspective of a student and seems to be a "willful" process of positioning herself as a student who is no longer part of the all-day structure. Nevertheless, this is only possible for her because she has had the freedom of choice – or at least it seems to be like that because it is not clear whether the decision to no longer participate in the optional afternoon programme was made by her or her mother. Following her narration, she can leave and re-enter the field and thus oscillate between participation and exclusion from afternoon-care.

In any case, it is noticeable that she mentions the devices and facilities of the all-day programme but talks less about friendships and the opportunity to be with peers during afternoon activities in OGS, which many other interviewed children pointed out in our study. Thus, it appears that she seems to be exploring the process of being (seen as) a peer and a student at the same time, so that the "backstage" (managing social roles) becomes the "frontstage", which has also been shown to be relevant in existing studies (e.g., Deckert-Peaceman 2009; De Boer 2009). From this perspective, the interview could also point to the internalisation of the role of a schoolgirl. This also seems to reflect standardised types of learning where interest and willingness to discuss is limited. This suggests that Hedda has a desire to be self-directed in her learning and to engage with issues and questions in an atmosphere of recognition and social affiliation – across all activities from morning to afternoon in OGS.

Taking this up it can be said that the all-day programme has the potential to offer children the opportunity for self-directed learning and exploring with friends. However, Hedda's assertions show that the potential does not yet seem to be exploited. With a view to the aim of creating educational justice through all-day school (Züchner/Fischer 2014), the question arises to what extent the afternoon is at risk of being subjected to school regulations and output orientation. Following Hedda's narration, it could be assumed that afternoon activities tend to be realised as standardised playful activities, which meets her resistance. Regarding the policy-related goal of strengthening educational justice by all-day-school structures with a compensating approach, it can be assumed that the perspective of formal education seems to dominate and to influence types of non-formal education in this facultative structure of all-day school. Here, the contradiction between compulsory morning activities, which Hedda associates with joy and fun, and voluntary participation in afternoon activities, whose structure she criticises, seems to complicate the situation.

This seems to be reinforced when participation in education is thought of in terms of performance-enhancement. The idea of reducing inequities by improving performance seems to lead to an increasing focus on competence in the entire school day while friendship, play, and pleasure seem to move into the background – which is criticised here by Hedda. It is therefore necessary to ask how educational conditions such as participation, voluntariness, and subject formation can be given a stronger focus. This could succeed together with a socio-educational perspective that focuses on subject formation in relation to empowerment for autonomy (cf. Rother 2019: 107).

In trying to gain a better understanding of children's experience of time and space at an OGS, a further aspect emerges concerning their feeling good, namely well-being at all-day school.

4.2   Feeling good all day through

In this interview passage, Samuel, fourth grade, expresses his perception of all-day school in a particularly vivid way.

Interviewer: Can you describe your day in OGS?

Samuel: First we go in the morning circle [...]. Right after the morning circle they tell us what to do. We go back to our seats and do the tasks and sometimes there are also tasks that we do with others, I think it's called a reading conference. And there we do something on our table, mark our texts and ask each other questions about that text. Then we learn during the day and then we have a breakfast break, then a break and then we play games, which I think is great. Well, students who are still new have to find their way around first but then they're fine, that's how it was for me too. And when the break is over, we go back to class, and we're supposed to be on time. And then we do what the teacher tells us from her seat. And actually, that's how it is, that we then learn on our own. And then we have a break, we play again and on all days except Tuesday and Friday we continue learning after the break. Except, for example, today and Friday, when we simply have free time after the big break, that is, after the second break, which is longer. And when we have lessons, on Mondays or so, we go back to class and do what she tells us to do, which is not so creative, so we tend to stick to learning [...]. Sometimes we do other things, even art, and maybe when we've done a page, we do something else that's maybe nicer, that the children like more or that they have more fun with, I think. I think that the children have a lot of fun with sports, art, and swimming [...]. We also have afternoon care and many clubs (OG), which I also find very nice. And there is yoga, programming, gardening, everything that is very important for me and for children and that is just very great.

Interviewer: Is there also something you don't like so much?

Samuel: I don't like English so much because it is often just learning what toys mean and stuff. I would like to learn what to say at work, when you write a song and stuff like that. And I just don't think that toys are that important.

Interviewer: Can you tell me three wishes you could think about, to make your school a better school?

Samuel: My wish would be that we all play together, the whole school ... that everyone plays together, so even more. It's often the case that the class plays together. And sometimes a few classes argue and say that their class is better, and I would like that to change. What else I would wish for, that is a similar wish, that everyone loves each other, and everyone feels good. The third wish is that we all help everyone else too, when the whole school is playing and one is out, that everyone goes to him and asks him what is wrong if we want to help him. That would also be a wish that I/ I just don't know how to say it.

When asked about OGS, Samuel does not name contents or topics like Hedda did but the power to decide about them. The mentioned circle-time seems to be perceived as a transition between a time phase in which children can decide for themselves and contribute content and time phases in which they are exposed to the decisions of others (Heinzel 2016). The morning circle is followed by a time phase that Samuel cannot decide for himself. For then, as he describes, "they tell us" what they are supposed to do, as opposed to learning that involves the children's interests. The unspecific "they" refers to an organisational knowledge of role-related decision-making power in OGS. The pattern "adults say what children have to do" seems to determine the experience of teaching. There is no clear criticism of the fact that there are adults who tell children what to do, but the consequences of this are described: children depend on adults to make educational decisions that are in their best interest.

In terms of learning, therefore, a distinction is made between working on "pages; getting done", which refers to working the whole time, and activities that for Samuel are associated with freedom for creativity and fun such as swimming and art. Samuel is obviously referring to classroom learning here. Here, working is juxtaposed with creative activity and fun as a negative counter-horizon. From here, the thread continues to educational activities that are attributed to "afternoon care", such as programming, gardening, etc. Samuel affirms that whenever activities meet a child's own interest – "something that the children like more or that they have more fun with" – their pleasure is higher, and they are thus more involved. This is particularly the case when a topic is offered "that is very important for me and for children and that is just very great", like experience-based activities. In his description, Samuel does not distinguish between morning and afternoon activities but repeatedly makes a distinction between him as a person and his point of view, on the one hand, and "children" on a generalised level, on the other. Here, he takes on the role of speaking on behalf of children about what moves and motivates them. This is also implicit in his criticism of English lessons. For him "toys" are an unmotivating content and he firmly states his wish for what he considers appropriate and important content for primary school children: how to communicate at work and songwriting. He had already expressed this just as clearly for yoga, programming, etc.: "everything that is very important for me and for children".

He describes in detail what, from his point of view, enables children to learn in a motivated way: he calls for turning away from working through worksheets, for learning in serious situations, for taking creativity and movement into account. He associates this learning with fun and meaningfulness.

Samuel's narratives and reflections lead us to the hypothesis that in the primary school day as a whole, opportunities for co-determination about the design of educational activities are a central orientation, regardless of whether this can be structurally attributed to the sphere of "teaching" or "care". Instead, in the interviews we did with the adults, the dichotomy of all-day school is conceived often since a clear separation between the morning and the afternoon (Seitz/Hamacher 2022) can be found: as in a taxonomy, this over-category encapsulates activities, which are themselves appropriate or inappropriate according to A or B. A is generally the time to learn and B the leisure activities (i.e., the break and the activities in the afternoon).

Summarising, listening to the children's voices, the essence of meaningful activities, the pleasure linked to an activity, which allows creativity and therefore the pleasure of being at OGS is put into focus. What emerges here can be seen as the quality of the experience (Dewey 1938), of children in OGS beyond a dichotomy of morning and afternoon. If we take the experience as a reciprocal interaction of an individual with the environment, opposed to "making an experience", "having an experience" is characterised by emotions and implies a final fulfilment. Referring to a child in all-day school to simply say that they "make experiences" does not imply that these are educative. An experience should thus have the quality to arouse curiosity, strengthen initiative and "set up desires and purposes that are sufficiently intense to carry a person over dead places in the future". When in the interaction with the environment the individual's internal condition and his previous experiences "intercept and unite", then also interaction is in place. Only in this case does the experience become a moving force for the child and they do *have* an experience (Dewey 1938: 24), in other words, an experience that is qualitatively significant. For Samuel, such quality has to do with the own interest, creativity, fun, real-life-situations and the meaningfulness of content. The school is experienced in all its spaces, indeed, whenever there is the possibility to explore and education is experienced as playing freely.

From here, it can be said that Samuel points out the importance of play for quality, child-centred education in all-day schools, since during play, a child is devoted to the game on its own will and for its own pleasure, choosing "silence, meditation, idle solitude or creative activity" (Caillois 1981: 22). This highlights the pleasure dimension of immersing oneself in an activity with interest and the lightness needed to feel good, also in relationships between peers.

5   Concluding discussion and perspectives

Summarising it can be said that the children's perspectives shed light on some meaningful ambivalences within all-day schooling.

From a methodological point of view, our findings indicate that it is not sufficient to reconstruct contrasting spheres of formal education (in the classroom) and non-formal education (in after-school care) in the empirical approach to all-day primary school from the children's perspectives, as they do not distinguish in this regard. Approaching a child-appropriate all-day school is possibly more related to the challenge of empirically grasping both spheres simultaneously in their interaction in order to be able to approach the children's perspective in the first place.

In light of the educational justice outlined at the beginning, our findings imply bringing together the children's self-determination with the adults' attention to a dimension of well-being appropriate to a play-oriented concept-tion of OGS in general. For teachers and educators, this means recognising and encouraging creative actions performed through play as an educational practice, and creating a climate of recognition and attention to the stories and suggestions that come from the children. On a concrete level this would mean, for example, the shared planning of activities with children and adults to meet their interests. The all-day school offers a high potential for such planning since it offers a more relaxed time during morning and afternoon for being together – and also more spaces for moments not mediated by the adults.

On a structural level, an optional format of the afternoon as opposed to a compulsory morning activity (OGS), which is often seen in socio-educational discourse as fundamental to the conception of all-day schooling (Sauerwein 2018), can be questioned as it raises aspects of inequity in terms of children's choice or non-choice of participation (Sauerwein 2019; see below), as reconstructed from Hedda's narratives. This seems to lead to some paradoxes. For as can be read in the political discourse, the further development of all-day schooling is primarily about reducing inequality through more effective promotion of children's competencies, specifically of children who are seen as being situated in disadvantaged living conditions. Hedda's reflections lead us, on the one hand, to the hypothesis that this narrow focus towards achieve-ment and educational success of children as "good" students may be a barrier for a child-oriented quality of all-day schooling because this way the recogni-tion of children as personalities who are recognised as subjects within educational processes may move into the background. On the other hand, it can be questioned if the voluntary nature of the afternoon at the level of implementation does not lead to more participation of the children in the sense of having a real choice but rather undermines it, as they act as family members on that level and different life situations play a role here (see also Sauerwein 2018).

Accordingly, Samuel's voice suggests that children have a positive attitude towards educational processes as being playful in OGS in the sense of positioning himself as a motivated learner if meaning can be found in the activity and the opportunity for creativity and participation is given. Following him, children seem to benefit from formats in which they can actively engage with the subject in a self-determined manner and in a respectful learning atmosphere. However, this requires that participation in education is no longer oriented toward the standardised acquisition of skills, as it was stated above for Germany, which implies goal-oriented support. Instead, all-day schools are called upon to emphasise educational processes in which children are recognised as personalities and can combine formal and informal learning in new child-oriented formats (Staudner 2018: 222).

However, the organisation of OGS is not detached from the hidden agenda of compensation along standardised educational expectations, as our results show from the children's point of view. Research on competencies and on performance-enhancing effects of all-day participation (cf. Sauerwein/ Heer 2020) show the impact of narrowing the concept of education towards a competence-oriented outcome with a view to educational success, while participation as a fundamental goal is given less attention (cf. Rother 2021: 100). This is linked with the responsibility for education throughout the day being left to the families, as it is their responsibility to decide whether to participate in the all-day programme or not, while hidden motives (such as lack of money) remain concealed. At the same time, the normative claim of competence orientation and the claim of self-determined learning processes, in which children move into the centre as active actors, stand isolated next to each other, and the latter is seen by children as particularly significant.

Regarding the introduction of the legal right to all-day care at primary school age in Germany, it must be asked how the children's right to play can be secured. The accompanied completion of homework so often positively emphasised in political and academic discourse about educational justice in the children's views is negatively connotated and linked with a lack of participation – as our analyses show and as has already been shown in different studies (e.g., Deckert-Peaceman 2009; Staudner 2018). It is obvious, however, that the conclusion not to offer children any educational support in the afternoon but to let them follow their interests on their own responsibility falls short as teachers and educators are responsible gatekeepers for children's educational success (Becker/Birkelbach 2013) and children cannot be made solely responsible for their learning (Stojanov 2011). It also turns out that a one-sided orientation towards formal education throughout the day goes hand in hand with positioning children mainly as students and neglects their role as children and peers, to which the children react with resistance and criticism, as described by Hedda and Samuel. Conversely, the vivid descriptions of an all-day school of well-being, where children feel recognised and "everyone plays together", as described by Samuel, point to the potential of linking formal and non-formal education in a child-centred way. This would then contribute to educational justice by recognising all children as personalities endowed with equal rights – to education and to play – and equal basic needs – for social belonging and for the unfolding of potentials. Being recognised as capable of creating sense and knowledge of one's own life then also means to be recognised as a person who is reliant on space to develop within institutions. That means that educational institutions are to be taken into responsibility for education in a broad sense.

In this way, the institution of all-day school could make a developmental leap towards an institution for children that focuses on participation, play and meaningful learning. And these aspects could possibly – despite the differences between the two educational systems – provide guidance for both Germany and Italy.

References

Ackeren, Isabell van/Kühn, Svenja M. (2017): Homogenität und Heterogenität im Schulsystem. In: Bohl, Thorsten/Budde, Jürgen/Rieger-Ladich, Markus (eds.): Studienbuch Umgang mit Heterogenität in Schule und Unterricht. Bad Heilbrunn: Klinkhardt, pp. 175–190.

Alanen, Leena (1992): Modern Childhood? Exploring the 'Child question' in Sociology. Publication Series A. Research Reports 50. Jyvaskyla: University of Jyvaskyla, Institute for Educational Research.

Alanen, Leena (2005): Kindheit als generationales Konzept. In: Hengst, Heinz/Zeiher, Helga (eds.): Kindheit soziologisch. Wiesbaden: VS Verlag für Sozialwissenschaften, pp. 65–82.

Allemann-Ghionda, Christina (2009): Ganztagsschule im europäischen Vergleich. Zeitpolitiken modernisieren – durch Vergleich Standards setzen? In: Stecher, Ludwig/Allemann-Ghionda, Christina/Helsper, Werner/Klieme, Eckhard (eds.): Ganztägige Bildung und Betreuung. Zeitschrift für Pädagogik, Beiheft 54. Weinheim: Beltz, pp. 190–208.

Allemann-Ghionda, Christina (2013): Bildung für alle, Diversität und Inklusion: Internationale Perspektiven. Leiden: Schöningh.

Baader, Meike S. (2014): Die reflexive Kindheit (1968-2000). In: Baader, Meike S./Eßer, Florian/Schröe, Wolfgang (eds.): Kindheiten in der Moderne. Eine Geschichte der Sorge. Frankfurt: Campus, pp. 414–455.

Baader, Meike (2016): Tracing and contextualising childhood agency and generational order from historical and systematic perspectives. In: Esser, Florian/Baader, Meike S./Betz, Tanja/Hungerland, Tanja (eds.): Reconceptualising Agency and Childhood. New Perspectives in Childhood Studies. Oxfordshire: Routledge, pp. 135–150.

Baur, Siegfried (2005): Verlängerte Unterrichtszeit in Italien. In: Otto, Hans-Uwe/Coelen, Thomas (eds.): Ganztägige Bildungssysteme – Innovation durch Vergleich. Münster: Waxmann, pp. 73–80.

Becker, Dominik/Birkelbach, Klaus (2013): Lehrer als Gatekeeper? Eine theoriegeleitete Annäherung an Determinanten und Folgen prognostischer Lehrerurteile. In: Becker, Rolf/Schulze, Alexander (eds.): Bildungskontexte. Strukturelle Voraussetzungen und Ursachen ungleicher Bildungschancen. Wiesbaden: Springer, pp. 207–237.

Bellin, Nicole/Tamke, Fanny (2010): Bessere Leistungen durch Teilnahme am offenen Ganztagsbetrieb? In: Empirische Pädagogik 24, 2, pp. 93–112.

Beher, Karin/Hänisch, Hans/Hermens, Claudia/Nordt, Gabriele/Prein, Gerald/Schulz, Uwe (eds.) (2007): Die offene Ganztagsschule in der Entwicklung. Empirische Befunde zum Primarbereich in Nordrhein-Westfalen. Weinheim: Beltz Juventa.

Berti, Maria Cristina (2013): La buona scuola: l'esperienza del tempo pieno nella scuola primaria. In: Roni, Riccardo (ed.): Le competenze del politico. Persone, ricerca, lavoro, comunicazione. Place: Firenze University Press, pp. 77–80.

Betz, Tanja/Eßer, Florian (2016): Kinder als Akteure – Forschungsbezogene Implikationen des erfolgreichen Agency-Konzepts. In: Diskurs Kindheits- und Jugendforschung 11, 3, pp. 301–314.

Bohnsack, Ralf (2017): Praxeologische Wissenssoziologie. München: UTB.

Breidenstein, Georg/Kelle, Helga (1996): Kinder als Akteure. Ethnographische Ansätze in der Kindheitsforschung. In: Zeitschrift für Sozialisationsforschung und Erziehungssoziologie 16, 1, pp. 47–67.

Breidenstein, Georg/Prengel, Annelore (2005): Schulforschung und Kindheitsforschung – ein Gegensatz? Wiesbaden: VS Verlag.

Burow, Olaf-Axel/Pauli, Bettina (2006): Ganztagsschule entwickeln. Von der Unterrichtsanstalt zum Kreativen Feld. Schwalbach: Wochenschau Verlag.

Butschi, Corinne/Hedderich, Ingeborg (2021): Kindheit und Kindheitsforschung im Wandel. In: Hedderich, Ingeborg/Reppin, Jeanne/Butschi, Corinne (Eds.): Perspektiven auf Vielfalt in der frühen Kindheit. Mit Kindern Diversität erforschen. Bad Heilbrunn: Klinkhardt, pp. 19–40.

Caillois, Roger (1981): I giochi e gli uomini. La Maschera e la vertigine. Milano: Bompiani.

Cambi, Franco (2003): Manuale di storia della pedagogia. Gius: Laterza.

Cerini, Giancarlo (2004): Il tempo scuola come variabile pedagogica. In: Catarsi, Enzo (ed.): La scuola a tempo pieno in Italia. Una grande utopia. Pisa: Edizioni del Cerro, pp. 58–83.

Capperucci, Davide/Piccioli, Marianna (2015): L'insegnante di scuola primaria. Identità, competenze e profilo professionale. Milano: FrancoAngeli.

Clark, Alison/Moss, Peter (2001): Listening to Young Children. The mosaic approach. London: National Children's Bureau.

Clark, Alison/Moss, Peter (2005): Spaces to Play. More listening to young children using the Mosaic approach. London: National Children's Bureau.

Clark, Alison/Moss, Peter (2011): Listening to Young Children. The mosaic approach. (2nd ed.). London: National Children's Bureau.

Clark, Alison/Statham, June (2005): Listening to young children. Experts in their own lives. In: Adoption and Fostering 29, 1 pp. 45–56.

Coelen, Thomas/Stecher, Ludwig (2014): Die Ganztagsschule. Eine Einführung. Weinheim: Beltz.

Dalhaus, Eva (2011): Bildung zwischen Institution und Lebenswelt. Zur Differenz von lebensweltlicher Bildungspraxis und schulischer Leistungsanforderung. In: Zeitschrift für Soziologie der Erziehung und Sozialisation 31, 2, pp. 117–135.

Damiano, Elio (2003): Idee di scuola a confronto. Un bilancio. In: Damiano, Elio (ed.): Idee di scuola a confronto. Contributo alla storia del riformismo scolastico in Italia. Roma: Armando Editore, pp. 239–288.

De Boer, Heike/Deckert-Peaceman, Heike (2009): Kinder in der Schule. Zwischen Gleichaltrigenkultur und schulischer Ordnung. Wiesbaden: VS Verlag.

De Boer, Heike (2006): Ganztagsschule als soziales Ereignis. In: Burk, Karlheinz/ Deckert-Peaceman, Heike (eds.): Auf dem Weg zur Ganztags-Grundschule. Frankfurt: Grundschulverband, pp. 55-66.

De Boer, Heike (2009): Peersein und Schülersein – ein Prozess des Ausbalancierens. In: De Boer, Heike/Deckert-Peaceman, Heike (eds.): Kinder in der Schule. Zwischen Gleichaltrigenkultur und schulischer Ordnung. Wiesbaden: VS Verlag, pp. 105–117.

Deckert-Peaceman, Heike (2006a): Ganztagsschule aus der Perspektive von Kindern. In Burk, Karl-Heinz (ed.): Auf dem Weg zur Ganztags-Grundschule. Frankfurt am Main: Grundschulverband (pp. 114–125).

Deckert-Peaceman, Heike (2006b): Raum und Räume in der Ganztagsschule. In: Burk, Karlheinz/Deckert-Peaceman, Heike (eds.): Auf dem Weg zur Ganztags-Grundschule. Frankfurt a.M.: Grundschulverband, pp. 90-100.

Deckert-Peaceman, Heike (2009): Zwischen Unterricht, Hausaufgaben und Freizeit. Über das Verhältnis von Peerkultur und schulischer Ordnung in der Ganztags-schule. In: De Boer, Heike/Deckert-Peaceman, Heike (eds.): Kinder in der Schule. Zwischen Gleichaltrigenkultur und schulischer Ordnung. Wiesbaden: VS Verlag, pp. 85–103.

Deinet, Ulrich/Gumz, Heike/Muscutt, Christina/Thomas, Sophie (2018): Offene Ganztagsschule – Schule als Lebensort aus Sicht der Kinder. Studie, Bausteine, Methodenkoffer. Opladen: Budrich.

Derecik, Ahmet (2018): Bedarfe und Möglichkeiten bei der Gestaltung von Bewe-gungs-, Spiel- und Ruheräumen in Ganztagsgrundschulen – Folgerungen aus der Studie „Offene Ganztagsschule aus Sicht der Kinder". In: Deinet, Ulrich/Gumz, Heike/Muscutt, Christina/Thomas, Sophie (eds.): Offene Ganztagsschule – Schu-le als Lebensort aus Sicht der Kinder. Studie, Bausteine, Methodenkoffer. Op-laden: Budrich, pp. 113–136.

Dewey, John (1910): How We Think. Boston: Heath & Co.

Dewey, John (1938): Experience and education. New York: Kappa Delta Pi.

Dewey, John (2000): Demokratie und Erziehung: Eine Einleitung in die philosophi-sche Pädagogik. Weinheim: Beltz (1949).

Ditton, Hartmut (2004): Der Beitrag von Schule und Lehrern zur Reproduktion von Bildungsungleichheit. In Becker, Rolf/Lauterbach, Wolfgang (eds.): Bildung als Privileg? Erklärungen und Befunde zu den Ursachen der Bildungsungleichheit. Wiesbaden: VS, pp. 251–279.

Ditton, Hartmut (2013): Kontexteffekte und Bildungsungleichheit. Mechanismen und Erklärungsmuster. In: Becker, Rolf/Schulze, Alexander (eds.): Bildungskontexte.

Strukturelle Voraussetzungen und Ursachen ungleicher Bildungschancen. Wiesbaden: Springer VS, pp. 173-206.

Dzengel, Jessica/Stein, Doreen (2015): Zur Schülersicht auf Freizeitangebote im offenen Ganztag. In: Reh, Sabine/Fritzsche, Bettina/Idel, Till-Sebastian/Rabenstein, Kerstin (eds.): Lernkulturen. Rekonstruktion pädagogischer Praktiken an Ganztagsschulen. Wiesbaden: Springer VS, pp. 283–296.

Edelstein, Wolfgang (2006): Bildung und Armut. Der Beitrag des Bildungssystems zur Vererbung und zur Bekämpfung von Armut. In: Zeitschrift für Soziologie der Erziehung und Sozialisation 26, 2, pp. 120–134.

Edelstein, Wolfgang (2007): Der Beitrag der Ganztagsschule zur Überwindung von Armut und Entwicklungsdefiziten. In: Kahl, Heike/Knauer, Sabine (eds.): Bildungschancen in der neuen Ganztagsschule. Lernmöglichkeiten verwirklichen. Weinheim: Beltz, pp. 30–45.

Enderlein, Oggi (2015): Schule ist meine Welt. Ganztagsschule aus Sicht der Kinder. Berlin: Deutsche Kinder- und Jugendstiftung. https://www.dkjs.de/fileadmin/ Redaktion/Dokumente/news/Themenheft-08-we150331_b.pdf.

Fischer, Nathalie/Holtappels, Heinz Günther/Klieme, Eckhard/Rauschenbach, Thomas/Stecher, Ludwig/Züchner, Ivo (eds.) (2011): Ganztagsschule. Entwicklung, Qualität, Wirkungen. Längsschnittliche Befunde der Studie zur Entwicklung von Ganztagsschulen (StEG). Weinheim: Beltz Juventa.

Fischer, Natalie/Kielblock, Stephan (2021): Was leistet die Ganztagsschule? Grundlagen, Designs und Ergebnisse der Ganztagsschulforschung. In: Hascher, Tina/ Idel, Till-Sebastian/Helsper, Werner (eds.): Handbuch Schulforschung. Wiesbaden: SpringerVS, pp. 1–21.

Fölling-Albers, Maria (2003): Grundschulpädagogik, Grundschulforschung und Kindheit. In: Panagiotopoulou, Argyro/Brügelmann, Hans (eds.): Grundschulpädagogik meets Kindheitsforschung. Opladen: Leske + Budrich, pp. 34–43.

Fölling-Albers, Maria/Schwarzmeier, Katja (2005): Schulische Lernerfahrungen aus der Perspektive von Kindern – Empirische Grundschulforschung mit Methoden der Kindheitsforschung. In: Breidenstein, Georg/Prengel, Annedore (eds.): Schulforschung und Kindheitsforschung – ein Gegensatz? (pp. 95–115) Wiesbaden: VS Verlag für Sozialwissenschaften.

Friebertshäuser, Barbara (2008): Verstehen und Anerkennen. Aspekte pädagogischer Beziehungen in Schule und außerschulischer Jugendarbeit. In Henschel, Angelika/Krüger, Rolf/Schmitt, Christof/Stange, Waldemar (eds.): Jugendhilfe und Schule. Handbuch für eine gelingende Kooperation (pp. 113–124). Wiesbaden: VS.

Fukkink, Ruben/Boogaard, Marianne (2020): Pedagogical quality of after-school care. Relaxation and/or enrichment? In: Children and Youth Services Review 112, 104903.

Geißler, Gert (2004): Ganztagsschule in der DDR. In: Appel, Stefan/Ludwig, Harald/ Rother, Ulrich/Rutz, Georg (eds.): Investitionen in die Zukunft. Schwalbach: Wochenschau-Verlag, pp. 160–170.

Gomolla, Mechthild/Radtke, Frank-Olaf (2007): Institutionelle Diskriminierung. Die Herstellung ethnischer Differenz in der Schule. Wiesbaden: Verlag für Sozialwissenschaften.

Harring, Marius/Rohlfs, Carsten/Palentien, Christian (eds.)(2007): Perspektiven der Bildung. Kinder und Jugendliche in formellen, nicht-formellen und informellen Bildungsprozessen. Wiesbaden: VS Verlag für Sozialwissenschaften.

Heinzel, Friederike (2005): Kindheit irritiert Schule – Über Passungsversuche in einem Spannungsfeld. In: Breidenstein, Georg/Prengel, Annedore (eds.): Schulforschung und Kindheitsforschung – ein Gegensatz? Wiesbaden, pp. 37–54.

Heinzel, Friederike (2011): Kindgemäßheit oder Generationenvermittlung als grundschulpädagogisches Prinzip? In: Heinzel, Friederike (ed.): Generationenvermittlung in der Grundschule. Ende der Kindgemäßheit. Bad Heilbrunn: Klinkhardt, pp. 40–68.

Heinzel, Friederike (2012) (ed.): Methoden der Kindheitsforschung. Ein Überblick über Forschungszugänge zur kindlichen Perspektive. Weinheim: Beltz Juventa.

Heinzel, Friederike (2016): Der Morgenkreis. Klassenöffentlicher Unterricht zwischen schulischen und peerkulturellen Herausforderungen. Opladen: Budrich.

Hengst, Heinz/Zeiher, Helga (2005): Kindheit soziologisch. Wiesbaden: VS Verlag für Sozialwissenschaften.

Honig, Michael-Sebastian (1999): Entwurf einer Theorie der Kindheit. Frankfurt am Main: Suhrkamp.

Honig, Michael-Sebastian/Lange, Andreas/Leu, Hans Rudolf (1999): Eigenart und Fremdheit. Kindheitsforschung und das Problem der Differenz von Kindern und Erwachsenen. In: Honig, Michael-Sebastian/Lange, Andreas/Leu, Hans Rudolf (eds.): Aus der Perspektive von Kindern? Zur Methodologie der Kindheitsforschung. Weinheim: Juventa, pp. 9–32.

Hunner-Kreisel, Christine/Kuhn, Melanie (2011): Children's Perspectives. Methodological Critiques and Empirical Studies. In Andresen, Sabine/Diehm, Isabell/Sander, Uwe/Ziegler, Holger (eds.): Children and the Good Life. New Challenges for Research on Children. Vol. 4. London: Springer, pp. 115–118.

Joos, Magdlena/Betz, Tanja/Bollig, Sabine/Neumann, Sascha (2018): Gute Kindheit als Gegenstand der Forschung. Wohlergehen, Kindeswohl und ungleiche Kindheiten. In: Betz, Tanja/Bollig, Sabine/Joos, Magdalena/Neumann, Sascha (eds.): Gute Kindheit. Wohlbefinden, Kindeswohl und Ungleichheit. Weinheim: Beltz Juventa, pp. 7–29.

Kaufmann, Elke (2007): Individuelle Förderung in ganztägig organisierten Schulformen im Primarbereich. https://www.dji.de/fileadmin/user_upload/bibs/ Abschlussbericht_Individuelle_Foerderung.pdf.

Kelle, Helga (2005): Kinder in der Schule. Zum Zusammenhang von Schulpädagogik und Kindheitsforschung. In: Breidenstein, Georg/Prengel, Annedore (eds.): Schulforschung und Kindheitsforschung – ein Gegensatz? Weinheim: Beltz, pp. 139–160.

Kramer, Rolf-Torsten/Helsper, Werner (2010): Kulturelle Passung und Bildungsungleichheit – Potentiale einer an Bourdieu orientierten Analyse der Bildungsungleichheit. In: Krüger, Heinz-Hermann/Rabe-Kleberg, Ursula/Kramer,

Rolf-Torsten/Budde, Jürgen (eds.): Bildungsungleichheit revisited. Bildung und soziale Ungleichheit vom Kindergarten bis zur Hochschule. Wiesbaden: Springer, pp. 103–125.

Kricke, Meike/Remy, Miriam/Seitz, Simone/Hamacher, Catalina (2022): „Qualitätsoffensive Ganztag" – Inklusive ganztägige Bildung mit allen Akteuren und Akteurinnen im Dialog gestalten. In Tusche, Simone/Webs, Tanja (eds.): Potenziale der Ganztagsschule nutzen. Forschung – Praxis – Transfer. Münster: Waxmann, pp. 245–267.

Ludwig, Harald (2005): Ganztagsschule und Reformpädagogik. In: Hansel, Toni (ed.): Ganztagsschule. Halbe Sache – großer Wurf? Schulpädagogische Betrachtung eines bildungspolitischen Investitionsprogramms. Herbolzheim: Centaurus Verlag, pp. 33–53.

Müller-Kuhn, Daniela/Herzig, Pascale/Häbig, Julia/Zala-Mezö, Enikö (2021): Student participation in everyday school life – Linking different perspectives. In: Zeitschrift für Bildungsforschung 11, pp. 35–53.

Nordt, Gabriele (2017): Die Ganztagsgrundschule auf dem Weg zum inklusiven Bildungsort. In: Amirpur, Donja/Platte, Andrea. (eds.): Handbuch inklusive Kindheiten. Opladen: Verlag Barbara Budrich, pp. 502–517.

OECD (2019): PISA 2018 Results. Where All Students Can Succeed (Volume II). Paris: OECD Publishing. https://doi.org/10.1787/b5fd1b8f-en.

Panesar, Rita (2020): Institutionen als Inklusionsförderer. Abbau von Bildungsbarrieren und Interkulturelle Öffnung von Schulen. In: Genkova, Petia/Rieken, Andrea (eds): Handbuch Migration und Erfolg. Psychologische und sozialwissenschaftliche Aspekte. Wiesbaden: Springer, pp. 331–348.

Petillon, Hanns (ed.) (2002): Individuelles und soziales Lernen in der Grundschule. Kinderperspektive und pädagogische Konzepte. Opladen: Leske & Budrich.

Petillon, Hanns (2017): Soziales Lernen in der Grundschule – das Praxisbuch. Weinheim, Basel: Beltz.

Prüß, Franz (2008): Didaktische Konzepte von Ganztagsschulen. In: Coelen, Thomas/Otto, Hans-Uwe (eds.): Grundbegriffe Ganztagsbildung. Wiesbaden: VS, pp. 538-547.

Rabenstein, Kerstin/Nerowski, Christian/Rahm, Sibylle (2015): Basiswissen Ganztagsschule. Konzepte, Erwartungen, Perspektiven. Weinheim: Beltz.

Rauschenbach, Thomas (2008): Bildung im Kindes- und Jugendalter. Über Zusammenhänge zwischen formellen und informellen Bildungsprozessen. In: Deutsches Jugendinstitut (ed.): Jugend und Bildung. Modernisierungsprozesse und Strukturwandel von Erziehung und Bildung am Beginn des 21. Jahrhunderts. München: Deutsches Jugendinstitut, pp. 17-34.

Reh, Sabine/Fritsche, Bettina/Idel, Till-Sebastian/Rabenstein, Kerstin (2015): Einleitung. Lernkultur- und Unterrichtsentwicklung in Ganztagsschulen. In: Reh, Sabine/Fritsche, Bettina/Idel, Till-Sebastian/Rabenstein, Kerstin (eds.): Lernkulturen. Rekonstruktion pädagogischer Praktiken an Ganztagsschulen. Wiesbaden: Springer VS, pp. 13–18.

Rogers, Margaret (2018): Listening to children's voice through art. Communicating experiences and understandings in mosaic research. In: International Art in Early Childhood Research Journal 1, 1, pp. 1–19.

Rother, Pia (2019): Sortieren als Umgang mit Bildungsbenachteiligung. Orientierungen pädagogischer Akteure in einem kooperativen Ganztags-Setting. Weinheim: Beltz Juventa.

Rother, Pia (2021): Rechtsanspruch auf Ganztagsbetreuung als Hoffnungsträger? Zur Rolle der Kooperation von Kinder- und Jugendhilfe mit Schule für den Abbau von Bildungsbenachteiligung. In: Graßhoff, Gunther/Sauerwein, Markus (eds.): Rechtsanspruch auf Ganztag. Zwischen Betreuungsnotwendigkeit und fachlichen Ansprüchen. Weinheim: Beltz, pp. 96–111.

Rüsing, Olaf (2006): Kindgerechtigkeit. Ideen zur kindgerechten Forschung. Saarbrücken: VDM.

Sauerwein, Markus (2018): Partizipation in der Ganztagsschule – vertiefende Analysen. In: Zeitschrift für Erziehungswissenschaft 22, pp. 435–459. https://doi.org/10.1007/s11618-018-0844-9.

Sauerwein, Markus (2019): Wie steht es mit der Ganztagsschule? Ein Forschungsreview mit sozialpädagogischer Kommentierung. In: Soziale Passagen 11, 1, pp. 81-97.

Sauerwein, Markus/Heer, Jana (2020): Warum gibt es keine leistungssteigernden Effekte durch den Besuch von Ganztagsangeboten? – oder über die Paradoxie individueller Förderung. In: Zeitschrift für Pädagogik 1, pp. 78–101.

Schütz, Sandra/Böhm, Eva Theresa (2021): Forschungsmethodische Vielfalt. Der Mosaic Approach. In: Hedderich, Ingeborg/Reppin, Jeanne/Butschi, Corinne (eds.): Perspektiven auf Vielfalt in der frühen Kindheit. Mit Kindern Diversität erforschen. Bad Heilbrunn: Verlag Julius Klinkhardt, pp. 172–186.

Scott, W. Richard (2014): Institutions and Organizations: Ideas, Interests and Identities. Los Angeles: SAGE.

Seitz, Simone (2014): Inklusion in der Grundschule. In: Franz, Eva-Kristina/Trumpa, Silke/Esslinger-Hinz, Ilona (eds.): Inklusion – Eine Herausforderung für die Grundschulpädagogik. Hohengehren: Schneider, pp. 21–29.

Seitz, Simone/Hamacher, Catalina (2022): Wie die Arbeit am Bildungsverständnis zum Motor von Kooperation in Ganztagsgrundschulen werden kann. In: Demo, Heidrun/Cappello, Silver/Macchia, Vanessa (eds.): Emergenze educativa. Neue Horizonte. Bozen/Bolzano: bu'press, pp. 1–16.

Sgritta, Giovanni B. (2005): Kindheitssoziologie und Statistik. Eine generationale Perspektive. In: Hengst, Heinz/Zeiher, Helga (eds.): Kindheit Soziologisch. Wiesbaden: VS Verlag für Sozialwissenschaften, pp. 49–64.

Staudner, Stephanie (2018): Bildungsprozesse im Ganztag. Wahrnehmung und Wertung erweiterter Bildungsgelegenheiten durch Kinder. Wiesbaden: Springer VS.

Stojanov, Krassimir (2011): Bildungsgerechtigkeit. Rekonstruktionen eines umkämpften Begriffs. Wiesbaden: Springer VS.

Sturzenhecker, Benedikt (2018): Demokratische Partizipation im Ganztag – Folgerungen aus der Studie „Offene Ganztagsschule aus Sicht der Kinder" für Bedarfe,

Inhalte und Ansätze demokratischer Mitbestimmung. In: Deinet, Ulrich/Gumz, Heike/Muscutt, Cristina/Thomas, Sophie (eds.): Offene Ganztagsschule – Schule als Lebensort aus Sicht der Kinder. Studie, Bausteine, Methodenkoffer. Opladen: Budrich, pp. 71–96.

Toppe, Sabine (2010): Ungleiche Kindheiten. Ganztagsbildung im Spannungsfeld von sozial-, bildungs- und kinderpolitischen Anforderungen. In: Diskurs Kindheits- und Jugendforschung 5, 1, pp. 63-76.

Triani, Pierpaolo (2018): Die Ganztagsschule in der italienischen Primarstufe. In: Maschke, Sabine/Schulz-Gade, Gunild/Stecher, Ludwig (eds.): Lehren und Lernen in der Ganztagsschule. Grundlagen – Ziele – Perspektiven. Schwalbach: Debus Pädagogik, pp. 225–236.

United Nations (UN) (1989): Convention on the Rights of the Child. http://www.ohchr.org/Documents/ProfessionalInterest/crc.pdf.

United Nations (UN) (2006): Convention on the Rights of Persons With Disabilities. New York: United Nations.

Wagener, Anna Lena (2012): Partizipation von Kindern an (Ganztags-)Grundschulen. Ziele, Möglichkeiten und Bedingungen aus Sicht verschiedener Akteure. Weinheim: Beltz Juventa.

Walther, Bastian/Nentwig-Gesemann, Iris (2021): Ganztag aus der Perspektive von Kindern im Grundschulalter. In: Graßhoff, Gunther/Sauerwein, Markus (eds.): Rechtsanspruch auf Ganztag. Zwischen Betreuungsnotwendigkeit und fachlichen Ansprüchen. Weinheim, Basel: Beltz, pp. 234–255.

Walther, Bastian/Nentwig-Gesemann, Iris/Fried, Florian (2021): Ganztag aus der Perspektive von Kindern im Grundschulalter. Eine Rekonstruktion von Qualitätsbereichen und -dimensionen. Gütersloh: Bertelsmann.

Wiere, Aandreas (2011): Wie wirkt die Ganztagsschule? Forschungsfragen und Befunde. In: Gängler, Hans/Markert, Thomas (eds.): Vision und Alltag der Ganztagsschule. Die Ganztagsschulbewegung als bildungspolitische Kampagne und regionale Praxis. Weinheim, München: Juventa, pp. 33–58.

Zeiher, Helga (1996): Kinder in der Gesellschaft und Kindheit in der Soziologie. In: Zeitschrift für Sozialisationsforschung und Erziehungssoziologie 16, 1, pp. 26–46.

Züchner, Ivo/Fischer, Natalie (2014): Kompensatorische Wirkungen von Ganztagsschulen – Ist die Ganztagsschule ein Instrument zur Entkopplung des Zusammenhangs von sozialer Herkunft und Bildungserfolg? In: Zeitschrift für Erziehungswissenschaft 17, 2, pp. 349–367.

On the Inclusiveness of the Education System in a Multination State from the Perspective of Primary School Children and Teachers' Values

Petra Auer

1   Introduction

Values have become a widely – sometimes even hotly – debated topic in public. Whether it is the problem of value erosion, the discussion of value relativism (i.e., the culturally or group-dependent different weighting of specific values) or the phenomenon of value scepticism, the concept of values seems to be very present in current social discourses of the public sphere (Bambauer 2019). According to Verwiebe (2019), the debate on values in Europe has intensified alongside the increase in immigration, especially following the humanitarian crisis of 2015, whereby it now mainly concerns the "right", the "extra" and the agreement on common values. Such a nego-tiation is not only conducted on the level of individual lifestyles but also on the superordinate level of social changes in the 21st century. He further reasons that it was in these public discussions that the notion of value education emerged – primarily, in relation to the integration of migrants and refugees in terms of "learning" fundamental values which are considered a prerequisite for successful social cohesion. In fact, common values and their transmission to the next generation are discussed to ensure consistency for cultures and societies (Döring et al. 2015; Kochanska 1994), and raising awareness of shared values is considered as a key competence of citizenship skills by the European Union (Council of the European Union 2018). Therefore, in a world of increasing diversification, it seems that values can be an important foundation for successful social inclusion, but conversely, they can also become a source of social conflict and exclusion (Thome 2019). As the exemplary and among many scholars controversially discussed case of the promotion of the so-called "fundamental British values" (i.e., democracy, the rule of law, individual liberty, and mutual respect and tolerance of those with different faiths and beliefs; Department for Education 2014; Sant 2021) has recently shown, schools seem to be put on the frontline when it comes to the education of these so-called right values (Crawford 2017). But even when no state guidelines for the education of values are laid down, school can never be considered as a value vacuum. Instead, it can be understood as a pedagogically shaped space for learning and experiencing, which is connected to a clear educational mandate and where every teacher embodies certain values, be it consciously or unconsciously (Schubarth 2019). To put it in other words, schools can be defined as key socialisation agents, with one of their main aims being to socialise values which are considered desirable by society (Daniel/Hofmann-Towfigh/Knafo 2013).

But what about what Kymlicka (2011) refers to as multination states? That is, "[...] states that have restructured themselves to accommodate significant sub-state nationalist movements, usually through some form of territorial devolution, consociational power-sharing, and/or official language" (Kymlicka 2011: 282)? Which values do schools socialise in such territories? The common values of the overall society or rather the values of each sub-society? The present contribution tries to partly investigate this broad question by venturing a step into the under-researched area of children's values within the school context considering the sociocultural background of the region data was collected in: a Northern-Italian, multilingual and autonomous province characterised by its formative history and the socio-political reality, which, for instance, shows up in a tripartite division of the school system. Specifically, against the backdrop of the overarching theme of this edited volume, some selected results of a larger doctoral dissertation project (Auer 2021) will be presented and discussed alongside the concept of educational justice with the aim of establishing a connection to inclusion from the perspective of socialisation in the school context.

2   Values

2.1   The Basic Human Values Theory by Shalom H. Schwartz

As is often the case in human sciences when it comes to defining concepts to be researched, there has long been a lack of a consensus definition of the construct of values, even though, since its inception, it assumed a central role in different disciplines (Schwartz 2012). It was the socio-psychologist researcher Shalom H. Schwartz, who, at the beginning of the 1990s, published an article introducing a theory of basic human values. Schwartz (1992, 1994) suggested a theory regarding the content and structure of personal values defined as "[...] trans-situational criteria or goals [...], ordered by importance as guiding principles in life" (Schwartz 1999a: 25). Concretely, he generated a set of 10 value types differing in terms of their underlying motivation and

Table 1:   Value types, their underlying motivational goal, and examples of specific values (Adapted from Schwartz 1994: 22; Schwartz, 2012).

Higher order value	Value type	Motivational goal (specific values)
Self-Enhance-ment	Power (PO)	Social status and prestige, control or do-minance over people and resources (social power, authority, wealth)
	Achievement (AC)	Personal success through demonstrating competence according to social standards (successful, capable, ambitious)
Openness to Change	Hedonism (HE)	Pleasure and sensuous gratification for one-self (pleasure, enjoying life)
	Stimulation (ST)	Excitement, novelty, and challenge in life (daring, varied life, exciting life)
	Self-direction (SD)	Independent thought and action – choosing, creating, exploring (creativity, curious, freedom)
Self-Trans-cendence	Universalism (UN)	Understanding, appreciation, tolerance, and protection for the welfare of all people and for nature (broad-minded, social justice, equality, protecting the environment)
	Benevolence (BE)	Preservation and enhancement of the wel-fare of people with whom one is in frequent personal contact (helpful, honest, forgiving)
Conservation	Tradition (TR)	Respect, commitment, and acceptance of the customs and ideas that traditional cul-ture or religion provide for the self (humble, devout, accepting my portion in life)
	Conformity (CO)	Restraint of actions, inclinations, and im-pulses likely to upset or harm others and violate social expectations or norms (polite-ness, obedient, honouring parents, and elders)
	Security (SE)	Safety, harmony, and stability of society, of relationships, and, of the self (national security, social order, clean)

being common to humans all over the world and therefore named as "basic human values" (see Table 1). These can be further summarised into the four higher order values *self-enhancement, openness to change, self-transcendence,* and *conservation.* Specifically, he first gathered the numerous words used to talk about values in various languages and then summarised them based on a common motivational goal (Döring/Cieciuch 2018).

Figure 1:   Theoretical circular model of dynamic relations among the 10 value types and the four higher order value types (personal illustration according to Schwartz 1992, 1994, 2012).

Moreover, Schwartz's theory not only identified these different value types, but he also specified the dynamic relations among them: they can harmonise or conflict with each other (Davidov/Schmidt/Schwartz 2008). These relationships show up graphically in the quasi-circumplex structure of the value system (Schmidt et al. 2007; see Figure 1). Values lying next to each other are in harmony (i.e., compatible with each other), while those lying on the opposite side are in conflict (i.e., incompatible with each other). The circular model was examined in cross-cultural research involving samples from more than 70 countries (i.e., students, teachers, and representative samples) by means of Multidimensional Scaling (MDS; Borg/Groenen/ Mair 2013), indicating that the value system can be understood as universal in terms of content and structure across cultures (Roccas/Sagiv 2010). Nevertheless, single persons or groups of persons (i.e., societies, cultures) can prioritise the values differently, which leads to contrasting value priorities or hierarchies (Schwartz 2012). The latter refer to the relative importance of a value within the value system. Hence, individuals share the same set of values with its universal structure, but individuals can differ according to which values are more important to them and which ones are less within the value system creating diverse value hierarchies. In this regard, it has been found, however, that in most nations around the world values of self-transcendence are rated as the most important, whereas those of self-enhancement as the least important. This is referred to as the "pancultural pattern of value priorities" (Schwartz 2006). Yet, the nation, society, or context to which a person belongs can lead to differences in the importance of specific values. That is, values can be ranked in the same position of the hierarchy from person to person or culture to culture, but when comparing the importance of a specific value, there might be differences between persons or culture. According to Schwartz (2012), people adapt most of their value priorities to life circumstances by ascribing more importance to accessible or socially accepted values and less importance to the ones that are inaccessible or socially not accepted.

Schwartz's theory has given a considerable impetus to values research – presumably also because alongside the theoretical work on the definition of the concept, it provided reliable instruments to measure values (Schwartz 2012) – leading to the fact that research on values in adulthood nowadays can be considered as very extensive. A different picture emerges, however, in the field of values research in childhood, which is currently only beginning to evolve. Therefore, in the upcoming section, key findings from the so far existing studies on values in primary school children (i.e., middle childhood) will be summarised to present the state of the art of this under researched field.

2.2   Values at primary school age

Even if there is still a long way to go in the field of values research at such an early age, some fundamental aspects of Schwartz's theory could be proven so far, thus providing a good basis for the further development of the research area. First, many studies (e.g., Bilsky et al. 2013, 2015; Cieciuch/Döring/ Harasimczuk, 2013; Döring 2010; Döring et al. 2010;) were able to confirm the existence of value structure in children at primary school age, that is, they hold a value structure – the value types with their dynamic relationships – comparable to the one of adults. Some studies (Bilsky et al. 2013; Cieciuch/ Döring/Harasimczuk 2013; Döring et al. 2015) could further provide cross-cultural evidence of value structure in children, which can also be interpreted as empirical evidence for the universality of Schwartz's basic human values in content and structure at an early age. Second, since socio-demographics and context variables are discussed to impact on an individual's values, their relationship with values has been recently investigated also for children: the relationship between values and age (e.g., Döring/Daniel/Knafo-Noam 2016), values and gender (e.g., Döring et al. 2017; Lee et al. 2017; Makarova et al. 2012), or values and culture, nation, or context (e.g., Döring et al. 2015, 2017; Daniel/Schiefer/Knafo 2012). In summary, the results show that value priorities change from openness to change to conservation and from self-enhancement to self-transcendence as age increases. Boys ascribe more importance to self-enhancement than girls do, whereas the latter rate self-transcendence more important than boys do. Overall, children in most nations around the world consider values of self-transcendence as the most important, whereas those of self-enhancement as the least important following the pancultural pattern of value priorities[1] (Döring et al. 2015). Rare, instead, is research investigating the influence of the school context on students' values and, even not existing to date are studies on this topic involving primary school children. Considering that schools next to families can be considered as primary socialisation agents who among others follow the aim to socialise to those values considered as desirable by the society (Daniel/Hofmann-Towfigh/Knafo 2013), it seems surprising that only few scholars have addressed this field so far. Daniel, Schiefer and Knafo (2012), for instance, found that adolescents' value hierarchies remained always the same despite changing the context (i.e., family, school, country). Instead, the importance of specific values changed according to the context, that is, some values were even more/less important in the family context, whereas others in the school context. In a different vein, Daniel, Hofmann-Towfigh and Knafo (2013) examined school-level value structure in schools of two different ethnic backgrounds (i.e., Israeli Jewish and Arab) and found the same value structure for both of them as for the overall sample, suggesting cross-cultural evidence of school-level values. In terms of the importance attributed to specific values, the two ethnic school types differed significantly from each other with Jewish schools giving higher importance to dominance, egalitarianism, and autonomy values, whereas Arab schools give higher importance to compliance, harmony, and achievement (Daniel/Hofmann-Towfigh/Knafo 2013). The research group thereupon accomplished a second study in the European context, which involved students and teachers. Next to a replication

---

1   This empirical evidence could also be replicated within the larger investigation underlying the present contribution. As reported elsewhere (Auer, 2022), children rated self-transcendence as most important and self-enhancement as least important. This pancultural pattern also showed to be consistent when the sample was differentiated according to the language of the school they attended or the children's mother tongue. This can be interpreted as a further confirmation of the pattern and, at the same time, shows that children – even though they can differ in the importance they attribute to specific values as will be shown within this contribution – they show similarities in their value hierarchies.

of the findings of their first study, they further found the structure in both the students' and the teachers' sample supporting their theoretically hypothesised value dimensions for the school context. Moreover, results indicate that school level values are consistent across age groups and across students and teachers.

Starting from these very few existing findings, it was one of the aims of the research project to investigate a possible impact by school-context-related variables on primary school children's values venturing a step into this still under-researched field. To make clear what is meant with school-context-related variables, the school system and sociocultural background the research project was embedded in will be illustrated in more detail in the upcoming section.

3   School in the Autonomous Province of Bolzano

The Autonomous Province of Bolzano is a northern Italian border region characterised by a particular socio-political reality showing up, for instance, also in its school system. To better understand this contemporary reality, it is necessary to recap the history of the territory.

3.1   Historical backdrop

Since ancient times the province has been cohabitated by three language groups, namely German, Italian, and Ladin. After belonging to the Austro-Hungarian Empire for several centuries, with the peace treaties of Saint Germain in 1919, the Province of Bolzano was annexed to the Italian Kingdom (Alcock 2001), leading to the fact that the German- and Ladin-speaking population became minorities within the Italian nation state. When, the fascists took over power in 1922 (i.e., *March on Rome*), a forced assimilation of these minorities began, which is also known as the time of *Italianization* (Voltmer et al. 2007). For instance, schooling in German language was prohibited and non-complying teachers were sentenced to imprisonment or exiled to Italian provinces in the South (Steininger 2004). In 1939, through an agreement between Hitler and Mussolini, the population of the Province of Bolzano then had the choice to opt for Germany and the expatriation to German territory, or Italy and a full acceptance of the Italianization. Pressured by war propaganda from both sides Fascist and Nazi organisations, the majority (more than 80%) opted for leaving the province (Alcock 2001), but due to the course of the war only a few did so, and many returned after the end of World War II (Wisthaler 2013). The post-war time (i.e., the 20th century) was then characterised by the striving for autonomy to gain the certainty that German and Ladin minorities will be protected after the events of the past. Contradictorily, this struggle for becoming more independent from the Italian nation state at times also took on violent dimensions (Alcock 2001), such as in the acts of some extremist separatists in the 1960s and 1970s leading to a deterioration of the tense situation between the different language groups (Zinn 2017). When in 1972 the Second Autonomy Statute came into force, a series of provisions were started to be implemented, among them the establishment of a quota system[2] (i.e., *Proporz*) regulating access to public jobs and resources or the tripartition of the school system according to the three languages (Alcock 2001). However, a full implementation of all provisions was completed only in 1992 (Steininger 2004). On the one hand, the autonomy guaranteed the protection of the minorities and after the events of the past helped in achieving a peaceful coexistence. On the other hand, recently, many scholars discuss that some provisions of the autonomy lead to a situation of social division according to the languages, which is seen as problematic (Baur 2013; Zinn 2017). Such a perspective will be incorporated and discussed in the following illustration of the school system of the province.

3.2   The organisation of the school system

Overall, the educational system in the province follows the structure prevailing at the state level (Augschöll 2011), that is, primary education comprises five years, which is followed by a uniform lower secondary education for three years, and two main routes of upper secondary education with its various school types varying from three to five years (MIUR n.d.). Consequently, children in Italy share the same educational pathway for eight years – from primary school to the end of lower secondary school no tracking is intended – which can be seen as one of the central pillars of an important characteristic of the Italian school system: its inclusiveness steeped in tradition. In the early 1970s, the legal right of children with disabilities to attend mainstream schools was established by law and at the end of the same decade the special school system was dissolved (Pavone 2012). Finally, as another characteristic the regulation of the *autonomy of the schools* should be mentioned as it considerably affects the organisation of schooling in Italy.

---

2   Public positions and resources are assigned based on the language groups' respective numerical strength, tied to the condition that the employees have to demonstrate a certain level of both languages in an exam (Voltmer et al. 2007). The proportional distribution underlying the quota system is determined by the individually declared belonging or affiliation to one of the three language groups through the general census (Carlà 2019).

This latter autonomy, which was implied in 2000, assigns schools the status of independent legal entities, giving them didactic, administrative, and financial autonomy (Augschöll 2011) leading to the fact that schools in Italy can respond flexibly to a variety of educational needs (D'Alessio 2011). Concerning all these characteristics, school in the Province of Bolzano is organised in the same way as all schools in Italy. However, some deviations can be found in some areas. First, it is important to make clear that the autonomy of the schools at the state level should not be confused with the *school autonomy* on the provincial level, which instead refers to special authorities of the province in the field of education as laid down in the Second Autonomy Statute (Steininger 2004). Overall, the development of the educational system in the province is closely connected to the development of the autonomy and, as mentioned above, clearly shows up in the tripartite division according to the three language groups (Verra 2008). This means that schools of the province are organised through three parallel school systems with their own administrations, three education authorities, directing bodies, and evaluation boards (Wisthaler 2013). Consequently, all educational institutions from kindergarten to secondary education are separated by language. Furthermore, schools in the territory differ not only in their language of instruction but also in the school model they follow when it comes to the use of the second or third language: German and Italian schools apply "school separatism", whereas in the Ladin schools a "parity model" is active (Rautz 1999). After the forced assimilation of the German and Ladin speaking population under the fascist regime such a division had the aim to guarantee to the minorities the right to education in their mother tongue. Therefore, the educational system can be considered, on the one hand, as a key foundation of the minority-protection policies but, on the other hand, as a mirror of the events and trauma of the past (Wisthaler 2013). The latter recently lead to the fact that many scholars address this organisation of school in the province also as potentially problematic since creating parallel worlds, linguistic division, and a fragmentation of society (cf. Gross 2019: 159; Baur 2013; Zinn 2017).

Given the organisation of school in the province, it seemed very promising to investigate primary school children's and their teachers' values in the school context. Due to the connectedness of language and culture (Kramsch 2000), it was possible to do so also from the perspective of possible ethnolinguistic differences in value priorities – like the above-mentioned study by Daniel, Hofmann-Towfigh and Knafo (2013) – on which the present contribution focuses. In what follows, the school-context-related variable under question is the *school system*, a denomination or variable, which refers to the three different systems the schools on the territory belong to, that is, schools of German, Italian, or Ladin language.

4   Methodology

4.1   The present study

Starting from the theoretical underpinnings, the empirical evidence, and the extant research gap outlined above, the present study investigated possible differences in children's and teachers' value priorities based on the school system they attend or work in. Since different studies were able to show a relationship between values and language or values and the environment not only in adults but also in children (Yang/Bond 1982; Döring et al. 2017; Ralston/Cunniff/Gustafson 1995; Verwiebe 2019), the main aim was to answer the following research questions for both participant groups (i.e., primary school children and teachers):

Does the importance children/teachers attribute to the higher order values differ according to the school system they attend/work in?

4.2   Participants

Based on the number of pupils in fourth and fifth grades for the 2018/19 school year[3], a sample was calculated, which was representative of the three school systems and stratified according to the territorial distribution of the different schools (i.e., stratification was carried out separately for each school system because their territorial distribution differs widely). Overall, 450 primary school children (M_{age} = 9.81, SD = 0.73; 217 girls, 233 boys) from 32 classes participated. Of these, 112 (24.9%) attended a Ladin school, 130 (28.9%) an Italian and 208 (46.2%) a German school. The children were distributed rather evenly among rural (n = 245, 54.4%) and urban (n = 205, 45.6%) located schools. Additionally, 79 of their teachers (N = 79, M_{age} = 42.77, SD = 10.54) participated in the study, whereby the number of participating teachers per class ranged from 1 to 4 teachers, and in two classes none of the teachers filled out a questionnaire. The gender distribution was unbalanced (74 females, 5 males) but corresponds to the population of primary school teachers in the Province of Bolzano (cfr. ASTAT, 2019). Further, since the Italian school system is characterised by the integration of children with disabilities, learning disabilities or other Special Educational Needs (SEN) in mainstream schools, appropriate measures were taken to ensure that the research respected this general principle of the schools: after a short

---

3   Overall, in the school year 2018/19, 11,068 children attended a fourth or fifth grade class. From these, 458 children attended Ladin, 2,582 Italian, and 8,028 German schools.

consultation with the teacher, children with SEN received any individual support that was necessary to complete the questionnaire by taking care to maintain the image of the child as an expert as well as their independence in answering the questions.

4.3   Procedures and measures

Written questionnaires were elaborated for the two participant groups. Children were guided step by step through the completion of the questionnaire, whereas teachers filled it out at home. All questionnaires were labelled with alphanumerical codes providing information on school context (i.e., school system) and asked for some socio-demographic characteristics (i.e., sex, age, first language, birthplace). For the children, the second part consisted in the *Picture Based Value Survey for Children* (PBVS-C; Döring et al. 2010), a well-established, standardised instrument to gather children's values (Cieciuch/Döring/Harasimczuk 2013). It is based on Schwartz's (1992, 1994) theory and consists of 20 pictures with short captions representing the 10 basic human values to be ranked in a five-graded Q-sort ranging from *very important* to *not at all important*. The questionnaire was provided in the language of the school but for some classes bilingual instructions were given as teachers deemed it necessary to allow all children to follow. Next to parents' formal consent, children were asked for their assent and ongoing consent (i.e., informed about their voluntary participation and the possibility of opting out at any time) as foreseen by ethical practice in research with children (Mertens 2015; see also Graham et al. 2013). Within the parents' questionnaire, values were gathered with the *Portraits Value Questionnaire* (PVQ; Schwartz 1992), which due to the multilingual reality of the territory, was provided in its German and Italian version (Schmidt et al. 2007; Capanna/Vecchione/Schwartz 2005). The PVQ consists of 40 Items describing a person in a short portrait. Participants then need to indicate how similar the respective person is to themselves on a 6-point Likert scale ($1 = not\ like\ me\ at\ all$, $6 = very\ much\ like\ me$) (Schwartz 2006).

4.4   Data Analysis

First, it was ensured that children from the three school systems understood values similarly and according to the theoretically postulated value theory by Schwartz (1992, 1994). For this purpose, multidimensional scaling (MDS; Borg/Groenen/Mair 2013) was performed for the participants of each school system. The results indicated that values are construed in similar ways and following Schwartz' theory (see Auer 2022 for the MDS for the children's sample).

Further, priority scores have been computed as the means of all item scores belonging to the respective higher order values as proposed by Schwartz (2003) and Döring et al. (2010). For the PVQ, as indicated by Schwartz (2003), individual response tendencies were corrected for by centring each participant's responses around their mean score. These centred value scores were then used for following statistical procedures.

A one-way ANOVA was conducted to explore the impact of the school system on children's or teachers' value priorities. Homogeneity of variances was asserted using Levene's Test, and where the assumption was not met, Welch's F-ratios was considered and reported. Post-hoc comparisons were conducted by using the Tukey HSD test or Games-Howell test in the case equal variances could not be assumed. Effect sizes were calculated as omega squared (ω^2) and interpreted as small, medium, and large if $\omega^2 = 0.01$, $\omega^2 = 0.06$ and $\omega^2 = 0.14$, respectively (Cohen 1988). For the cases where Welch's F ratio has been reported, an adjusted omega squared (*est.* ω^2) was calculated.

5   Findings

5.1   Differences in children's value priorities based on the school system

Levene's Test showed that equal variances could be assumed for self-trans-cendence ($p = .307$), conservation ($p = .548$) and openness to change ($p = .067$), but not for self-enhancement ($p < .001$). Therefore, for the latter higher order value type Welch's F-ratios is reported. One-way ANOVA revealed statistically significant differences in mean scores for all four higher order values for the different school systems: self-transcendence, $F(2, 447) = 3.26$, $p = .039$, $\omega^2 = .01$, conservation, $F(2, 447) = 10.10$, $p < .001$, $\omega^2 = .04$, self-enhancement *Welch's* $F(2, 256.43) = 11.38$, $p < .001$, *est.* $\omega^2 = .04$, and openness to change $F(2, 447) = 7.94$, $p < .001$, $\omega^2 = .03$). The reported effect sizes can be considered as indicating a small effect (Cohen 1988). Post-hoc comparisons using the Tukey HSD test[4] revealed that children attending German schools ($M = 3.67$, $SD = 0.46$) significantly differed in their mean score for self-transcendence from children attending Italian schools ($M = 3.53$, $SD = 0.52$). Children attending German schools ($M = 2.97$, $SD = 0.35$) also showed a significantly different mean score in conservation from

---

4   In addition, as the sample size was not equal, the Gabriel post hoc test was run and checked for differing results.

Table 2:   Children's means and standard deviations of higher order values by school systems.

School System	n	Self-Transcendence		Conservation		Self-Enhancement		Openness to change	
		Mean	SD	Mean	SD	Mean	SD	Mean	SD
German	208	3.67	0.46	2.97	0.35	2.01	0.44	3.24	0.38
Italian	130	3.53	0.52	3.05	0.36	2.25	0.56	3.10	0.43
Ladin	112	3.65	0.46	3.15	0.33	1.96	0.39	3.09	0.34

children attending Ladin schools ($M = 3.15$, $SD = 0.33$). Furthermore, they differed significantly in their mean score ($M = 3.24$, $SD = 0.38$) for openness to change from children attending Italian ($M = 3.10$, $SD = 0.43$) and Ladin schools ($M = 3.09$, $SD = 0.34$). For the higher order value self-enhancement Games-Howell test was used for post-hoc comparisons. It revealed that the mean score for children attending Italian schools ($M = 2.25$, $SD = 0.56$) was significantly different from children attending German ($M = 2.01$, $SD = 0.44$) as well as Ladin schools ($M = 1.96$, $SD = 0.39$). Means and standard deviations across the different groups are shown in Table 2.

5.2   Differences in teachers' value priorities based on the school system

According to Levene's test, homogeneity of variance across groups could be assumed for self-transcendence ($p = .429$), conservation ($p = .256$), self-enhancement ($p = .693$) and openness to change ($p = .182$). One-way ANOVA showed statistically significant differences in mean scores across the different school systems for two out of the four higher order values: conservation $F(2, 76) = 2.18$, $p = .028$, $\omega^2 = .06$, and openness to change, $F(2, 76) = 2.40$, $p = .039$, $\omega^2 = -.08$. Effect sizes indicate that both differences in means are of medium magnitude (i.e., $\omega^2 > .06$; Cohen 1988). The Tukey HSD test was used for post-hoc comparisons and results indicate that teachers at German schools differ significantly in their mean score for conservation ($M = -0.99$, $SD = 0.53$) when compared to teachers at Italian schools ($M = 0.33$, $SD = 0.54$). Moreover, concerning their mean values in openness to change values, teachers from German schools ($M = 0.06$, $SD = 0.62$) differed significantly from teachers at Italian schools ($M = -0.34$, $SD = 0.61$). Means and standard deviations across the different groups are shown in Table 3.

Table 3:   Teachers' means and standard deviations of higher order values by groups of school system.

School System	n	Self-Transcendence		Conservation		Self-Enhancement		Openness to change	
		M	SD	M	SD	M	SD	M	SD
German	40	0.68	0.42	−0.06	0.48	−1.21	0.77	0.06	0.57
Italian	27	0.87	0.53	0.29	0.64	−1.61	0.83	−0.31	0.70
Ladin	12	0.65	0.45	−0.05	0.50	−1.17	0.78	0.04	0.38

6   Discussion

6.1   Summary of the results

In summary, the results show that the children differ in their value priorities depending on the school system they attend and so do the teachers. For the children, differences in value priorities for all four higher order values emerged. Specifically, children attending German schools attribute more importance to self-transcendence than those attending Italian schools, less importance to conservation than children attending Ladin schools, as well as more importance to openness to change than children attending Italian and Ladin schools. Instead, children attending Italian schools rate self-enhancement as more important than children attending German and Ladin schools do. For the teachers, school system-based differences emerged only in the two higher order values conservation and openness to change. Teachers working at German schools rate conservation lower and openness to change higher than teachers from Italian schools do. In the following, some of these differences will be discussed in more detail by integrating them into the results of previous studies.

6.2   School system-based differences in value priorities

As the results of the present study show, the school system seems to impact on the attributed importance of both children and teachers even though children show more and sometimes also divergent differences when compared with the results in the teacher sample. On the one hand, this might be attributed to the size and composition of the teacher sample (i.e., 12 teachers from a Ladin, 27 from an Italian, 40 from a German school; see limitations of the study in section 7). On the other hand, it might be attributed to overall differences in value priorities according to the participants' life spans (Döring/Daniel/Knafo-Noam 2016). Döring et al. (2015), for instance, also found a greater variation across countries in children's self-enhancement values rather than in conservation values as it was reported in prior studies in adults. However, both children and teachers from German schools rated openness to change higher than children and teachers from Italian schools. Concerning the higher order value of self-transcendence, which children from German schools rated as being more important than children from Italian schools, Verwiebe (2019) also showed that German-speaking countries attribute more importance to benevolence and universalism than the Italian population does. This might be attributed to the fact that most of the German-speaking population in the Province of Bolzano is oriented more towards the culture of German-speaking countries, that is Austria, Germany and Switzerland, (e.g., through television programmes, literature, newspapers, etc.; cf. Baur 2009). Zinn (2019) describes this reality as the living "[...] within a German-speaking 'bubble' inside of the Italian national imagined community [...]" (p. 57). Therefore, value orientations of the German-speaking population are very likely to be influenced more by German-speaking countries across the borders than by the nation the province is located in. Consequently, it can be argued that value differences within the province follow value differences as they have been shown in prior studies at a nation-level (Verwiebe 2019; Schwartz 1999b). This result of school system-based differences seems to be in accordance with Daniel, Hofmann-Towfigh and Knafo's (2013) study which also showed significant differences in value priorities in two ethnic school types (i.e., Israeli Jewish and Arab schools). Even though the authors addressed values at the school level, comparable to the present study they attained them by simply aggregating values of individuals belonging to the respective school. Within both studies, differences in the importance attributed to specific values according to the distinct school systems or school types, respectively, could be shown.

6.3   The school as a socialisation agent

What do these results tell us about the role of schools? It seems that the school as a socialisation agent clearly follows the aim of socialising those values which by a society – or, to put it in Kymlicka's (2011) words, by a "sub-state" – are considered as desirable (Daniel/Hofmann-Towfigh/Knafo 2013; Grusec/Hastings 2015; Hurrelmann 2006). As the results show, across the distinct school systems, individuals rate the importance they attribute to specific values differently. Conversely, this could be interpreted insofar as schools of the respective ethnolinguistic groups socialise those values that are considered desirable. To put it differently, ethnolinguistically based differences in values as they have been shown in prior research (Sagiv et al. 2017) seem to become evident within schools belonging to the different school systems. Such a result might be interpreted also in the vein of the above-mentioned critical voices by other scholars, who claimed that the organisation of the education system in the province leads to or further promotes the social division of the population of the three official languages of the territory (Baur 2013; Zinn 2017). Even though variation in value priorities within and across cultures has been empirically proven so far and should not be seen as problematic at all, the strict separation of schools according to the three languages hinders daily contacts between the children (Wisthaler 2013) and contributes to the creation of parallel worlds (cf. Gross 2019). And this, in turn, can lead to the fact that the values of the respective sub-society are socialised within the schools, but the socialisation of values on the super-ordinate level of the multilingual region might be prevented by such an organisation of schooling. Under the consideration that the transmission of common values ensures consistency for cultures and societies (Döring et al. 2015) and the awareness of shared values as a key competence of citizenship skills (Council of the European Union 2018), the organisation of the school system of the Autonomous Province of Bolzano might be reimagined through cross-linguistic collaboration between policy, school authorities, and teacher training or the creation of one single school system involving personnel from all three language groups (Baur 2000; Baur/Videsott 2012; Gross 2019). Instead, on the level of the single classroom, projects spanning across schools of all languages should be realised on a regular or even everyday basis with the aim of a meeting of diversities possibly leading to the development of additional value similarities in a way that children identify as residents of province, regardless of the language group they belong to (cf. *White Paper on Intercultural Dialogue* by the European Union 2008). However, in any case, further and more detailed studies are needed to be able to draw clear conclusions since the study had its limitations. These will be addressed in the following.

7   Limitations

Even though the present study contributed some empirical evidence to current value research in childhood and in the context of school, several limitations need to be addressed. The small sample size of teachers limits the conclusions that can be drawn for this group of participants, and a subsequent study based on a larger sample size is undoubtably necessary. Another limitation lies in the fact that children from the Ladin language schools as well as all children speaking a language other than German and Italian were only offered the questionnaire in their second or third language. Since prior studies showed that the language of the questionnaire impacts on the importance attributed to the values (Bond/Yang 1982), this might cause bias in the data. Further, since analysing school-system-based differences was not the first aim of the overall research project, the research design could be improved to better fit the research question presented here. Through the combination of quantitative and qualitative methods the phenomenon could be explored more in-depth, and it would allow to draw clearer conclusions. Additionally, such a design would also better meet the children's need for discussion, who showed a great desire to express themselves on what is important to them after completing the questionnaire.

8   Conclusions

The present study was able to demonstrate that schools in the Autonomous Province of Bolzano seem to impact on the importance children attribute to specific values. Even though cultural differences in value priorities have been proven so far by many prior studies (e.g., Daniel et al. 2013; Döring et al. 2015; Schwartz 1999b; Verwiebe 2019;) and should not be seen as problematic per se, one question may arise: even though schools in the territory, in a world-wide comparison, as all other Italian provinces can show a long-standing and quite unique tradition of school inclusion, how inclusive is the school system and its structures when taking the perspective of language? An organisation of schools through three parallel systems and the clear division of all educational institutions belonging to them seems to run counter to the idea and conception of inclusion as *one school for all*. Seen from the perspective of Special Educational Needs, the latter asked and still asks schools all over Europe and the world to be transformed through restructuring policies, practices, and cultures to respond to student population's diversity (Ainscow/Booth/Dyson 2006; Powell et al. 2019). Consequently, in order to work towards a more inclusive school system in the specific case of the Province of Bolzano, it might be necessary to also work in the direction of "a multinational conception of citizenship" and a "a more multicultural conception of multinationalism", that is, national groups, sub-state national groups, and immigrant groups (Kymlicka 2011: 282). This would promote a sense of common citizenship and therefore be more consistent with the understanding of inclusive education in terms of fair schools for all.

References

Alcock, Antony E. (2001): The South Tyrol Autonomy. A short Introduction. http://www.provinz.bz.it/news/de/publikationen.asp.

Ainscow, Mel/Booth, Tony/Dyson, Alan (2006): Improving schools, developing inclusion. London: Routledge.

ASTAT (2019): Öffentlich Bedienstete. In: astatinfo 11, pp. 1–24.

Auer, Petra (2021): Values in the classroom. A study on value differences and similarities in primary school children, their parents, and their teachers in a multilingual European border region. Diss. Bozen-Bolzano: Free University of Bozen-Bolzano.

Auer, Petra (2022): „Was uns wichtig ist." – Zu den Werten von Kindern im Grundschulalter in der Autonomen Provinz Bozen. In: Demo, Heidrun/Cappello, Silver/Macchia, Vanessa (eds.): Didattica e Inclusione scolastica – Inklusion im Bildungsbereich: Ermergenze educative: Neue Horizonte. Bozen-Bolzano: bu,press, pp. 33–51.

Augschöll, Annemarie (2011): Die Schule in Südtirol. In: Bündner Schulblatt = Bollettino scolastico grigione = Fegl scolastic grischun 73, 6, pp. 4–9.

Bambauer, Christoph (2019): Werte aus philosophischer Perspektive. In: Verwiebe, Roland (ed.): Werte und Wertebildung aus interdisziplinärer Perspektive. Wiesbaden: Springer, pp. 25–48.

Baur, Siegfried (2000): Die Tücken der Nähe. Kommunikation und Kooperation in Mehrheits-/Minderheitssituationen. Meran: alpha&beta.

Baur, Siegfried (2013): Schwierigkeiten und Möglichkeiten einer Erziehung für ein mehrsprachiges Europa am Beispiel der Grenzregion Südtirol. In: Synergies Pays germanophones 6, pp. 71–82.

Baur, Siegfried/Videsott, Gerda (2012): Klassenpartnerschaften zwischen deutschen und italienischen Grund- und Mittelschulen in Südtirol. In: Baur, Siegfried (ed.): Austauschpädagogik und Austauscherfahrung: Sprach- und Kommunikationslernen durch Austausch. Baltmannsweiler: Schneider, pp. 97–134.

Berman, Gabrielle/Hart, Jason/O'Mathúna, Dónal/Mattellone, Erica/Potts, Alina/O'Kane, Claire/Shusterman, Jeremy/Tanner, Thomas (2016): What We Know about Ethical Research Involving Children in Humanitarian Settings: An overview of principles, the literature and case studies. Florence: UNICEF Office of Research. https://www.unicef-irc.org/publications/pdf/IWP_2016_18.pdf.

Bilsky, Wolfgang/Borg, Ingwer/Janik, Michael/Groenen, Patrick J. F. (2015): Children's value structures – Imposing theory-based regional restrictions onto an ordinal MDS solution. In: Roazzi, Antonio/Campello de Souza, Bruno/Bilsky, Wolfgang (eds.): Facet Theory: Searching for Structure in Complex Social, Cultural and Psychological Phenomeny. Recife: Editora UFPE, pp. 23–37.

Bilsky, Wolfgang/Döring, Anna/van Beeck, Franka/Rose, Isabel/Schmitz, Johanna/Aryus, Katrin/Drögekamp, Lisa/Sindermann, Jeannette (2013): Assessment of Children's Value Structures and Value Preferences. Testing and Expanding the Limits. In: Swiss Journal of Psychology 72, 3, pp. 123–136.

Borg, Ingwer/Groenen, Patrick J. F./Mair, Patrick (2013): Applied Multidimensional Scaling. Heidelberg: Springer.

Yang, Kuo-Shu/Bond, Michael H. (1982): Ethnic affirmation versus cross-cultural accommodation. The variable impact of questionnaire language on Chinese bilinguals from Hong Kong. In: Journal of Cross-Cultural Psychology 13, 2, pp. 169–185.

Capanna, Cristina/Vecchione, Michele/Schwartz, Shalom H. (2005): La misura dei valori. Un contributo alla validazione del Portrait Values Questionnaire su un campione italiano. In: Bolletino di psicologia applicata 246, pp. 29–41.

Carlà, Andrea (2019): Fear of "Others"? Processes of Securitization in South Tyrol. In: Research and Science Today. International Relations, 2, 18, pp. 9–25.

Cieciuch, Jan/Döring, Anna K./Harasimczuk, Justyna (2013): Measuring Schwartz's values in childhood. Multidimensional scaling across instruments and cultures. In: European Journal of Developmental Psychology 10, 5, pp. 625–633.

Cieciuch, Jan/Schwartz, Shalom H./Davidov, Eldad (2015): Values, Social Psychology of. In: Wright, James D. (ed.), International Encyclopedia of the Social & Behavioral Sciences. Oxford: Elsevier, pp. 41–46.

Cohen, Jacob W. (1988): Statistical power analysis for the behavioral sciences. Hillsdale, NJ: Lawrence Erlbaum Associates.

Council of the European Union (2018): Council Recommendations of 22 May 2018 on key competences for lifelong learning (2018/C 189/01). In: Official Journal of the European Union. https://eur-lex.europa.eu/legal-content/EN/TXT/PDF/?uri=CELEX:32018H0604(01)&from=EN.

D'Alessio, Simona (2011): Inclusive Education in Italy. A Critical Analysis of the Policy of Integrazione Scolastica. Rotterdam: Sense Publishers.

Daniel, Ella/Hofmann-Towfigh, Nadi/Knafo, Ariel (2013): School Values Across Three Cultures. A Typology and Interrelations. In: SAGE Open, 3, 2, pp. 1–16. doi:10.1177/2158244013482469.

Daniel, Ella/Schiefer, David/Knafo, Ariel (2012): One and Not the Same. The Consistency of Values across Contexts among Majority and Minority Members in Israel and Germany. In: Journal of Cross-Cultural Psychology 43, 7, pp. 1167–1184.

Davidov, Ella/Schmidt, Patrick/Schwartz, Shalom H. (2008): Bringing Values Back in. The Adequacy of the European Social Survey to Measure Values in 20 Countries. In: The Public Opinion Quarterly 72, 3, pp. 420–445.

Department for Education (DfE) (2014): Promoting fundamental British values as part of SMSC in schools. In: Departmental advice for maintained schools. Department for Education. https://www.gov.uk/government/publications/promoting-fundamental-british-values-through-smsc.

Döring, Anna K./Blauensteiner, Andrea/Aryus, Katrin/Drögekamp, Lisa/Bilsky, Wolfgang (2010). Assessing values at an early age. The picture-based value survey for children. In: Journal of Personality Assessment 92, pp. 439–448.

Döring, Anna K. (2010): Assessing Children's Values. An Exploratory Study. In: Journal of Psychoeducational Assessment 28, 6, pp. 564–577.

Döring, Anna K./Cieciuch, Jan (2018): Die Theorie menschlicher Werte nach Shalom H. Schwartz und ihre Relevanz für die Erforschung der Werteentwicklung im Kindes- und Jugendalter. In: Döring, Anna K./Cieciuch, Jan (eds.): Werteentwicklung im Kindes- und Jugendalter. Warschau: Liberi Libri, pp. 21–27.

Döring, Anna K./Daniel, Ella/Knafo-Noam, Ariel (2016): Introduction to the Special Section Value Development from Middle Childhood to Early Adulthood – New Insights from Longitudinal and Genetically Informed Research. In: Social Development 25, 3, pp. 471–481.

Döring, Anna K./Makarova, Elena/Herzog, Walter/Bardi, Anat (2017): Parent-child value similarity in families with young children. The predictive power of prosocial educational goals. In: British Journal of Psychology 108, pp. 737–756.

Döring, Anna K./Schwartz, Shalom H./Cieciuch, Jan/Groenen, Patrick J. F./Glatzel, Valentina/Harasimczuk, Justyna/Janowicz, Nicole/Nyagolova, Maya/Scheefer, E. Rebecca/Allritz, Matthias/Milfont, Tacino L./Bilsky, Wolfgang (2015): Cross-cultural evidence of value structures and priorities in childhood. In: British Journal of Psychology 106, 4, pp. 675–699.

Council of the European Union (2008): White Paper on Intercultural Dialogue. Living Together As Equals in Dignity. https://search.coe.int/cm/Pages/result_details.aspx?ObjectId=09000016805d37c2.

Frey, Dieter (2016): Psychologie der Werte. Von Achtsamkeit bis Zivilcourage – Basiswissen aus Psychologie und Philosophie. Berlin, Heidelberg: Springer.

Graham, Anne/Powell, Mary Ann/Taylor, Nicola/Anderson, Donnah/Fitzgerald, Robyn (2013): Ethical Research Involving Children. Florence: UNICEF Office of Research – Innocenti. https://childethics.com/wp-content/uploads/2013/10/ERIC-compendium-approved-digital-web.pdf.

Gross, Barbara (2019): Further Language Learning in Linguistic and Cultural Diverse Contexts. A Mixed Methods Research in a European Border Region. London: Routledge.

Gross, Barbara/Dewaele, Jean-Marc (2018): The relation between multilingualism and basic human values among primary school children in South Tyrol. In: International Journal of Multilingualism 15, 1, pp. 35–53.

Grusec, Joan E./Hastings, Paul D. (2015): Handbook of socialization. Theory and Research. New J: Guilford.

Hunner-Kreisel, Christine/Kuhn, Melanie (2010): Children's perspectives. Methodological Critiques and Empirical Studies. In: Andresen, Sabine/Diehm, Isabell/Sander, Uwe/Ziegler, Holger (eds.): Children and the Good Life. New Challenges for Research on Children. Dordrecht: Springer, pp. 115–118.

Hurrelmann, Klaus (2006): Einführung in die Sozialisationstheorie. Weinheim: Beltz.

Kochanska, Grazyna (1994): Beyond cognition. Expanding the search for the early roots of internalization and conscience. In: Developmental Psychology 30, pp. 20–22. doi:10.1037/0012-1649.30.1.20.

Kymlicka, Will (2011): Multicultural citizenship within multination states. In: Ethnicities 11, 3, pp. 281–302. https://doi.org/10.1177/1468796811407813.

Lee, Julie A./Ye, Sheng/Sneddon, Joanne N./Collins, Patricia R./Daniel, Ella (2017): Does the intra-individual structure of values exist in young children? In: Personality and Individual Differences 110, pp. 125–130.

Makarova, Elena/Herzog, Walter/Weber, Katharaina/Frommelt, Manuela (2012): Werte und Wertetransmission. Wertevermittlung durch Erziehungsziele und Werthaltungen der Eltern. Bern: Uni Bern. Retrieved from https://www.elenama karova.ch/projects/value-transmission/.

Mertens, Donna M. (2015): Research and Evaluation in Education and Psychology. Integrating Diversity with Quantitative, Qualitative, and Mixed Methods (4th ed.). Los Angeles: SAGE.

MIUR (n.d.): Sistema educativo di istruzione e di formazione. https://www.miur.gov. it/sistema-educativo-di-istruzione-e-formazione.

Pavone, Marisa (2012): Inserimento, Integrazione, Inclusione. In: d'Alonzo, Luigi/ Caldin, Roberta (eds): Questioni, sfide e prospettive della Pedagogia Speciale. Naples: Liguori, pp. 145–158.

Powell, Justin J. W./Merz-Atalik, Kerstin/Ališauskienė, Stefanija/Brendel, Michelle/ Echeita, Gerardo/GuÐjónsdóttir, Hafdís et al. (2019): Teaching Diverse Learners in Europe. Inspiring Practices and Lessons Learned from Germany, Iceland, Lithuania, Luxembourg, Spain and Sweden. In: Schuelka, Matthew/Johnstone, Christopher/Thomas, Gary/Artiles, Alfredo J. (eds.): The Sage Handbook of Inclusion and Diversity in Education. London: SAGE, pp. 321–337.

Ralston, David A./Cunniff, Mary K./Gustafson, David J. (1995): Cultural Accomodation. The effect of language on responses of bilingual Hong Kong Chinese Managers. In: Journal of Cross-Cultural Psychology 26, 6, pp. 714–727.

Rautz, Günther (1999): Die Sprachenrechte der Minderheiten. Ein Rechtsvergleich zwischen Österreich und Italien. Baden-Baden: Nomos.

Roccas, Sonia/Sagiv, Lilach (2010): Personal Values and Behavior. Taking the Cultural Context into Account. In: Social and Personality Psychology Compass 4, 1, pp. 30–41. doi:10.1111/j.1751-9004.2009.00234.x.

Sagiv, Lilach/Roccas, Sonia/Cieciuch, Jan/Schwartz, Shalom H. (2017): Personal values in human life. In: Nature Human Behavior 1, pp. 630–639. doi:10.1038/ s41562-017-0185-3.

Sant, Edda (2021): Political Education in Times of Populism. Cham: Palgrave Macmillan. https://doi.org/10.1007/978-3-030-76299-5_8.

Schmidt, Peter/Bamberg, Sebastian/Davidov, Eladad/Hermann, Johannes/Schwartz, Shalom H. (2007): Die Messung von Werten mit dem „Portraits Value Questionnarie". In: Zeitschrift für Sozialpsychologie 38, 4, pp. 261–275.

Schubarth, Wilfried (2019): Wertebildung in der Schule. In: Verwiebe, Roland (ed.): Werte und Wertebildung aus interdisziplinärer Perspektive. Wiesbaden: Springer, pp. 79–96.

Schwartz, Shalom H. (1992): Universals in the content and structure of values. Theory and empirical tests in 20 countries. In: Zanna, Marc Z. (ed.): Advances in experimental social psychology. New York: Academic Press, pp. 1–65.

Schwartz, Shalom H. (1994): Are There Universal Aspects in the Structure and Contents of Human Values? In: Journal of Social Issues 50, 4, pp. 19–45.

Schwartz, Shalom H. (1999a): A Theory of Cultural Values and Some Implications for Work. In: Applied Psychology. An International Review 48, I, pp. 23–47.

Schwartz, Shalom H. (1999b): Cultural value differences. Some implications for work. In: Applied Psychology. An International Review 48, pp. 23–47.

Schwartz, Shalom H. (2003): Computing Scores for the 10 Human values. https://www.europeansocialsurvey.org/docs/methodology/ESS_computing_human_valu es_scale.pdf.

Schwartz, Shalom H. (2006): Les valeurs de base de la personne. Théorie, mesures et applications. In: Revue Française De Sociologie 47, 4, pp. 929–968.

Schwartz, Shalom H. (2012): An Overview of the Schwartz Theory of Basic Values. In: Online Readings in Psychology and Culture 2, 1. https://doi.org/10.9707/2307-0919.1116.

Steininger, Rolf (2004): Südtirol im 20. Jahrhundert. Vom Leben und Überleben einer Minderheit. Innsbruck: StudienVerlag.

Thome, Helmut (2019): Werte und Wertebildung aus soziologischer Sicht. In: Verwiebe, Roland (ed.): Werte und Wertebildung aus interdisziplinärer Perspektive. Wiesbaden: Springer, pp. 47–78.

Verra, Roland (2008): Die Entwicklung der drei Schulmodelle in Südtirol seit 1945. In: Ladinia 17, pp. 223–260.

Verwiebe, Roland (2019): Werte und Wertebildung – Einleitende Bemerkungen und empirischer Kontext. In: Verwiebe, Roland (ed.): Werte und Wertebildung aus interdisziplinärer Perspektive. Wiesbaden: Springer, pp. 1–24.

Voltmer, Leonhard/Lanthaler, Franz/Abel, Andrea/Oberhammer, Margit (2007): Insights into the Linguistic Situation of South Tyrol. In: Abel, Andrea/Stuflesser, Mathias/Voltmer, Leonhard (eds.): Aspects of Multilingualism in European Border Regions. Insights and Views from Alsace, Eastern Macedonia and Thrace, Lublin Voivodeship and South Tyrol. Bozen: LEO, pp. 197–258.

Wisthaler, Verena (2013): Identity Politics in the Educational System in South Tyrol. Balancing between Minority Protection and the Need to Manage Diversity. In: Studies in Ethnicity and Nationalism 13, 3, pp. 358–372.

Zinn, Dorothy L. (2017): Migrant Incorporation in South Tyrol and Essentialized Local Identities. In: F. Decimo, Francesca/Gribaldo, Alessandra (eds.): Boundaries within. Nation, Kinship and Identity among Migrants and Minorities. IMISCOE Research Series, Springer, pp. 93–114.

Evidence on Analysis and Reflections of Available Statistical Data in Italy

Rosa Bellacicco, Silver Cappello[1]

Introduction

During the past few decades, the definition of inclusive education has shifted from an approach to support and placement of pupils with disability/special needs to a notion of education for all (Messiou 2017; Wolff et al. 2021). Adopting this vantage point, inclusive education implies the need to dismantle complex barriers for learning and participation for all children and young people in schools (Artiles/Kozleski/Waitoller 2011). According to some authors (Ainscow 2016, 2020; IBE-UNESCO 2016), consequently, in research it is helpful to use a definition of inclusive education as a process: it is about addressing all forms of disparities and inequalities in students' presence, participation, and achievement, and at the same time, emphasising the attention to those groups of learners who may be at specific risk of marginalisation, exclusion, or underachievement. In practice, this results in a complex conceptual model in which an inclusive school can be defined as a system where structures in place and the processes operate to translate the inputs (e.g., the resources, the expertise available to the school, the student and teacher variables, and the supports available from the macro educational system, from external agencies and from the community) into the desired outputs (e.g., including the pupil's academic output) (Kinsella 2018).

A strong commitment reinforcing inclusion and equity in education was expressed by the United Nations' Convention on the Rights of Persons with Disabilities (UNCRPD; United Nations 2006). Since then, international agencies and supra-national organisations have tried to formulate and orchestrate national policies towards this global trend (Ball/Maguire/Braun 2011; Waldow 2009). Whilst many states took several efforts to make their education systems more and more inclusive (Smyth et al. 2014), like all major policy

---

1   The design of the text is equally attributable to both authors. As far as the drafting is concerned, Rosa Bellacicco is responsible for the introduction and paragraphs 1, 2, 6 and the conclusions, whereas Silver Cappello bears responsibility for the paragraphs 3, 4 and 5.

changes, the realisation and provision of this ideal vary significantly both in research and in practice between countries around the world and even within them (Amor et al. 2019; Artiles et al. 2006; Göransson/Nilholm 2014; Nilholm/Göransson 2017; Anastasiou/Keller 2014). The difficulty to implement inclusive education in practice is unsurprising given that it is a concept to be fulfilled in different settings with varying policy environments, resources, and organisational traditions (Magnússon/Göransson/Lindqvist 2019). Within this framework, data are required to evaluate the impact of inclusive interventions, to review the effectiveness of policies and processes, and inform future policies (Ainscow et al. 2012, 2020).

1   The role and shortcomings of data

A key passage in the UNCRPD stresses that its implementation and monitoring require the collection of data on the population with disabilities for the countries that have ratified it, "to enable them to formulate and implement policies to give effect to the [...] Convention" (article 31). Consistently, the *World Report on Disability* (WHO 2011) makes a strong case for research on disability and categorically points out that continued "lack of data and evidence [...] often impedes understanding and action" (p. 263) across the various sectors, including education. More recently, one of the main calls in the Sustainable Development Goals (SDG) of the *2030 Agenda target 17.18* is to support capacity-building in developing countries in the collection of disability statistics with the aim to ensure evidence-based formulation of inclusive development, policies and programmes (United Nations Department of Economic and Social Affairs 2019). Additionally, the policy agenda of the European Agency for Special Needs and Inclusive Education (EASNIE 2020) also clearly embraces the importance of gathering statistics, by stating that "access to valid and reliable data is essential as an evidence base to develop inclusive educational policy at the regional, national and international level" (p. 4).

A major impetus in this direction is given by the UNESCO Institute for Statistics (UIS), United Nations Statistics Division, the World Bank, and other international (e.g., Eurydice) and European networks (e.g., EASNIE itself) that try to collect internationally comparable indicators and statistics on education and literacy. A significant development in recent years, especially in relation to enhancing conceptual clarity around disability, has been also undertaken by the Washington Group on Disability Statistics. The Washington Group has built on the World Health Organisation's (WHO) conceptual framing of disability as a bio-psycho-social model of human functioning, developing a disability-related set of questions suitable for use in national censuses. This endeavour has meaningful implications in dealing with the challenge of disability definition and measurement in a culturally neutral and reasonably standardised way among the United Nations member states (Madans/Loeb/Altman 2011).

However, even though these bodies are monitoring the progress made concerning inclusion and the equity agenda on education systems (e.g., Blanck/Edelstein/Powell 2013; D'Alessio/Watkins 2009), this line of research should be further developed. On the one hand, the availability and reliability of statistics about inclusion differ between countries (Buchner et al. 2021). Rich information across all states is hard to obtain due to a limited collection of data on disability, particularly on the participation of children with disabilities in inclusive education in countries from the Global South. On the other hand, despite the Washington Group's work, definitions of disability still vary across countries covering different 'categories' of special needs (e.g., disability, learning difficulties, behaviour problems) (Bines/Lei 2011; Watkins/Ebersold/Lénárt, 2014). Of course, this leads to a series of issues in making international comparisons between statistics and, ultimately, between policies and practices of individual countries (D'Alessio and Watkins 2009).

Beyond this, data by international and European authorities present potential intrinsic limitations. For example, EASNIE still focuses on categories of Special Educational Needs (SEN), on placement of learners with SEN and the allocation of additional resources. Thus, the exclusion of students with SEN from mainstream schools is still a reliable indicator of the potential inclusiveness of education systems (Graham/Sweller 2011). In this regard, Buchner and colleagues (2021) have investigated EASNIE secondary data across several European countries to examine trends in placements (i.e., mainstream classes, special classes in mainstream schools and special schools) of students with SEN in general and, specifically, those with intellectual disability. Given their focus on this type of students, they had to integrate EASNIE datasets with the datasets from national education authorities. The authors conclude that it is problematic to track tendencies of the implementation of inclusive education in different countries since, for example, national policies sometimes do not precisely define the differences between an inclusive or segregated settings (e.g., special classes in mainstream schools could be considered inclusive) and this can reproduce some bias. Furthermore, in some countries, there are no official statistics about impairment-related forms of SEN at a national level. Similar concerns are reported in the analysis by Weedon and Lezcano-Barbero (2021) of EASNIE statistics and those publicly available on SEN students in mainstream education in four European jurisdictions. They argue that it is not sufficient to examine the EASNIE data to present a full picture but there is the need to add other national statistics and qualitative, contextual factors in order to gain an in-depth understanding of the provision of special educational needs in a country.

2   The research project

This contribution addresses some of these issues by examining statistical reports in Italy on a national and local level, specifically the indicators/ variables included in these analyses on students with SEN[2]. Subsequently, other variables as detected in a few other countries were explored to offer a more complete picture. While recognising the broader scope and meanings of inclusive policies, here we concentrate on data relating to students with SEN, as in all European education systems, as outlined above, the distribution of inclusive and special education refers to the administrative categories of SEN as an "inevitable variable" (Buchner et al. 2021: 10) for doing research in the sector.

The Italian school system has a long tradition of inclusive education, starting in the 1970s with the first experiences of integrating students with disabilities into mainstream schools. Then in particular from the '90s on-wards, the legislation has developed further to guarantee students with disabilities the right to individualisation and personalisation in mainstream schools, granting basically Individualised Educational Plans (IEPs) and additional personnel resources. While the Law no. 170/2010 introduces some reasonable accommodations also for students with certified specific learning disabilities (SLD), more recent legislations (Ministerial Directive of 27 December 2012; and Ministerial Circular no. 8 of 6 March) extend several rights to students having other SEN (i.e., disadvantages stemming primarily from cultural, linguistic, or socio-economic factors).

The Ministry of Education (MIUR)[3] as well as the national statistical office ISTAT[4] are responsible for collating and publishing statistical data and information on the performance of the national school system, including those on the population of pupils with disabilities/SEN. For a better understanding, the specific situation of the Autonomous Province of Bolzano, the seat of the university to which the authors are affiliated, must be briefly

---

2   We adopted here the term "SEN" as an umbrella term regarding disability (e.g., physical, sensorial, intellectual, etc.), specific learning disabilities or cultural, linguistic, and socio-economic disadvantages. However, as we will see, in our jurisdiction, the provision for these three categories of special needs provision relies on different laws.
3   Ministry of Education, University and Research (www.miur.gov.it).
4   National Institute of Statistics (www.istat.it).

explained hereafter. As its name already suggests, within the Italian nation state, the province holds the status of legislative and administrative autonomy in different fields. In brief, this autonomy can be understood as the result of the ethnolinguistic landscape (i.e., three official languages spoken in the province since ancient times) and the historical events which have shaped the territory (for a detailed discussion of the history of the region, see Alcock 2001). For example, the province has a few special authorities in the field of education as well as a Provincial Institute for Statistics (ASTAT), which represents ISTAT at the provincial level. Thus, the province implements here a specific survey to collect these data (ASTAT)[5], even if it is closely bound to the official ISTAT national statistical report[6].

We draw on the indicators/variables reviewed in the national reports and compare them with each other and with those presented in the local statistical report to highlight convergences and divergences. To obtain a complete picture, as outlined above, some international sources – published by both international organisations and different governmental institutions – were also investigated. These countries were selected based on two criteria: the researchers' linguistic skills and the similarity of the school systems with the Italian system, that is, where most children attend mainstream public schools.

Our key argument is that in addition to studying trends in national and international data, analysing the variables considered by individual countries could, on the one hand, offer insights into the type of information and, on the other hand, stress areas of concern at a political level by identifying topical foci related to the provision for inclusive education.

3   Method

First, a checklist was prepared to map and compare the variables present in the most recent and current national and local institutional documents published from the 2017-2018 to the 2020-2021 school year. Second, further relevant categories were identified through a review of the international reports, both for the school and academic level. The analysis of these documents was realised through a second check list, which kept track of the different existing variables.

---

5   Provincial Institute of Statistics of South Tyrol (https://astat.provincia.bz.it/it/default. asp).
6   The national reports do not include most of data related to the Autonomous Province of Bolzano.

The research process started in 2020 with an exploration of the web pages of the Italian sources, both national and local of the Province of Bolzano (MIUR, ISTAT and ASTAT), collecting documents dating back until 2010. In this first phase, a total of 24 reports were identified. Subsequently, the research process shifted to the international level and the following sources were investigated: EASNIE, Eurydice, OECD, WHO, UNESCO, Unicef. A total of 32 documents were collected at this stage. Finally, it was decided to focus on some specific European countries (England, Ireland, Norway, Spain) and this last step revealed another 25 documents.

At the end of the research process, a total of 81 documents were collected. In any case, we are strongly aware that the existing materials in the national and, above all, international context are many more. Therefore, it is unlikely that the documentation identified can guarantee any sort of "representativeness" in Italy and Europe, and this aspect also constitutes a limitation of the study, which the reader should consider in the following results section.

4   Results of national reports' mapping

The results of the national (MIUR and ISTAT) and local (ASTAT) reports refer to the most recent school year, and any information available only in previous reports is given in the footnotes. The three reports presented in this section are the following:

- MIUR (2018–2019). Main data on pupils with disabilities.
- ISTAT (2018–2019). School inclusion of pupils with disabilities[7].
- ASTAT (2018–2019). School inclusion[8].

For the sake of clarity, the items will be described according to four macro-categories of variables: pupils with SEN, school personnel, school context and school-family relationships.

---

7   There are two more recent ISTAT reports (2019–2020 and 2020–2021) presented in a very reduced form, in which only the following data are reported: number of pupils with disabilities, support teachers and autonomy and communication assistants; percentage of support teachers teaching support without a specialisation qualification; participation of support teachers in courses on educational technologies; number of schools (state and private) with specific technological equipment for inclusion, distinguished only by geographical area; accessibility of schools. Two new variables also appear: data on distance learning during the COVID-19 pandemic; aggregated percentage of the three categories of SEN.

8   There is a more recent report (19–20) only on distance learning during the COVID-19 pandemic.

4.1   Variables relating to pupils with SEN

The analysed reports consider pupils with SEN in different ways since the national reports contain only data on students with disabilities, while the ASTAT report presents all three categories of SEN. The number of pupils is reported from kindergarten to upper secondary school, with a distinction by gender and, only for the MIUR report, by region, geographical area, state and private schools and the degree of disability (i.e., mild or severe disability).

The number of students who have a support teacher is mentioned in the ISTAT[9] and ASTAT reports distinguishing by gender and school level, while only in the ISTAT report, exclusively for primary and lower secondary school, also the number of pupils with reduced autonomy (i.e., those with serious difficulties or limitations in moving around the building, eating and going to the bathroom on their own) for the respective geographical areas.

Unlike the provincial report, the two national ones provide more detailed information by also indicating the specific type of disability. The ISTAT report distinguishes these data by gender and primary and lower secondary school, whereas the MIUR report draws a detailed distinction from kindergarten to upper secondary school and by state and private schools. In addition, in the latter, among the state schools there is a section dedicated to the different pathologies (i.e., prevalent International Classification of Diseases [ICD] code), with a distinction between the three main types of upper secondary school (i.e., lyceums, technical institutes, vocational institutes). Moreover, the MIUR report is the only one that indicates the number of classes/sections with at least one pupil with a disability with a distinction by school level and by state and private schools. However, only the ISTAT report pays specific attention to the pupils' participation in educational trips and extracurricular activities (with and without overnight stay and indicating the relative reasons). Further, it reports the amount of time the students spent in and out of the classroom considering their level of autonomy and the geographical area of their school.

Finally, two documents out of three (i.e., MIUR and ASTAT reports) include the number of foreign pupils with disabilities, that is, those without Italian citizenship, whereby in the MIUR report the related numbers are presented by region, geographical area and school level.

It should also be pointed out that students with specific learning disabilities (SLDs) are not mentioned in these reports in detail (with the exception of the three categories of SEN provided by ASTAT). There is another different annual report by MIUR in which only the data on students with SLDs are

9   Data only available in the report of the school year 17–18, with a distinction also by type of disability.

reported, broken down by type of SLD (i.e., dyslexia, dysgraphia, dysortho-graphy, or dyscalculia), school level, geographical area and region with the relative presence in state and private schools from primary to upper secondary school (MIUR 2020b).

4.2   Variables relating to school personnel

The reports of the three institutes indicate the number of support teachers with a distinction by school level (MIUR, ASTAT), by region (ISTAT) and by gender (ASTAT). Moreover, all of them indicate the number of teachers but only two of the three (ISTAT and ASTAT) also offer the ratio in relation to pupils with disabilities[10]. Moreover, only one document (ISTAT) for primary and lower secondary school considers the continuity of the relationship between students with disabilities and support teachers as well as the average number of weekly support hours assigned to pupils with disabilities.

The ISTAT report also tracks support teachers' attendance of training courses on inclusive education, the percentage of support teachers who work without a specialisation qualification in inclusive education, the number of autonomy and communication assistants (by region and in relation to the number of pupils) and the number of working hours per week from this professional figure. In the Province of Bolzano, the autonomy and communication assistant finds its equivalent in the so-called "integration collaborator". In the ASTAT report, these figures are shown in relation to pupils with disabilities. Further, information on the integration collaborators' knowledge in Italian Sign Language is incorporated.

4.3   Variables relating to the school context and school-family relationships

The ISTAT and ASTAT reports provide some data on the school context: the number of schools that have specific technological equipment for inclusion. In the case of ISTAT data are distinguished by region, while in the case of ASTAT the school levels and the type of technological equipment are indicated. Additionally, both documents focus on the accessibility of schools, be it architectural and sensory (ISTAT) or internal and external (ASTAT).

---

10 This data is surprisingly missing in the most recent MIUR report referred to the 2018–2019 school year, but there is in the previous one (2017–2018 school year), the only one in which the type of contract of support teachers (fixed or permanent) is also reported.

Only one report (ISTAT) tracks the family participation indicating data on the frequency of meetings among parents, curricular and support teachers with a distinction by geographical area, and data on appeals to the Regional Administrative Court (the so-called *Tribunale Amministrativo Regionale – TAR*) by dissatisfied families (only for primary and lower secondary schools). The following table displays a summary of the main elements emerging from the analysis of the reports (Tab. 1).

Table 1:   Synthesis of the analysis of national and local reports

		MIUR 18–19	ISTAT 18–19	ASTAT 18–19
Pupils with Special Educational Needs	Number of pupils with SEN from pre-school to secondary school, by gender	X Only pupils with disabilities, by region, geographical area, state and private schools, degree of disability (mild or severe disability)	X Only pupils with disabilities[11]	X Three categories of SEN
	Number of pupils with a support teacher, by gender and school level		Report 17–18	X
	Number of pupils with reduced autonomy (they cannot move around the building, eat, and go to the toilet by themselves), by geographical area		X Only primary and lower secondary school	
	Number of so-called foreign pupils with disabilities (with non-Italian citizenship)	X By region, geographical area and school level		X

11 In the report of the 2019–20 school year there is only the total number of the three categories of SEN, from primary to secondary school.

		MIUR 18—19	ISTAT 18—19	ASTAT 18—19
Pupils with Special Educational Needs	Types of disabilities	X By school level, state and private schools, different pathologies (prevalent ICD code), in the three types of upper secondary school (lyceums, technical institutes, vocational institutes)	X By gender, primary and lower secondary school	
	Number of classes/sections with at least one pupil with disabilities, by school level (state and private schools)	X		
	Amount of school time spent by pupils with disabilities in and out of class, by level of autonomy and geographical area		X By primary and lower secondary school	
	Participation of pupils with disabilities in educational trips and extracurricular activities with and without overnight accommodation, by reasons and geographical area		X By primary and lower secondary school	
School personnel	Number of support teachers	X By school level	X By region	X By gender and school level
	Support teachers/pupils with disabilities (ratio)	Report 17—18	X	X
	The continuity of the relationship between students and support teachers, by geographical area		X By primary and lower secondary school	

		MIUR 18—19	ISTAT 18—19	ASTAT 18—19
School personnel	Number of weekly support hours assigned to pupils with disabilities, by geographical area		X By primary and lower secondary school	
	Type of contract of support teachers (fixed-term and permanent)	Report 17—18		
	Participation of support teachers in courses on inclusive teaching		X	
	Percentage of support teachers teaching support without a specialisation qualification		X	
	Number of autonomy and communication assistants, by region and in ratio of pupils		X	
	Number of hours per week worked by autonomy and communication assistants, by level of autonomy and geographical area		X	
	Number of integration collaborators, by gender, school level, with information on knowledge of Italian Sign Language (ISL) and in ratio of pupils with disabilities and those assisted by integration collaborators			X
School context and school-family relationships	Number of schools with specific technological equipment for inclusion, by school level and type of technological equipment		X By school region	X
	Accessibility of schools, by school level		X Physical and sensory accessibility, by region	X Internal and external accessibility

		MIUR 18—19	ISTAT 18—19	ASTAT 18—19
School context and school-family relationships	Frequency of meetings among family, curricular and support teachers, by geographical area		X	
	Data on appeals to the Regional Administrative Court by dissatisfied families, by geographical area (primary and secondary schools only)		X	

5   New variables from international reports

There are many variables explored in international reports and they partly overlap with those identified in the Italian scenario. In this paragraph we will only consider the "additional" ones, which are not included in the national documentation.

An important aspect that emerged from English reports is the one related to the periods of absence or permanent absence of pupils with SEN, with and without certification (statement), in terms of the number of days of non-attendance and related reasons (Department for Education 2016, 2019). They also consider the variables "ethnicity" and "English as a first language", focusing on the number of students who have these characteristics and, at the same time, special needs (Department for Education 2020a, 2020b). Closely related to this point, a report from Ireland (2020) indicates the number of pupils at risk of educational disadvantage and with SEN who are followed and supported by the Irish National Educational Psychological Service.

Finally, the area relating to the adult life project of pupils with SEN is considered in England and Ireland through some variables related to participation in apprenticeships (Department for Education 2020a) and the proportion of entrants with learning difficulties and/or disabilities to higher education (Department for Education 2020b; Department of Education 2020).

International reports often discuss information on the special school system, such as data on drop-out in special classes and special schools or the transition between mainstream and special system (Department of Education and Skills 2011). Such data can be considered less relevant to the Italian context.

6   Discussion

The three reviewed Italian statistical reports differ in the way they record inclusive education variables. All three datasets include data on the category of disability. The two national reports distinguish different degrees and types of impairment (e.g., physical, sensorial, intellectual, etc.). They also specify in detail the number of students accessing inclusive education at various school levels and the types of schools and their geographical distribution throughout the country. As a result, a general picture of the student population with disabilities is described.

However, only one national body publishes a specific report on the proportion of students with SLDs. Moreover, only the local report pays attention to data on cultural, linguistic, and socio-economic disadvantages (i.e., SEN students), describing them from pre-primary to upper secondary school and by gender (even if in a more recent ISTAT report there is a reference to the rate of students with SLDs and other SEN; see footnote 13). This is likely to be due to the traditional centrality of the disability category in the Italian context and the late identification of students as having specific learning disabilities or other SEN as caused by socioeconomic, cultural, and linguistic disadvantages. In general, the perspective of intersectionality – namely how different factors intersect to create multiple deep-rooted disadvantages – is partly missing as only gender and migrant status are included while other information is not published, for instance, the intersection between the category of disability and social class or first language or ethnicity. On the international level some of them are available.

However, what seems even least explored are data on students with disabilities with different types of impairments, with SLDs and with SEN that allow for comparison of the quality of inclusive education in terms of micro-exclusions. This is a widespread phenomenon also in Italy that implies the promotion of the teaching of students with SEN in regular schools yet in different settings, instead of classrooms with peers (Nes/Demo/Ianes 2018; Bellacicco et al. 2019). The broader view of inclusion now necessitates a wider consideration of students involved and not only a generic reference to the category of disability.

Moreover, results from this study show that also the area of social participation is covered only superficially and considered solely the student population with disability in one report.

Referring to Kinsella's model (2018), regarding inputs and especially the involved resources, data on physical accessibility and technological factors are available in two reports. However, in this dimension, the most in-depth analysis concerns the resource of support teacher. Their profile is tackled particularly in one report, the one by ISTAT, which outlines competence, previous training and specialisation, the continuity of their relationship with the student with disability, staff ratios, and so forth. The allocation of the number of support teachers' hours per pupil in the different regions covered by the report is another important element, given the many regional differences found in Italy in this regard (Fogarolo 2021).

The same report (ISTAT) and the local one (ASTAT) also discuss the figure of other professionals employed in case of severe disabilities alongside support teachers, the so-called "autonomy and communication assistants" or "integration collaborator". However, it would be necessary to take in other information related to these input variables, such as providing a comprehensive illustration of their profiles (in terms of their distribution, tasks assigned, professional development, etc.) but also embracing issues about mainstream classroom teachers' competence and their expertise in inclusive education. All this attention on support teachers and personnel is rooted in the influence and pervasiveness of a medical approach that leads to providing additional support to Italian students with disabilities rather than focusing on the expertise of mainstream classroom teachers and their ability to meet diverse student needs and employ differentiate instruction. This is confirmed by the fact that the relationship with students' families is only touched upon in one report (ISTAT) out of three and especially in relation to the request, through the Court, for additional hours of support teaching – another typical Italian issue (Ianes/Augello 2019). However, information on the support of external agencies and the community is absent.

Beyond this, the collection of data on inclusive processes is also regarded as needing a significant critical review about communication, consultation, collaboration and coordination amongst, for instance, school staff, since it is the starting point for developing inclusive practices (Ainscow 2016, 2020).

Finally, the results indicate an overwhelming lack of data on outputs, especially concerning students. In addition to a mere superficial engagement with SEN students' social achievements, academic outcomes for this population are lacking. However, in relation to children's performance on the basic learning tasks, the Global Monitoring Report (UNESCO 2014) clearly highlights that the global learning crisis is even more magnified for children with disabilities. Moreover, it is crucial to emphasise that within the various types of disabilities some are even more likely to be disadvantaged than others, and hence a homogenised discourse around disability would once again not be sufficient (Singal et al. 2018).

In Italy, in addition to traditional assessment mechanisms regarding pupil performance at the international level (e.g., PISA, perhaps the most well-known), further monitoring procedures were introduced, such as those guided by national research and evaluation public body "INVALSI" (*Istituto nazionale per la valutazione del sistema educativo di istruzione e di formazione*), which is now committed to the development of indicators and descriptors for the outcomes of students with disabilities – both in terms of learning and social participation. However, as Ianes, Demo and Dell'Anna (2020) noted, "the task is challenging because of the enormous variety of individualised learning goals defined in the IEPs" (p. 258).

Finally, it is worth noting the few "new" areas covered by international reports. As the analysis of these documents reveals, similarities in the variables published at the international level appear to suggest that statistical monitoring around the world is grappling with similar issues. Regarding new variables, the first one addresses the issue of students' absence from schools and the reasons behind them. The number of absences and the underlying rationales can be significant to understand, for example, the trend of disorder, its impact on student's daily functioning (if it requires hospitalisation, frequent check-up, etc.) or other contextual and personal factors potentially leading to a school drop-out. This data clearly would allow, whether explored, a better development of an individualised/personalised IEP also for the (Italian) pupils.

The second element refers to the relationships with psychological counselling service, which capture the collaboration between schools and public health system. The absence of these data in Italian reports, previously noted, may be a symptom that cooperation and dialogue between school and different stakeholders – in this case the health professionals – are underestimated or considered difficult to map because of the territorial disparities regarding provision of services outside of schools. It is of concern that in Italy 9.01% of funds are allocated at the regional level and even 10.27% at the local level (Ianes/Demo/Dell'Anna 2021; EASNIE 2019).

The last suggestion from international reports involves in-school learners' preparation for adult life (through internships; in Italy called *alternanza scuola-lavoro*) and their transition to higher education. More in general, we know that few studies analyse progression from school years towards adulthood and the extent to which inclusive education leads to independent living in the community (EASNIE 2018). However, according to the literature (Kefallinou 2019; Kefallinou/Symeonidou/Meijer 2020), a successful inclusive education can positively impact the transition to employment, financial independence, and stable adulthood. Thus, the collection of these data should be seen as a vital component of inclusive education and might be arguably integrated into Italian statistical reports.

7   Conclusions

Internationally, there is a considerable agreement on the need for the systematic collection of information to monitor progress toward greater educational inclusion and then improve the effectiveness of policies. However, this process has developed in multiple and varying directions in terms of approach and methods used across countries.

This study provides an overview of the current state of the type of statistical data gathered on inclusive education in Italy. The results of our study demonstrate that there are many components mapped in official reports, above all in terms of attendance of Italian schools, general profile, type and degree of impairment and other issues (e.g., participation in group class activities or some social experiences) related to students with disabilities. It is thus not surprising that we also found notable information about support teachers assigned to them and the relationship between these teachers and students' families. Notably, Italian reports shed light on how support teachers are treated as supplemental resources by the Italian state, highlighting, even though only through quantitative data, many of the recurrent problems found in the literature, such as a lack of teachers' continuity, legal disputes over the number of support hours assigned, recruitment of teachers without any specialisation qualification, high frequency of pull/push-out phenomena, etc.; (Nes/Demo/Ianes 2018; Fogarolo 2021).

Given this emphasis on the category of disability, the other categories (SLDs and disadvantaged learners) are not investigated or are not subject to different brief reports. All in all, the data gathered appear more closely connected to special education than inclusive education. Moreover, the data collection process seems fragmented in various documents and this does not allow to reach an integrated framework of evidence on Italian inclusive education.

Consequently, it is important to look beyond the current data and into other areas that should be covered in the years to come. Some of the most important further areas in this regard, also identified through the analysis of some international reports, are mainstream teachers' competence and their expertise in inclusive education; the intertwined relationships of (dis)ability with the socio-economic background; the collaboration and the provision from the territorial system. Of key importance, another area that is also missing in all our reports is a focus on students' long-term outcomes: social achievements (only mentioned), academic attainments, quality of life issues including self-reliance, autonomy, and transition to higher education/employment.

Two other issues concerning the data collection that would inform policymaking for inclusive education should also be raised here. First, at a national level, Fogarolo (2021) pointed out that there is also a lack of data on students with IEPs and, notably, on the number of students who graduate with a "full" diploma in high school or with a certificate of competence without possibility to access higher education (that is a result of an IEP in which the goals of the general curriculum are not achieved) (FISH 2021). It is thus impossible from the current data to provide evidence on the proportion of upper secondary students with SEN who apply or enter higher education. Moreover, the figure of support teachers who ask annually for a transfer to become curriculum teachers – another widespread phenomenon – is unknown.

Second, at an international level, Watkins, Ebersold and Lénárt (2014) also commented on these questions and added key strategies, some of which overlap with those just described. Summing up, one crucial suggestion is to align data gathered at the national level to the broader approach of inclusive education. This would encourage the examination of all students at risk of exclusion (i.e., students with other disadvantages) over the traditional 'target group' of students with disabilities. While the current distinction in different SENs and their placement was helpful, it did not consider the policy context of more systematic education systems reform (Florian 2019). Moreover, this broader view would support the contextualisation of specific data on inclusive education within all 'usual' educational data collection activities. From a methodological point of view, Watkins, Ebersold and Lénárt (2014) also argue for a regular and systematic collection of both quantitative and qualitative data and the triangulation of data from different points of view as a vital next step to implementing inclusive education policies based upon clearer and reliable information. There is considerable work to do, yet we hope this study, and other ones like this, can contribute to highlighting the development of the inclusive education field and offer invaluable insights.

Concluding, it is necessary to acknowledge some limitations in our study. The first one is that we reported only Italian statistical reports explicitly concentrated on students with SEN and we excluded the general education reports in which some relevant contextual variables could be found (e.g., the degree of decentralisation of the educational system). Yet, as we have argued, integrated reports should be warranted to connect the discourse between the fields of special and general inclusive education. Secondly, as noted above, results were limited to include only a few international reports. We did not conduct a systematic review on them or contact researchers of single countries. The low number of reports restricted a true comparison of findings.

References

Ainscow, Mel (2015): Struggles for equity in education: The selected works of Mel Ainscow. London, New York: Routledge.

Ainscow, Mel/Dyson, Alan/Goldrick, Sue/West, Mel (2012): Making schools effective for all: rethinking the task. In: School Leadership & Management 32, 3, pp. 197-213.

Ainscow, Mel (2020): Promoting inclusion and equity in education: Lessons from international experiences. In: Nordic Journal of Studies in Educational Policy 6, 1, pp. 7-16.

Alcock, Antony (2001): The South Tyrol Autonomy. A short Introduction. http://www.geography.ryerson.ca/wayne/Geo773-F2017/South-Tyrol-Autonomy.pdf [30.04.2022].

Amor, Antonio/Hagiwara, Mayumi/Shogren, Karrie/Thompson, James/Verdugo, Miguel Ángel/Burke, Kathryn/Aguayo, Virginia (2019): International perspectives and trends in research on inclusive education: a systematic review. In: International Journal of Inclusive Education 23, 12, pp. 1277-1295.

Anastasiou, Dimitris/Keller, Clayton (2014): Cross-national differences in special education coverage: An empirical analysis. In: Exceptional Children 80, 3, pp. 353-367.

Artiles, Alfredo/Kozleski, Elizabeth/Dorn, Sherman/Christensen, Carol (2006): Learning in inclusive education research: re-mediating theory and methods with a transformative agenda. In: Review of Research in Education 30, 1, pp. 65-108.

Artiles, Alfredo/Kozleski, Elizabeth/Waitoller Federico (2011): Inclusive Education: examining equity on five continents. Cambridge, MA: Harvard Education Press.

ASTAT (2020): Didattica a distanza durante l'emergenza Covid-19. Anno scolastico 2019/20. In: astatinfo 44, pp. 1-7.

ASTAT (2020): Inclusione scolastica. Anno scolastico 2018/19. In: astatinfo 15, pp. 1-12.

Ball, Stephen/Maguire, Meg/Braun, Annette (2011): How schools do policy: Policy enactments in secondary schools. London: Routledge.

Bellacicco, Rosa/Cappello, Silver/Demo, Heidrun/Ianes, Dario (2019): L'inclusione scolastica fra push-e pull-out, transizioni e BES: una indagine nazionale. In: Ianes, Dario (ed.): Didattica e inclusione scolastica. Ricerche e pratiche in dialogo. Milano: FrancoAngeli, pp. 175-218.

Bines, Hazel/Lei, Philippa (2011): Disability and education: the longest road to inclusion. In: International Journal of Educational Development 31, 5, pp. 419-424.

Blanck, Jonna Milena/Edelstein, Benjamin/Powell, Justin (2013): Persistente schulische Segregation oder Wandel zur inklusiven Bildung? Die Bedeutung der UN-Behindertenrechtskonvention für Reformprozesse in den deutschen Bundesländern. In: Swiss Journal of Sociology 39, 2, pp. 267–292.

Buchner, Tobias/Shevlin, Michael/Donovan, Mary-Ann/Gercke, Magdalena/Goll, Harald/Šiška, Jan/Janyšková, Kristýna/Smogorzewska, Joanna/Szumski, Grzegorz/Vlachou, Anastasia/Demo, Heidrun/Feyerer, Ewald/Corby, Deirdre (2021): Same progress for all? Inclusive education, the United Nations Convention on the rights of persons with disabilities and students with intellectual disability in European countries. In: Journal of Policy and Practice in Intellectual Disabilities 18, 1, pp. 7-22.

D'Alessio, Simona/Watkins, Amanda (2009): International comparisons of inclusive policy and practice: are we talking about the same thing? In: Research in Comparative and International Education 4, 3, pp. 233-249.

Department for Education (2016): Absence and exclusions additional analysis for pupils with special educational needs (SEN). Sheffield.

Department for Education (2019): A guide to absence statistics. London.

Department for Education (2020a): Progression to higher education or training, England, 2015/16 cohort. London.

Department for Education (2020b): Special educational needs and disability: an analysis and summary of data sources. Sheffield.

Department of Education and Skills (2011): National School Annual Census. Ireland: Statistics section of the Department of Education and Skills.

Department of Education (2020): Education Indicators for Ireland. Ireland.

European Agency for Special Needs and Inclusive Education (2018): Evidence of the link between inclusive education and social inclusion: a review of the literature. Denmark: European Agency for Special Needs and Inclusive Education.

European Agency for Special Needs and Inclusive Education (2019): Legislation updates 2019. Denmark: European Agency for Special Needs and Inclusive Education.

European Agency for Special Needs and Inclusive Education (2020): Key Principles – Supporting policy development and implementation for inclusive education: Policy Brief. Denmark: European Agency for Special Needs and Inclusive Education.

FISH – Federazione Italiana per il Superamento dell'Handicap (2021): Risultati sondaggio GLO e PEI. https://www.fishonlus.it/eventi/risultati-sondaggio-glo-e-pei/ [30.04.2022].

Fogarolo, Flavio (2021): Inclusione scolastica: così non va. Analisi e riflessioni sui dati statistici del Ministero dell'Istruzione (ottobre 2021). In: Ianes, Dario/Fogarolo, Flavio (eds.): Oltre la crisi della nostra inclusione scolastica. Verso un paradigma globale ed ecologico di supporto alla scuola inclusiva. Trento: Erickson, pp. 3-16.

Göransson, Kerstin/Nilholm, Claes (2014): Conceptual diversities and empirical shortcomings – a critical analysis of research on inclusive education. In: European Journal of Special Needs Education 29, 3, pp. 265-280.

Graham, Linda/Sweller, Naomi (2011): The Inclusion Lottery: Who's in and Who's Out? Tracking Inclusion and Exclusion in New South Wales Government Schools. In: International Journal of Inclusive Education 15, 9, pp. 941–953.

Ianes, Dario/Augello, Giuseppe (2019): Gli inclusio-scettici: Gli argomenti di chi non crede nella scuola inclusiva e le proposte di chi si sbatte tutti i giorni per realizzarla. Trento: Erickson.

Ianes, Dario/Demo, Heidrun/Dell'Anna, Silvia (2020): Inclusive education in Italy: historical steps, positive developments, and challenges. In: Prospects 49, 3, pp. 249-263.

IBE-UNESCO (2016): Training Tools for Curriculum Development – Reaching out to all learners: a resource pack for supporting Inclusive Education. Geneva: IBE-UNESCO.

Istituto Nazionale di Statistica (2020): L'inclusione scolastica degli alunni con disabilità. Anno scolastico 2018-2019. Italy: ISTAT.

Istituto Nazionale di Statistica (2020): L'inclusione scolastica degli alunni con disabilità. A.S. 2019-2020. Italy: ISTAT.

Istituto Nazionale di Statistica (2021): L'inclusione scolastica degli alunni con disabilità. A.S. 2020-2021. Italy: ISTAT.

Kefallinou, Anthoula (2019): Preventing school failure: examining the potential of inclusive education policies at system and individual levels. Denmark: European Agency for Special Needs and Inclusive Education.

Kefallinou, Anthoula/Symeonidou, Simoni/Meijer, Cor (2020): Understanding the value of inclusive education and its implementation: a review of the literature. In: Prospects 49, 3, pp. 135-152.

Kinsella, William (2018): Organising inclusive schools. In: International Journal of Inclusive Education 24, 12, pp. 1340-1356.

Madans, Jennifer/Loeb, Mitchell/Altman, Barbara (2011): Measuring disability and monitoring the UN Convention on the Rights of Persons with Disabilities: the work of the Washington Group on Disability Statistics. In: BMC Public Health 11, 4, pp.1-8.

Magnússon, Gunnlaugur/Göransson, Kerstin/Lindqvist, Gunilla (2019): Contextualizing inclusive education in educational policy: the case of Sweden. In: Nordic Journal of Studies in Educational Policy 5, 2, pp. 67-77.

Messiou, Kyriaki (2017): Research in the field of inclusive education: time for a rethink? In: International Journal of Inclusive Education 21, 2, pp. 146-159.

MIUR (2019): I principali dati relativi agli alunni con disabilità. Anno scolastico 2017/2018. Italy: MIUR – Ufficio Gestione Patrimonio Informativo e Statistica.

MIUR (2020a): I principali dati relativi agli alunni con disabilità. Anno scolastico 2018/2019. Italy: MI – DGSIS – Ufficio Gestione Patrimonio informativo e Statistica.

MIUR (2020b): I principali dati relativi agli alunni con DSA. Anno scolastico 2018/2019. Italy: MI – DGSIS – Ufficio Gestione Patrimonio informativo e Statistica.

Nes, Kari/Demo, Heidrun/Ianes, Dario (2018): Inclusion at risk? Push-and pull-out phenomena in inclusive school systems: the Italian and Norwegian experiences. In: International Journal of Inclusive Education 22, 2, pp. 111-129.

Nilholm, Claes/Göransson, Kerstin (2017): What is meant by inclusion? – An analysis of high impact research in North America and Europe. In: European Journal of Special Needs Education 32, 3, pp. 437–451.

Singal, Nidhi/Sabates, Ricardo/Aslam, Monazza/Saeed, Sahar (2020): School enrolment and learning outcomes for children with disabilities: findings from a household survey in Pakistan. In: International Journal of Inclusive Education 24, 13, 1410-1430.

Smyth, Fiona/Shevlin, Michael/Buchner, Tobias/Biewer, Gottfried/Flynn, Paula/Latimier, Camille/Šiška, Jan/Toboso-Martín, Mario/Díaz, Susana Rodríguez/Ferreira, Miguel (2014): Inclusive education in progress: policy evolution in four European countries. In: European Journal of Special Needs Education 29, 4, pp. 433–445.

UN (2006): Convention on the Rights of Persons with Disabilities. New York: United Nations.

United Nations Department of Economic and Social Affairs (2019): Disability and Development Report. Realizing the Sustainable Development Goals by, for and with persons with disabilities 2018. New York: United Nations.

UNESCO (2014): Teaching and learning: achieving quality for all. EFA Global Monitoring Report. France: UNESCO.

Waldow, Florian (2009): Undeclared imports: silent borrowing in educational policymaking and research in Sweden. In: Comparative Education 45, 4, pp. 477-494.

Watkins, Amanda/Ebersold, Serge/Lénárt, András (2014): Data collection to inform international policy issues on inclusive education. In: Measuring Inclusive Education. Bingley: Emerald Group Publishing Limited, pp. 53-74.

Weedon, Elisabet/Lezcano-Barbero, Fernando (2021): The challenges of making cross-country comparison of statistics on pupils with special educational needs. In: European Journal of Special Needs Education 36, 5, pp. 854-862.

Wolff, Charlotte/Huilla, Heidi/Tzaninis, Yannis/Magnúsdóttir, Berglind Rós/Lappalainen, Sirpa/Paulle, Bowen/Seppänen, Piia/Kosunen, Sonja (2021): Inclusive education in the diversifying environments of Finland, Iceland and the Netherlands: a multilingual systematic review. In: Research in Comparative and International Education 16, 1, pp. 3-21.

World Health Organisation (2011): World Report on Disability. Geneva: WHO Press.

Funding Models of Inclusion in an International Perspective

Joanne Banks, Silver Cappello, Heidrun Demo,
Rune Hausstätter, Simone Seitz[1]

1   Introduction

European policies on inclusive education show a general trend from a focus on disability and Special Educational Needs (SEN) towards a focus on the development of quality education for all learners (Meijer/Watkins 2016). Nevertheless, their implementation is challenged by the fact that, in many countries, conceptualisation of inclusive education has grown out of discussions around specialist segregated provision or integration (Meijer/Watkins 2019) and has produced confusing and sometimes contradictory overlapping of policies.

This becomes particularly visible in funding models. Recently, Meijer and Watkins (2019), basing on some comparative analysis conducted by the European Agency for Special Needs and Inclusive Education, have stated: "finding the best ways of financing special needs and inclusive education was and still is a challenge many European countries are facing" (716). In fact, several scholars have investigated the relationship between resource allocation and the implementation of inclusive practices (e.g., Parrish 2015; Ebersold 2016).

In many countries, besides a general orientation towards inclusive education policies, specific funding tracks for specific student groups considered eligible for special education exist. In the literature, this is described as the *Input model of funding* (Meijer 2003): funding is based on the identification of learners' needs at school level, municipalities, or local regions. Over the

---

1   The authors planned and elaborated the contents for the article together. The contribution refers to the Symposium "Financing Inclusive Education: Implications for the Implementation of Inclusive Education" organised within the Conference ECER 2021. Simone Seitz is author of the theoretical framework. The Introduction is written by Silver Cappello. Joanne Banks wrote the analysis of the Irish context. Rune Hausstätter is the author of the section about the Norwegian context. Heidrun Demo is the author of the section about the Italian context and of the discussion.

past decade, however, research from different European countries suggest that this funding model runs counter to the development of inclusion this funding model implies some risks for the development of inclusion (Ebersold/Meijer 2016). Countries using the input model are reporting a increase in the requests for funding and a growing prevalence of identified needs. Furthermore, the increased funding is often used for "outsourcing" strategies, where identified students are delegated to specific professionals or, in some systems, are placed in special classes or schools (Ebersold et al. 2019).

For this reason, many countries currently are moving towards funding models that combine the Input model with the *Throughput model* (Meijer 2003), where funding is based on specific formulas and on the condition that specific services will be organised at school or local level. The latter model is a form of funding that leaves the responsibility of resource allocation to schools, without the need for identification or assessment. Therefore, it potentially reduces the risk of labelling in schools and supports the implementation of inclusive practices (Ebersold et al. 2019).

In this chapter, we will describe how funding for inclusion is conceived in three different countries: Ireland, Italy, and Norway. The countries differ in their history in inclusive policies: Norway and Italy since the 1970s have a "school for all" and almost no special schools, while in Ireland special schools operate parallel to mainstream schools, of which many have special classes attached. The countries also differ in the way Throughput and Input funding models are balanced: in Norway almost no specific funding track for inclusion exists, in Italy mainly an Input model is in place, whereas Ireland mixes the Input, Throughput and Output models, as part of the funding depends also on the learning results obtained by students.

2   Theoretical framework

Taking a comparative perspective encourages critical reflection on how inclusive education is conceived and funded. As later comparative works have contributed to rethinking terms such as "disadvantage", "need", "ability" and "disability", in this paper we examine how the idea of funding inclusion-related resources has been culturally constructed, questioning 'taken for granted' conceptualisations (Scott 2014).

The international comparative character of our analysis requires a structuring of the research object on the different levels of governance and organisation of education systems – knowing that national policies and discourses are deeply interwoven with international ones. Impulses on an international level like the Agenda 2030 (UNESCO 2015) are part of different and overlapping national and international discourses on education but meeting different system conditions on national and regional levels.

In the context of the concern pursued here, neo-institutionalism, a sociological organisation theory, will therefore be used to structure our argumentation, specifically the three-pillar model according to Scott (2014). In this way, the interrelationships of governance, funding and educational practice can be brought into an overview and discussed.

This is possible because the sociological theory of organisation, neo-institutionalism, focuses not only on organisations themselves but also on the relationship between organisations and their social environment (Wohlfart 2020; Biermann/Powell 2014). Characteristic for early works of neo-institutionalism in the 1950s and early 1960s is the recognition that organisations cannot be regarded as autonomous social units but as "open systems" (Senge/Hellmann 2006: 12), which are embedded in and influenced by society. The focus in this context is not on society *per se* but on the connection between organisation and society: the social conditions of organisations. This is done by identifying functional relationships between organisations and various social institutions.

From the (early) perspective of neo-institutionalism, schools as organisations tend to a dynamic that their socially constructed norms are in "harmony" with the institutional environment – or at least in relation to them. Hence, this approach can be used to explain why reforms and regulations can also have non-intended conservative effects (cf. Scott 2014: 71; DiMaggio/Powell 1991). This provides the approach with specific explanatory value for our internationally based analysis.

Neo-institutionalism is often seen as a primarily macro-sociological approach (Mense-Petermann 2006: 71). It considers that institutional influences are often not based on the actor's or organisational level but on a broader social environment. Of primary importance then are not intra-organisational actors and internal decision-making processes. Instead, institutionalised rules and roles, as well as assumptions of self-evidence that are located "above" the individual actors or the individual organisation for institutions, provide patterns or systems of rules (cf. Senge/Hellmann 2006: 17). They are endowed with power and organisations cannot completely escape the influences of these but can react to them differently. In fact, organisations are affected by many different contradictory and institutionally anchored social contexts that are causally related to processes and decisions in organisations. However, institutions can also be shaped by organisations in the opposite way, as organisations are embedded in social environments and form institutionalised rules themselves. From that perspective, the comparative analyses of how inclusion and funding for inclusion is conceived within the organisation of school in different countries offers more than just a synthesis of different policies. Hints to the way the concepts are culturally institutionalised in the different contexts can be detected and contribute to a deeper understanding of the phenomenon.

According to Scott (2014), institutionalisation, understood as the developmental process of the consolidation of social norms and patterns of behaviour, can be analysed via three dimensions or pillars, given that institutions are built on 1) cognitive, 2) normative and 3) regulative structures and behaviours. "Institutions comprise regulative, normative, and cultural-cognitive elements that, together with associated activities and resources, provide stability and meaning to social life" (Scott 2014: 56).

Regulative institutions generate actions through explicitly formulated rules, laws, or contracts. These aspects of institutions limit and regulate action. Rulemaking, observation, control and sanctions influence the behaviour of actors consciously or unconsciously. Compliance is thus guided by the criteria of rational choice (e.g., strategic behaviour in case of Input model), coercion is defined as the source of institutional power (e.g., no diagnosis, means no additional money) (cf. Senge 2006: 38).

Normative institutions generate actions via norms and values. They are shaped by prescriptive, evaluative, and obligatory dimensions and they are mainly followed for two reasons: firstly, because the actors have internalised the norms and values and thus made them their own, and secondly, because of the assessment that one's own behaviour corresponds to social norms and values and is thus appropriate. A moral, abstract authority acts as a control mechanism. The effect of this depends on the degree of internalisation or on the pressure of expectations created by others. Legitimate organisations are those that fulfil – or give the appearance of fulfilling – values and norms accepted in society (cf. Merkens 2011: 36).

The cultural-cognitive dimension describes "the shared conceptions that constitute the nature of social reality and create the frames through which meaning is made" (Scott 2014: 67). For example, routines of action, regulated by cognitive institutions, run naturally and quasi-automatically. They are taken for granted as "the way we do these things" (Scott 2014: 68). Alternative ways of perceiving, acting, or thinking are therefore often inconceivable. This form of knowledge thus differs from discursive, conscious, or explicit knowledge. Unquestioned routine action is thus based on tacit knowledge (cf. Senge 2006: 38). Culturally cognitive institutions gain their legitimacy from the fact that they are considered culturally supported and conceptually correct. They are particularly sustainable because they are taken for granted.

Table 1:   Regulative, normative, and cultural-cognitive dimensions of institutions (Modified from Scott 2014; Senge 2006: 39; Wohlfart 2020: 99)

Dimensions	I Regulative: rules, laws, contracts	II Normative: norms, values	III Cultural-cognitive: Shared conceptions of social reality, belief systems, meaning systems
Basis of consent/ acceptance	expediency, appropriateness, practicality	Social obligation (social commitment)	Taken for granted; shared views/ not questioned
Indicators	Rules, laws, sanctions	Recognition, confirmation	Common beliefs (General convictions, shared beliefs)
Legitimacy	legally sanctioned	Morally controlled	Culturally supported, conceptually correct/ understandable

Using the dimensions of the neo-institutionalist model, it can be investigated how regulative, cultural-cognitive, and normative institutions affect organisational practices. This leads to questioning institutionalised rules, roles and "taken for granted-knowledge" within organisations (cf. Mense-Petermann 2006; Senge/Hellmann 2006: 17). In the specific case of this paper, cultural assumptions that lie behind the way inclusion and funding of inclusion are constructed in laws and policies can be unveiled and offer new perspectives on how funding hinders or strengthens inclusion and equity in education.

For the comparative analysis of this chapter, we will use a simplified version of the model, also considering that Scott's three dimensions have been criticised for the difficulty of separating clearly one from the other (cf. Senge 2006; Wohlfart 2020). For each country the regulative dimension will be described and then the normative and cultural-cognitive dimension will be considered jointly, in the awareness that single indicators can only rarely be assigned exclusively to one dimension.

3   Analysis of the Irish context

3.1   The historical policy context: the development of the regulative dimension

Current education policies in Ireland are, like in any country, guided by legacy and the historical development of its education system over time. Following the formation of the Irish state in 1919 and the establishment of the Department of Education in 1924, the education of students with disabilities became the remit of religious organisations who operated residential schools for specifics disabilities (such schools for blind or deaf children) or homes for 'mentally defective children' (Cussan Commission 1936). It was not until the 1960s that the Irish State began to consider the educational provision for these students with establishment of special schools for children with physical, sensory or mental disabilities. During this period, several policy reports were published reflecting, perhaps, a growing pressure on the government to provide an education for children with disabilities. The Report on Commission of Inquiry on Mental Handicap (1965) highlighted the lack of settings available for students with cognitive or intellectual disabilities. Alongside the growth in special schools during this time, the government began to open special classes located in mainstream 'national' or primary schools. Many of these classes were designated for students with Mild General Learning Disabilities and allowed students, previously at home or attending a special school, to attend their local school. Despite these developments throughout the 1960s and 1970s in Ireland, and the influential policy developments by its closest neighbour, the United Kingdom, with the publication of the Warnock Report (1978), Irish special education policy and development remained relatively stagnant. It was not until the early 1990s and the publication of the report from the Special Education Review Committee (SERC) (Government of Ireland 1993) that the educational provision for students with 'special educational needs' was fully addressed. Significantly, the report documented serious shortcomings in special educational provision at the time and acknowledged the need for greater government (instead of voluntary) involvement in the provision of education for students with disabilities (Shevlin/Banks 2021). SERC introduced the idea, which remains today, of a 'continuum of educational provision' that included mainstream classes, special classes and special schools (Merrigan/Senior 2021). The SERC Report was closely followed by a series of government acts including the Education Act (1998) which provided a statutory basis for policy and practice relating to all educational provision and the Equal Status Act (2000) which prohibited discrimination on nine grounds, including disability.

In addition to government reports and legislation of the time, a number of key legal cases were brought by parents of children who had autism and/or severe/profound intellectual disabilities who the State claimed to be 'ineducable' (Meegan/MacPhail 2006). These cases highlighted how these children had been systematically ignored by the state, and that the educational provision at the time was seriously inadequate. Following this, the state was obliged to recognise that these children had the right to receive an appropriate education based primarily on their learning needs rather than their medical needs, which had been the case.

The publication of the Education for Persons with Special Educational Needs (EPSEN) Act (2004) remains, however, the most influential policy with respect to children and young people with disabilities in Ireland. This Act fundamentally changed practices in mainstream education for students with disabilities as it required that "a child with special educational needs shall be educated in an inclusive environment with children who do not have such needs" but only if this was considered to be in the best interest of the child and their peers (Government of Ireland 2004). It broadened the definition of who was considered to have a 'special educational need'. This subsequently changed the profile of the mainstream school population as the prevalence of students with disabilities increased (Banks/McCoy 2011). The Act led to the development of a new organisation, the National Council for Special Education (NCSE), which was primarily responsible for resource allocation in schools which took the form of 'resource hours' for students with disabilities and Special Needs Assistants depending on the assessment of need.

3.2   Provision for students with disabilities

Ireland has 3,241 primary schools serving 560,000 students aged 5 to 12 years and 730 secondary schools catering for 380,000 students between 12 and 19 years of age (Education Statistics 2021). Measuring the prevalence of students with disabilities is complex. Rates often depend on how disability is defined, the reason for data collection, the individual reporting (parent or teacher, for example) and the context in which the identification takes place with some evidence to suggest identification may be socially stratified depending on the disadvantaged status of the school (McCoy/Banks 2012). Despite these difficulties, Growing Up in Ireland data shows the prevalence rate of students with disabilities is somewhere between 25 and 28 per cent of the mainstream school population (Banks/McCoy 2011; Cosgrove et al. 2014).

Students with disabilities can attend several different settings depending on their diagnosis and the availability of special school and class placements.

Students can attend one of Ireland's 123 special schools located around the country and operate separately to mainstream schools. They can also be placed in one of almost 2,000 special classes which are located in mainstream schools but generally designated for students with Autistic Spectrum Disorders (Shevlin/Banks 2021). Students can also attend mainstream schools and classes and receive in-class supports by having a Special Needs Assistant or can be withdrawn for individual or small-group work in specific areas of teaching and learning. There is little evidence from research, however, that students placed in special schools or classes gain from being placed in those settings compared to mainstream school settings (McCoy et al. 2014; Banks et al. 2016). While our understanding of student experiences in special schools is limited, research on special classes suggests much variability in how these classes operate with little evidence of progression out of these settings once students are placed in them (McCoy et al. 2014; Banks et al. 2016). Research has also highlighted some difficulties in initial teacher education and the extent to which it prepares teachers for working in mainstream settings with little emphasis on teaching more diverse student groups including those with disabilities (Hick et al. 2018). For teachers working in more specialised settings, there is no requirement to have specific special education qualifications and research indicates that teachers lack confidence and capacity in these settings with some experiencing overwhelm and burnout (Banks et al. 2016; Hick et al. 2018; NCSE 2019).

3.3   The intertwining of the regulative and normative/ cultural-cognitive dimension

Tensions in the inclusion debate

Since the publication of the EPSEN Act (2004), there have been significant changes in the education landscape in Ireland. Changes in culture and attitudes towards inclusion, language around special education and dramatic increases in funding and the provision of supports for special education have led to a rethinking about the extent to which the EPSEN Act is fit for purpose. The Act is now under review (DES 2021) to address these changes. In particular, there has been a shift in thinking, among some policy-makers, educators, parents and children and young people that 'additional' supports and accommodations for students with disabilities should be provided for every student regardless of their level of need through an inclusive or universal system of supports (NCSE 2019; Shevlin/Banks 2021; Flood/Banks 2021). Parallel to this conversation, however, there has been a policy push towards segregated provision, or special classes, since 2011 (Shevlin and Banks 2021). Despite the increase in this type of provision, there has been no decrease in the numbers of special schools in Ireland over the same period.

Ireland's ratification of the UNCRPD in 2018 has led to much of this discussion about how we can create an inclusive education system (UN 2006). Article 24 on Education, and more specifically, General Comment 4, have highlighted how Ireland is not meeting its obligations under the convention in relation to inclusive education. An NCSE public consultation (NCSE 2019) on Ireland's possible move to a fully inclusive education system in 2019 provided a timely insight into the nature of this increasingly polarised philosophical debate. On one side are education stakeholders who wish to retain a parallel system of special education (supports in the mainstream class or placement in special classes or special schools) and a mainstream school system, and on the other are voices which advocate for adopting a fully inclusive and rights-based approach where every child can attend their local school. This perspective views the provision of special education for some students as a form of segregation that is not in the best interests of the students in terms of their academic and social outcomes.

Changes to Ireland's special education funding model

The cost of 'special education' and the special education funding formula in place in Ireland has come under much scrutiny in recent years (DPER 2017; 2019) due mainly to 'spiralling costs' (Banks 2021). Some argue that the current spending on special education in Ireland is unsustainable, whereas others have suggested that it may simply be a form of 'catch-up' given the lack of investment over the past decades (Banks/McCoy 2017). The funding mechanism used to support students with disabilities has changed a number of times since the mid-2000s as the profile of the mainstream school population has become more diverse. Given the growth in prevalence of students with disabilities, the NCSE moved away from its Input or individualised student funding model and began to operate a mix of Input (individual funding) and Throughput funding (block grant to schools based on perceived levels of need) known as the General Allocation Model or GAM. This meant that schools received a general allocation of funding for students considered to have 'high incidence' needs which removed the need for individual assessment. Students with 'low incidence' needs were, however, still required to have a diagnosis in order to receive support. This model was criticised, however, for requiring labelling and diagnosis of students in order to receive support, leading to a burden of administration for schools and long waiting lists for parents unable to pay assessments privately. In an attempt to address these inequities, the NCSE undertook a lengthy consultation and, in 2017, introduced a new 'more equitable' model of funding known as the Special Education Teaching (SET) Model (NCSE 2014). The new model seeks to target funds more effectively and combines different elements of Input (individual), throughout (baseline funding) and Output (funding based on student grades) funding formula.

Input funding continues to be used for students with 'complex needs' or those with enduring conditions that "significantly affect their capacity to learn" (NCSE 2014: 32). In identifying these students, however, the model no longer uses categories of disabilities so as to avoid 'inappropriate diagnosis' and the 'unnecessary labelling of children" (NCSE 2013; NCSE 2014). A particularly innovative part of this model is the way in which the Throughput funding formula is allocated. Baseline funding is provided to all schools regardless of the level of demand and is weighted based on the school's characteristics or 'educational profile'. This includes the school's disadvantaged status, its gender-mix in addition to its 'social context' which is based on survey data from school principals about students' socioeconomic and family background. Elements of the Output funding model are also present in the SET model which measures student progress through standardised test results (NCSE 2014). The SET model is almost 5 years old but to date there has been no evaluation of its effectiveness. A couple of key issues have emerged since its introduction that warrant examination.

Despite increased autonomy around the spending and allocation of resources at school level, the model operates without any system of accountability. The equitable and inclusive targeting of various resources such as the allocation of a Special Needs Assistant or resource hours with special education teachers, for example, will therefore vary by school leaders' and teachers' views of inclusive education. Without a model of accountability there is little understanding around whether students requiring resources are receiving them under the new funding model. Without a clear understanding of what makes this model effective or how it can reach its objectives (DPER 2019), it raises broader questions about the outcomes for students with disabilities both while they are in school and when they leave. Again, there is a gap in our understanding of these students' experiences while in school and their post-school pathways. Other issues exist around the criteria used in the model such as the use of standardised tests, which may create perverse incentives in schools where achievement (or lack of) is linked to funding.

Aside from possible difficulties in the structure and implementation of this newly introduced model, perhaps the bigger issue is that Ireland continues to operate parallel funding streams of special and general education and is thus adhering to a medical understanding of disability where support is required to 'include' or 'integrate' students with disabilities into a pre-existing mainstream system. The system of special education is continually reinforced through the increased use of separate educational settings (special classes and schools) and specific staff (Special Education Teachers and Special Needs Assistants). It is another example of how a funding model can directly impact on the extent to which schools can be inclusive (Ebersold/ Óskarsdóttir/Watkins 2018; Ebersold et al. 2019; Sharma/Furlonger/Forlin 2019; Slee 2018).

4   Analysis of the Italian Context

4.1   Regulative dimension

The Constitution of the Italian Republic of 1947 lays the foundations of the Italian school system. Three articles of the Constitution are crucial in order to understand the way school was already conceived at that time as "open, inclusive and plural" (Matucci 2020). Article 34 states that "Education shall be open to everyone" in the sense that all children and youth have the right to get access to school. Article 3 declares that: "It shall be the duty of the Republic to remove those obstacles of an economic or social nature which constrain the freedom and equality of citizens, thereby impeding the full development of the human person and the effective participation". Both together state the expectation towards an inclusive school, understood as a contribution to compensate individual obstacles experienced by single students.

Later, in the time of the 1968 movements, characterised in Italy by the alliance of the Catholic and left wing in social and political movements that harshly challenged dominant ideologies and the power of traditional institutions, the legislative framework for an inclusive school was reinforced (Canevaro/Ciambrone/Nocera 2021). Law 1859/1962 introduced the "Scuola media unica" (unitarian lower secondary school), limiting de facto tracking to upper secondary school (age 14-19). From the 1970s, driven by the movement of deinstitutionalisation of psychiatry initiated by Franco Basaglia, the pressure actions for students with disabilities to attend regular school became successful and the laws for school integration (i.e., *Integrazione Scolastica*) entered into force (Law 118/71; Law 517/77). It was by means of this legislation that the current school system with all children attending the school in their neighbourhood under the same roof for 8 years was created. Linked with it was an expanded understanding of education in (all-day) schools as a "house of learning", which is interdisciplinary and concerns the entire development of the personality (Damiano 2003: 244).

After that period, the focus moved from placement to quality (Ianes, Demo and Dell'Anna 2020). A significant impulse was given for collaboration between professionals by establishing the multi-classroom teacher principle. In this way, pedagogical-didactical responsibility was organised in teams, although its realisation could not be sustained throughout. At the same time, within a broader law dedicated to the support, social integration, and rights of "handicapped persons" (using the wording of the time) (Law 104/ 1992), specific measures for school integration of students with disabilities were introduced: Individual Educational Plans (IEPs) became compulsory to ensure meaningful participation to curricular activities and the roles of support teachers in teacher teams of classes attended also by a student with a disability were defined. The idea was to introduce specific measures to be implemented into the regular school context in case of presence of a student with a motor, sensory or intellectual disability (Matucci 2020). The compensative approach to inclusion introduced already in the Constitution and described above can be recognised also in this more recent law. Moreover, it was confirmed also by successive legislative measures that enlarged the group of students for whom specific measures are ensured, comprehending students with specific learning disabilities (Law 170/2019) and more in general students with Special Educational Needs (Ministerial Directive of 27 December 2012; and Ministerial Circular no. 8 of 6 March 2013).

Summing up, the regulative Italian framework forms the basis for an inclusive school that is open for all learners in terms of presence and treats inclusion as a personal right for students experiencing obstacles to be compensated by means of specific measures and resources.

4.2   Educational institutions and organisational form and paradigms

In order to describe the Italian School System in its complexity, it is important to keep in mind that the Italian public administration has a decentralised organisation. This means that schools have administrative and managing autonomy. They design their own 'Three-year educational offer plan' (i.e., *Piano triennale dell'offerta formativa – PTOF*) which sets out the cultural and planning identity of the school and defines the school curriculum (in line with the national curriculum), and organises learning processes (time, grouping, allocation of personnel resources within the school...) (Eurydice 2022).

In Italy compulsory education lasts 10 years, from 6 to 16 years of age. All students aged between 6 and 14 years regardless of their individual or socio-economic characteristics attend primary and lower secondary school, one mainstream for all. Before and after that age, the educational career of children and students is not unified, as nursery school and kindergarten are not compulsory and in upper secondary school students choose between three types of schools (lyceums, technical institutes, vocational institutes). Nevertheless, nobody can be excluded because of individual characteristics or social background from the age of zero up to university.

Valuing diversity and inclusion is part of the educational principles that the Ministry of Education has shared with all Italian schools by means of the national curriculum for all school grades. Coherently to this, also the documents structuring the compulsory self-evaluation and development three-years process require to consider, among other aspects, also "inclusion and differentiation" (INVALSI 2014).

Against this background, school legislation assures specific measures and resources to support some groups of students. As described above, these are reserved to students with Special Educational Needs (SEN). Students with diagnosed disabilities (category A of SEN) have the right for an IEP that is conceived as the adaption of the class curriculum to the needs of the student with a disability. Furthermore, on the basis of decisions taken in the IEPs, support teachers are assigned to the whole class for some hours and are expected to take responsibility for the whole class in co-teaching with the subject teachers, while personal assistants are assigned to the single student and have tasks related to personal care, autonomy and communication. Also, students with diagnosed learning disabilities like dyslexia or dyscalculia (category B of SEN) and students with so-called "cultural, linguistic and socio-economic disadvantages" (category C of SEN) have the right to learn according to an IEP with teaching/learning strategies that take into consideration their individual characteristics, whereas, differently than in case of category A-disability, curricular goals need to be achieved and cannot be adapted. Nevertheless, no extra personnel resources are foreseen for their classes.

Research shows ambivalences in the use of these compensative forms of support in everyday practices and suggests that the same regulative framework legitimises both practices that support all children's and students' participation, but also practices with a segregating character. For example, it has been shown how the IEP, in some settings, works as an instrument that makes class activities accessible for the student with a disability and that facilitates participation. In others, however, it puts the legitimate basis for forms of micro-exclusion within an inclusive school system in the name of 1:1 interventions (D'Alessio 2011; Demo et al. 2021). Another line of thought has reflected the impact of the compensative support structures in relation to the representation of differentiation. Whereas education scholars from different perspectives call for differentiation – understood as a general demand for high quality teaching based on the assumption that diversity is the norm in learning processes – connecting the idea of Individualised Educational Plans exclusively to some students with SEN implicitly conveys the idea that differentiation is directed only at selected students. Seen in this way, specific measures as IEPs become add-on solutions that legitimate a resistance for a deeper change of learning contexts towards differentiation for all (Alves 2018). This can produce a loss of the potential of inclusive didactics oriented towards valuing all children's diversity and look at differentiation in terms of enrichment for all (Seitz 2020).

4.3   Funding model and paradigm

Coherently with the decentralised structure of the school system, also school funding is provided at several levels: state, regions, and municipalities. The Ministry of Education (State) provides 80% of general school funding that covers core services such as school functioning, salaries of the teaching and administrative staff, compulsory in service-training, technical equipment. Regions allocate the resources to the single schools or to networks of schools. Municipalities are responsible for funding of school infrastructures and meals for kindergartens, primary school, and lower secondary schools.

For what specific measures for students identified as students with SEN, the Italian funding system has many similarities to the Input model of funding. Coherently with the compensative approach to inclusion adopted in the regulative framework, the main resource for inclusion is conceived in terms of hours of specialised professionals (support teachers and personal assistants, mainly) to be allocated to students that are recognised as belonging to the category A of SEN, the one of disability. The entitlement occurs by means of a medical diagnosis produced by the healthcare. The diagnosis constitutes the legal prerequisite to draw up an IEP for the student with a certified disability. In the IEP then a multi-professional team that involves teachers, health professionals, the school principal and the family of the student defines the amount of hours of support teacher or personal assistance to be assigned. Allocation of resources to the school occurs by means of a request done by the school principal to the region, in which the sum of hours of all the school IEPs is considered.

Looking at statistical data on funding, Italy is the European country that, considering the percentage of its public expenditure, invests the least in 'education': 8%, while the European mean is 10.3%. Looking retrospectively at the years 2010-2018, the budget for education has decreased by 7% (statistics of Eurostat[2]). Around two thirds of the education budget is spent for teacher salaries. Looking more in the details of that, it's interesting to note that out of the total teacher population, the percentage of support teachers is constantly increasing: from 11.67% in the school year 2010/2011 to 20.76% in 2018/2019 and 25.15% in 2020/2021 (annual statistics of the Ministry of Education). This is tightly bound to a parallel constant increase of students identified as having a disability. This means that, in front of expenditure contraction for education in general, the main expenditure for the specific funding for inclusion is constantly growing. In literature regarding funding for inclusion, the trend is not new. Ebersold and colleagues (2019)

---

2   https://ec.europa.eu/eurostat/databrowser/view/GOV_10A_EXP__custom_
     1618171/default/table?lang=en (22.09.2022).

describe how financial austerity has reduced resources for education in many European countries, whereas expenditure for meeting the additional or special educational needs of learners in mainstream education has increased and put forward the idea that this is influenced by mechanisms that link funding to the identification of a learner's needs (Input funding model). In these systems, referring more learners to specialist support and provision is encouraged by a "strategic behaviour" aimed at obtaining more resources at the cost of a medicalisation of some individual students' characteristics (Dovigo/Pedone 2019; Ianes/Augello 2019).

Furthermore, the fact that resources for inclusion are defined in an individual document embodies the constitutional principle that sees inclusion as a subjective right and contributes to an individual understanding of provision for inclusion that compensate the obstacles experienced by certain students because of their individual characteristics. Research shows that the risk of this is a "double segregation" (Mura 2015) where both the student with disability and the support teacher experience specific provision in form of individual work, separated from the other teachers and classmates. Also, this phenomenon is present in different countries with Input models of funding where the increased funding is often used for "outsourcing" strategies: identified students are delegated to specific professionals (Ebersold et al. 2019).

4.4   Shared hidden conceptions: the normative and cultural-cognitive dimensions

Summing up, the Italian school system's legislative framework and its organisational structures embody the idea of a school that is open to all and sensitive to diversities. Autonomy is intended as a way for schools to develop an institutional unique identity that connects the national curriculum with the characteristics of the student group and social context of that specific institution. Also, the national curriculum principles call for valuing diversity.

The right for inclusion is defined in terms of a subjective right of some students to get personal obstacles for full development and participation compensated. The structures of the school system and funding procedures, which are commonly referred to as inclusive structures and funding, ensure the right: 1) defining mainly by means of medical diagnosis the entitled students (SEN), 2) granting them the IEP as an instrument that adapts the school curriculum to the personal student characteristics, 3) allocating personnel resources to students who are recognised being part of category A of SEN, disability. Research shows, as described in some of the paragraphs above, that this framework leads to ambivalent practices: these kinds of specific measures and resources can become both means for inclusive or for segregating practices.

In line with the Country Report by the European Agency (EASNIE 2017), we agree that "Challenges relate to the prevalence of an Input model of funding, which connects support to an official decision". A development towards a combination of the Input model with Throughput models of funding could stop the constant increase of students identified as SEN and support teachers. Going further, we see the Input model as strictly connected with the compensative idea of inclusion rooted in the legislative framework and in structures developed for funding and organising inclusion. For this reason, a change of the funding procedures needs to be accompanied by a rethinking of the legislative and normative framework of inclusion. A possible direction is outlined by the constitutionalist Matucci (2020) when she writes that the active commitment that Article 3 of the Constitution requires from the institutions must not be limited to the *ex-post* recognition of measures but can (and should) also be expressed through preventive actions that reduce, *ex ante*, the very formation of inequalities. From this perspective the focus shifts from specific measures for specific students identified as disadvantaged to a comprehensive development of a school that can offer a democratic learning environment where, ideally, inequalities are not reproduced.

5   Analysis of the Norwegian context

The development of special education and later inclusion in Norway is closely linked to the historical growth of Norway as an independent nation (Hausstätter/Thuen 2014; Takala/Hausstätter 2012). Major changes in the educational system were highly influenced by the development of European, mainly Swedish, educational reforms both in general and special education. Politically, Norway is a strong social democratic country with a dominant focus on social equality through the Nordic welfare state model. Education is a central element in the national strive towards social fairness, and the educational history is generally understood as the development of a system where equal opportunities for all is the central argument for change. Creating opportunities was also part of the special educational system, but it was not before the 1970s that real and important changes in this part of the educational system were introduced, first by introducing the theoretical foundations of normalisation, secondly by a political wave of integration, and thirdly by changing the focus towards inclusive education.

5.1   History towards inclusion

Norway got the first school law regulating children with special needs in 1881 (the Abnormal School Act) and the second in 1896 (the Child Welfare Council Act). These were used to create the Special School Act in 1951 that established the basis for a national special educational system in Norway. The general education for all, as part of one educational system, was established in Norway through a common school law for all in 1975 (incorporating the special school act of 1951 with the general school act) (Hausstätter/Thuen 2014). The goal was to give all children educational support in their local school and this goal was reached in a second reform in 1993 where nationally owned special schools and nursing homes were closed down and replaced with local solutions (Haug 1999). The education for all structure was further developed in 1994 when the right to education was increased to cover higher secondary education. Further to strengthen the education for all, the individual right to "adapted education" was added to the legislation in 2008 and the right to early intervention in 2018. These historical elements have led to a central division in the structure of Norwegian education: a discussion of an education for all as part of a social strategy for equality in the Norwegian society and secondly a debate about the need for special education. Inclusive education has been linked to the strategy for education for all and used as an argument against special education (Hausstätter/Jahnukainen 2014).

5.2   Regulative dimension

There are 635,000 students and 2,760 schools in the primary education system in Norway with a ratio of 15.8 students per teacher. Norwegian compulsorily primary education starting from age 6 (K1–K10) is mainly a public education system covering 96% of all children and voluntary secondary education (K11–K13/14) 94% of all youth. All children and youth have the right to 14 years of education in Norway. The primary and secondary educational system has both support systems for special education (local systems for primary education and regional systems for secondary education). Alternatives to the public-school system are private schools based on Waldorf or Montessori education and a few religious based schools. However, all private schools must follow the national curriculum and the national school law and they can use the public support system for special education. This description of the Norwegian special and inclusive education system will focus on the situation in primary public education; however, the systems are more or less the same.

About 8% of the student population receive special education support – most of them as part-time support (0.5% full time support) in particular subjects or as general support. However, research suggests that the real number of students in need of extra support is over 20% (Hausstätter 2013; Nordahl et al. 2018). Hausstätter (2013) claims that this huge discrepancy between children getting the support and children needing support is mainly due to the "gate keeping" process by the pedagogical psychological office.

There is no specific requirement for teachers to have special education knowledge in order to support children with special educational needs (SEN), and it is expected that teachers have the necessary pedagogical knowledge to support all learners. However, a lot of the support is given by school assistants (Nordahl/Hausstätter 2009). The school can seek pedagogical support from a local pedagogical psychological support system (PPS) or in challenging cases from a national pedagogical support system (STATPED).

The number of students receiving special education is statistically defined through the number of students receiving an individual educational plan (IEP). For the student defined as SEN the Norwegian school legislation (§5) states that the child does not benefit from ordinary education. With necessary approval by parents, the PPS can go into the school and through observations and individual assessments evaluate if, and to what extent, the child is able to benefit from ordinary education. This should be a pedagogical, and not psychological/medical, assessment – however, in many cases medical arguments are used as a basis for the assessment. The evaluations of whether a child benefits or not from ordinary education vary from area to area and are highly dependent on the assessment made by the local PPS – therefore, there are huge variations between regions in Norway on the number of children with SEN.

The pedagogical psychological support system is an independent office placed administratively between school leader (principal) and school owner (politicians and administration). The intention is that the PPS should be an independent evaluation agent that can work unbiased with the sole interest of supporting the student. When the PPS have made their evaluation, it is up to the school owner to decide if they want to follow the proposals presented by the PPS. In general, they do, but changes are made based on the financial and practical situation. There are two main strategies used to help students, first as described to assess the learning potential for the child and secondly to support and help teachers to develop teaching strategies for supporting all learners. This last element, to offer support to teachers, has been the central focus for policy development within this area for the last ten years (white paper: meld.st. 6 [2019-2020]) – the main argument is that resources should be used to support learners, not to evaluate them.

Resources for special educational support vary from community to community. In most cases there is no extra financial support for covering increased expenses in special education, that is, the resources have to be moved from general education support to special education support. In other cases, teacher hours can be replaced with assistant hours to cover the need for extra support (Nordahl/Hausstätter 2009).

5.3   Normative and cultural-cognitive dimension

The right to special education is highlighted in the school law. However, this right has been extensively debated since Norway ratified the Salamanca statement in 1994. The argument is that this special education has to be replaced with a general goal of education for all through adapted education (Nordahl et al. 2018). The argument is that all teachers should have the necessary knowledge to support and adapt the learning process for most children in education.

As part of the strong focus on education for all, adapted education and inclusion, there are no national requirements for schools to hire teachers with special education knowledge. The idea is, as presented, that all teachers should have the necessary pedagogical knowledge to support all learners. To meet these requirements, there is a strong focus on teamwork and collaborative strategies among teachers. In cases where teachers need extra help, they can seek support at the PPS or from STATPED.

As stated by Hausstätter and Jahnukainen (2014), the Norwegian focus on inclusive education is mainly a debate on the strategies of education. The integration reforms in the 1980s and early 1990s had already made structural changes so that most children were part of their local school and lived in their local community. The challenge in the 1990s and in the beginning of 2000 was how to develop educational strategies for all children. Child-centred approaches became very popular, and strategies of adapted teaching were highlighted as the necessary solution. Adapted teaching and inclusion were presented as "two sides of the same coin" and theoretical and practical strategies developed (Haug/Bachman 2007).

As the focus on inclusion developed in the 1990s, the interest for special education diminished. The introduction of inclusive education was followed by criticism of special education (its segregated effect and very resource demanding sides) and it became a political goal to reduce the need of special education. Two changes in the last part of the first decade of 2000 started the process of changing attitudes towards special education. The first major change was the participation in the PISA test where Norwegian students preformed "shockingly bad" (Hausstätter 2007), leading to a huge debate about why Finland was much better than Norway – one argument here was that Finland had a much more developed special educational system (Hausstätter/ Takala 2011). The second major change, supported by weak PISA results, was the implementation of a national curriculum in 2006 – the Knowledge Promotion Reform. This reform was followed up by a national school test – a test that for the first time revealed differences between regions and clearly described which children struggled at school. The PISA and the Knowledge Promotion Reform created a new interest for special education and the role of special educational knowledge in the educational system in Norway. More resources and research programmes were established in order to understand the role of special education (e.g., The Function of special education – SPEED project: https://www.hivolda.no/Forsking/Forskingsprosjekt/speed-prosjektet), and the debate changed from a focus on children with SEN towards a stronger focus on teachers' competence and ability to support all learners (Nordahl et al. 2018).

In the 1990s and first decade of 2000, inclusive education was clearly linked to the content and didactic of ordinary education and the goal of supporting good education for all – and also with a clear ambition of reducing the need for special educational solutions. However, looking at the development over the last decade, it seems that special educational knowledge to a greater extent is accepted as a central part of inclusive education, and in today's debate inclusion and special education is more closely connected than it was two decades ago. One example of this new link between special and inclusive education in Norway is the establishment of a national centre "Special Needs Education and Inclusion for the 21st Century – Achieving an inclusive special education System of Support". However, the battle around the role of special education in the Norwegian educational system is not finished – in a proposal for the new school law the term special education is deleted and the term "individual adapted education" is introduced as the future description of how the educational system shall meet students that do not benefit from ordinary education (NOU 2019: 23).

5.4   Normativity and bureaucracy

For 50 years there has been a strong focus on establishing an educational system for all in Norway. This clear aim has created a political axiom supporting inclusive education in the Norwegian culture. There is no alternative, no arguments against inclusion in the political debate of the future of the Norwegian educational system. However, the strategy towards inclusion has been altered during the 30 years of inclusive education in Norway – from a general idea towards more a part of special education.

This national attention on inclusion seems to be less important at the local educational level where practical and resource debates are the reality. The political system supports local governance and differences are therefore expected. At the local level, the number of segregated school solutions for children with special needs is increasing both as a pragmatic organisational solution and pedagogical arguments based on historical categories in special education (mainly related to behaviour and "spectrum" disabilities). This is partly also supported by interest organisations and parents who argue that special solutions are the safest way of giving some children the best education.

In this short presentation of the status of inclusion and special education in Norway the point has been to describe how inclusion is established as a normative and essential part of the national educational system. However, it is also important to be aware of the fact that there are huge differences on the local level on how inclusive education is incorporated into the educational system. It is also necessary to understand that the relationship between general education, inclusion and special education is challenging and that the relationship and understanding of these areas is constantly changing in Norway.

6   Some concluding reflections

Against the background of the dimensions explored in the analysis of the three countries, in the final section of this chapter we comment on a summarising synoptic representation of the way inclusive education and its funding is conceived in Ireland, Italy and Norway. This simplified visualisation of key-ideas makes the intertwining of the inclusive education concept of a country with its funding model particularly evident. Norway and Italy are apparently very similar in terms of inclusive education structures: the presence of all children and students is (more or less completely) granted in mainstream learning settings. With this communality in mind, at first sight the difference of funding in the two countries looks apparently inconsistent and not fully understandable. With a deeper analysis, looking at the way inclusive education is conceptualised in both countries, it becomes clear that similar structures do not "automatically" correspond to similar conceptualisations of inclusion. The Norwegian idea that inclusive education contributes to equity in society in general and requires the development of the learning context differs strongly from the Italian idea of inclusive education as an individual right of students who experience obstacles that should be compensated. Through these lenses, also the fact that Norway has no specific funding for inclusive education, whereas Italy has an Input model on the basis of mainly medically defined categories, becomes more comprehensible, as it mirrors the two conceptualisations of inclusion.

Table 2:   Synoptic representation of the ways inclusive education and funding models for inclusion are conceptualised in Ireland, Italy and Norway

	Ireland	Norway	Italy
Idea of inclusive education (IE)	IE represents one way, together with special schools and classes, to respond to SEN; it is discussed in terms of effectiveness for students' learning outcomes.	IE is understood in terms of a strategy for contributing to equality in society. It comprehends the idea that adapted education responds to those that do not benefit from ordinary education. It has been long conceived in opposition to special education, while recently special education tends to be perceived as part of IE.	A contradiction exists between a general education system sensitive to equity and differences, on one side, and IE understood as the right of some students to get personal obstacles for full development and participation compensated, on the other.
Funding model for inclusion (FI)	Mixed Output, Throughput and Input model based on a non-categorical medical understanding of SEN. Autonomous decisions for funding on school level.	No specific funding for inclusion or special education; only funding for general education. Autonomous decisions for funding on school level.	Input model based on a category-based medical understanding of SEN. National funding rules, common to all schools.

The coherence between funding model and conceptualisation of inclusion becomes visible also in the Irish context. Here, inclusive education needs to seek for a legitimisation in terms of effectiveness for students' learning outcomes, in a constant comparison to special schools and special classes. This is very different from Norway and Italy, where inclusive education was established as an ethical choice, based on values like equity and democracy and therefore legitimate in itself. Also in this case, the funding model for inclusion reflects the importance attributed to outcomes; in fact, Ireland is one of the very few countries that allocate funding on the basis of achieved results.

Moreover, Ireland and Italy share the Input model at least for a part of the funding strategy. Going back to the sections of text that refer to the analysis of these countries, we can see that this orientation is also connected with a narrow understanding of resources for inclusion. In both countries funding for inclusion consists mainly in the allocation of special education teachers or teachers specialised for the inclusion of students with diagnosed SEN. The situation is strongly different in Norway, where no specific funding for inclusion is foreseen, and where the first resources activated for inclusion is a counselling that sustains teachers in "adapting" their teaching and learning environment (Pedagogical Psychological Support System). Only at a second stage are special education personnel resources allocated, if necessary. From this point of view, the analysis confirms that the Input model is connected with a narrow, SEN-oriented understanding of resourcing for inclusion that facilitate an "outsourcing" of the responsibility for inclusive processes, whereas a broader understanding of resources sustains the intertwining of inclusive and more general school development processes that promote change for the whole context.

Finally, in all countries evaluative processes explicitly or implicitly play a role in the discourse on inclusive education and funding models. We have already discussed the role of evaluation of students' learning results for Ireland, understood as legitimation of inclusive education. Evaluation, in this country, focuses on the outcomes for single students. But evaluation of inclusion-related quality of educational practice can focus on different aspects and have different aims. Accountability is just one of the possibilities, quality development can be a different one with very different effects. The latter could be an interesting means to support the development of reflective practices of school communities and single teachers in cases where, as described for the Italian and in the Norwegian system, under the same legislative framework very different practices take place. The definition of quality criteria of inclusive processes that guide self-evaluation and self-development, like, for example, the indicators and questions of the Index for Inclusion (Booth/Ainscow 2011), can encourage a critical rethinking of practices, and support a more unitarian understanding of inclusive (funding) practices.

In conclusion, our analysis suggests that a deeper understanding of institutions is possible if the comparative analysis of different countries manages to capture the normative and cultural assumptions behind the idea of inclusive education embodied in laws and educational structures, as outlined here with recourse to the neo-institutional approach. In the specific case of funding models for inclusion, the analysis of Ireland, Italy and Norway shows that funding structures are strictly intertwined with conceptualisations of inclusive education constructed in educational laws. This implies for future research that inclusive funding structures and models cannot be explored, developed, or reformed in an isolated manner, because their understanding is strictly interconnected with a more general understanding of inclusion and equity within education.

References

Alves, Ines (2018): The transnational phenomenon of individual planning in response to pupil diversity: A paradox in educational reform. In: Hultqvist, Elisabeth/Lindblad, Sverker/Popkewitz, Thomas (eds.): Critical Analyses of Educational Reforms in an Era of Transnational Governance. Cham: Springer, pp. 151-168.

Banks, Joanne (2021): Examining the Cost of Special Education. In: Sharma, Umesh/Salend, Spencer J. (eds.): Oxford Research Encyclopedia of Education. New York: Oxford University Press.

Banks, Joanne/McCoy, Selina (2011): A Study on the Prevalence of Special Educational Needs. Trim: NCSE.

Banks, Joanne/McCoy, Selina (2017): Playing catch-up or overspending? Managing the cost of Special Education. In: Ireland's Yearbook of Education, 2017-2018, pp. 236-242.

Banks, Joanne/McCoy, Selina/Frawley, Denise/Kingston, Gillian/Shevlin, Michael/Smyth, Fiona (2016): Special Classes in Irish Schools, Phase 2: A Qualitative Study. Dublin/Trim: ESRI/NCSE.

Biermann, Julia/Powell, Justin J. (2014): Institutionelle Dimensionen inklusiver Schulbildung–Herausforderungen der UN-Behindertenrechtskonvention für Deutschland, Island und Schweden im Vergleich. In: Zeitschrift für Erziehungswissenschaft 17, 4, pp. 679-700.

Booth, Tony/Ainscow, Mel (2011): Index for Inclusion: Developing Learning and Participation in Schools. Bristol: Centre for Studies on Inclusive Education.

Canevaro, Andrea/Ciambrone, Raffaele/Nocera, Salvatore (Eds) (2021): L'inclusione scolastica in Italia. Trento: Erickson.

Cosgrove, Jude/McKeown, Caroline/Travers, Joseph/Lysaght, Zita/Ní Bhroin, Órla/Archer, Peter (2014): Educational Experiences and Outcomes for Children with Special Educational Needs, A Secondary Analysis of Data from the Growing Up in Ireland Study. Trim: NCSE.

Cussen Report (1936): Commission of Enquiry into the Reformatory & Industrial School system 1934-36. In: Kilcommins, Shane/O'Donnell, Ian/O'Sullivan, Eoin/Vaughn, Barry (eds.) (2004): Crime and Punishment and the Search for Order in Ireland. Dublin: The Institute for Public Administration.

D'Alessio, Simona (2011): Inclusive education in Italy. A critical analysis of the policy of Integrazione Scolastica. Springer Science & Business Media.

Damiano, Elio (2003): Idee di scuola a confronto. Un bilancio. In: Damiano, Elio (ed.): Idee di scuola a confronto. Contributo alla storia del riformismo scolastico in Italia. Roma: Armando Editore, pp 239-288.

Demo, Heidrun/Nes, Kari/Somby, Hege Merete/Frizzarin, Anna/Dal Zovo, Sofia (2021): In and out of class – what is the meaning for inclusive schools? Teachers' opinions on push-and pull-out in Italy and Norway. In: International Journal of Inclusive Education pp. 1-19.

Department of Education (2021): Minister Josepha Madigan launches review of the Education for Persons with Special Educational Needs (EPSEN) Act 2004. In:

https://www.gov.ie/en/press-release/69020-minister-josepha-madigan-launches-review-of-the-education-for-persons-with-special-educational-needs-epsen-act-2004/ [23.06.2022].

Department of Health (1965): Report of the Commission of Inquiry on Mental Handicap. Dublin: Stationery Office.

DiMaggio, Paul J./Powell, Walter W. (1991): The iron cage revisited. In: DiMaggio, Paul J./Powell, Walter W. (eds.): The New Institutionalism in Organizational Analysis. University of Chicago Press, pp. 63-82.

Dovigo, Fabio/Pedone, Francesca (2019): I bisogni educativi speciali. Roma: Carocci.

DPER (2017): Spending Review 2017 Special Educational Needs provision. Dublin: Department of Public Expenditure and Reform.

DPER (2019): Spending Review 2019 Monitoring Inputs, Outputs and Outcomes in Special Education Needs Provision. Dublin: Department of Public Expenditure and Reform and Department of Education.

Ebersold, Serge (2016): Financing of Inclusive Education: Mapping Country Systems for Inclusive Education. Denmark: European Agency for Special Needs and Inclusive Education.

Ebersold, Serge/Meijer, Cor (2016): Financing Inclusive Education: Policy Challenges, Issues and Trends. In: Watkins, Amanda/Meijer, Cor (eds.): Implementing Inclusive Education: Issues in Bridging the Policy-Practice Gap. Bingley: Emerald Group, pp. 37–62.

Ebersold, Serge/Óskarsdóttir, Edda/Watkins, Amanda (2018): Financing Policies for Inclusive Education Systems, Final Summary Report. Denmark: European Agency for Special Needs and Inclusive Education.

Ebersold, Serge/Watkins, Amanda/Óskarsdóttir, Edda/Meijer, Cor (2019): Financing Inclusive Education to Reduce Disparity in Education: Trends, Issues and Drivers. In: Schuelka, Matthew/Johnstone, Christopher/Thomas, Gary/Artiles, Alfredo (eds.): The Sage Handbook of Inclusion and Diversity in Education. London: Sage Publications Ltd, pp. 232-248.

European Agency for Special Needs and Inclusive Education (2017): Financing Policies for Inclusive Education Systems. Country Study Visit Report: Italy. European Agency for Special Needs and Inclusive Education. In: https://www.european-agency.org/sites/default/files/agency-projects/FPIES/CSV/FPIES%20Italy%20Country%20Study%20Visit%20Report.pdf [23.06.2022].

Eurydice (2022): National Education Systems. In: https://eacea.ec.europa.eu/national-policies/eurydice/national-description_en [23.06.2022].

Flood, Margaret/Banks, Joanne (2021): Universal Design for Learning: Is It Gaining Momentum in Irish Education? In: Education Sciences 11, 7, 341.

Haug, Peder (1999): Spesialundervisning i grunnskulen. Grunnlag, utviklng og innhold. Oslo: Abstrakt forlag.

Haug, Peder/Bachmann, Kari (2007): Grunnleggjande element for forståing av tilpassa opplæring. In: Berg, Grete/Nes, Kari (eds.): Kompetanse for tilpasset opplæring. Oslo: Utdanningsdirektoratet, pp. 15-38.

Hausstätter, Rune Sarrormaa (2007): På sporet av den gode lærer i finsk essensialisme. In: Bedre skole, 3.

Hausstätter, Rune Sarrormaa (2013): 20 prosentregelen i spesialundervisningen. In: Spesialpedagogikk 6, pp. 4-13.

Hausstätter, Rune Sarrormaa/Jahnukainen, Markku (2014): From integration to inclusion and the role of special education. In: Kiuppis, Florian/Hausstätter, Rune Sarrormaa (eds.): Inclusive education twenty years after Salamanca. New York: Peter Lang, pp. 119-131.

Hausstätter, Rune Sarrormaa/Takala, Marjatta (2011): Can special education make a difference? Exploring the differences of special educational systems between Finland and Norway in relation to the PISA results. In: Scandinavian Journal of Disability Research 13, 4, pp. 271-281.

Hausstätter, Rune Sarrormaa/Thuen, Harald (2014): Special education today in Norway. In: Rotatori, Anthony/Bakken, Jeffrey/Burkhardt, Sandra/Obiakor, Festus/ Sharma, Umesh (eds.): Special education international perspectives: Practises across the globe vol.28. Bingley: Emerald Group Publishing Limited, pp. 181-207.

Hick, Peter/Solomon, Yvette/Mintz, Joseph/Matziari, Aikaterini/Ó Murchú, Finn/ Hall, Kathy/Cahill, Kevin/Curtin, Catriona/Margariti, Despoina (2018): Initial Teacher Education for Inclusion Phase 1 and 2 Report. Trim: NCSE.

Ianes, Dario/Augello, Giuseppe (2019): Gli inclusio-scettici: Gli argomenti di chi non crede nella scuola inclusiva e le proposte di chi si sbatte tutti i giorni per realizzarla. Trento: Erickson.

Ianes, Dario/Demo, Heidrun/Dell'Anna, Silvia (2020): Inclusive education in Italy: historical steps, positive developments, and challenges. In: Prospects 49, 3, pp. 249-263.

INVALSI (2014): I percorsi valutativi delle scuole. Inquadramento teorico del RAV. In: https://www.invalsi.it/snv/docs/271114/Inquadramento_teorico_RAV.pdf [23.06.2022].

Matucci, Giuditta (2020): Ripensare la scuola inclusiva: una rilettura dei principi costituzionali. In: Sinappsi X, 3, pp. 3-16.

McCoy, Selina/Banks, Joanne (2012): Simply academic? Why children with special educational needs don't like school. In: European Journal of Special Needs Education 27, 1, pp. 81-97.

McCoy, Selina/Banks, Joanne/Frawley, Denise/Watson, Dorothy/Shevlin, Michael/ Smyth Fiona (2014): Understanding Special Class Provision in Ireland. Trim/ Dublin: National Council for Special Education/The Economic and Social Research Institute.

Meegan, Sarah/MacPhail, Ann (2006): Inclusive education: Ireland's education provision for children with special educational needs. In: Irish Educational Studies 25, 1, pp. 53-62.

Meijer, Cor (2003): Special Across Europe in 2003. Trends in Provision in 18 European Countries. Middelfart: European Agency for Development in Special Needs Education.

Meijer, Cor/Watkins, Amanda (2016): Changing Conceptions of Inclusion Underpinning Education Policy. In: Watkins, Amanda/Meijer, Cor (eds.): Implementing Inclusive Education: Issues in Bridging the Policy-Practice Gap. Emerald Publishing Limited, pp. 1-16.

Meijer, Cor/Watkins, Amanda (2019): Financing Special Needs and Inclusive Education–from Salamanca to the Present. In: International Journal of Inclusive Education 23, 7-8, pp. 705-721.

Meld.st. 6 (2019-2020): Tett på – tidlig innsats og inkluderende fellesskap i barnehage, skole og SFO. Ministry of education.

Mense-Petermann, Ursula (2006): Micro-political or inter-cultural conflicts? – An integrating approach. In: Journal of International Management 12, 3, pp. 302-317.

Merkens, Hans (2011): Neoinstitutionalismus in der Erziehungswissenschaft. Opladen: Barbara Budrich.

Merrigan, Catherine/Senior, Joyce (2021): Special schools at the crossroads of inclusion: do they have a value, purpose, and educational responsibility in an inclusive education system? In: Irish Educational Studies.

Mura, Antonello (2015): L'insegnante specializzato: radici e ali. In: de Anna, Lucia/ Gaspari, Patrizia/Mura, Antonello (eds.): L'insegnante specializzato. Itinerari di formazione per la professione. Milano: FrancoAngeli, pp. 27-41.

National Council for Special Education (2013): Supporting Students with Special Educational Needs in Schools. Trim: NCSE.

National Council for Special Education (2014): Delivery for Students with Special Educational Needs. A better and more equitable way. Trim: NCSE.

National Council for Special Education (2019): Policy Advice on Special Schools and Classes. An Inclusive Education for an Inclusive Society? Progress Report. Trim: NCSE.

Nordahl et al. (2018): Inkluderende fellesskap for barn og unge: Ekspertgruppen for barn og unge med behov for særskilt tilrettelegging. Bergen: Fagbokforlaget

Nordahl, Thomas/Hausstätter, Rune Sarrormaa (2009): Spesialundervisningens forutsetninger, innsatser og resultater: situasjonen til elever med særskilte behov for opplæring i grunnskolen under Kunnskapsløftet. Hamar: Høgskolen i Hedmark.

NOU (2019): Ny opplæringslov. Ministry of education.

Parrish, Thomas (2015): How Should we Pay for Special Education? In: Bateman, Barbara/Lloyd, John Wills/Tankersley, Melody (eds.): Enduring Issues in Special Education: Personal Perspectives. New York: Routledge, pp. 410-428.

Seitz, Simone (2020): Dimensionen inklusiver Didaktik – Personalität, Sozialität und Komplexität. In: Zeitschrift für Inklusion 15, 2.

Senge, Konstanze (2006). Zum Begriff der Institution im Neo-Institutionalismus. In: Senge, Konstanze/Hellmann, Kai-Uwe (eds.): Einführung in den Neo-Institutionalismus. Wiesbaden: VS Verlag für Sozialwissenschaften, pp. 35-47.

Senge, Konstanze/Hellmann, Kai-Uwe (Eds.) (2006): Einleitung. In: Senge, Konstanze/Hellmann, Kai-Uwe (eds.): Einführung in den Neo-Institutionalismus. Wiesbaden: VS Verlag für Sozialwissenschaften.

SERC (1993): Report of the Special Education Review Committee. Dublin: The Stationary Office.

Scott, Richard W. (2014): Institutions and Organizations: Ideas, Interests and Identities (4th ed.). London: SAGE.

Sharma, Umesh/Furlonger, Brett/Forlin, Chris (2019): The Impact of Funding Models on the Education of Students with Autism Spectrum Disorder. In: Australasian Journal of Special and Inclusive Education 43, 1, pp. 1-11.

Shevlin, Michael/Banks, Joanne (2021): Inclusion at a crossroads: Dismantling Ireland's system of special education. In: Education Sciences 11, 4, 161.

Slee, Roger (2018): Defining the scope of inclusive education. Think piece prepared for the 2020 Global Education Monitoring Report. Inclusion and Education. UNESCO.

Takala, Marjatta/Hausstätter, Rune Sarrormaa (2012): Effects of history and culture on attitudes toward special education: A comparison of Finland and Norway. In: ISRN Education, pp. 1-7.

UN (2006): Convention on the Rights of Persons with Disabilities. New York: United Nations.

Wohlfart, Anja (2020): Uneingeschränkt Kindsein durch inklusive Förderung? Ein Vergleich der Frühförderung in Mecklenburg-Vorpommern (Deutschland) mit der Habilitation in Skane (Schweden) unter den Zielsetzungen der Inklusion und Partizipation. Wiesbaden: Springer VS.

Part III:
Doing Inclusion —
Doing Difference

Inclusive Education from the DisCrit Perspective

Valentina Migliarini

"At last, you'll know with surpassing certainty that only one thing is more frightening than speaking your truth. And that is not speaking".

Audre Lorde

1   Introduction

When I started my doctoral research project in 2014 on the limits of integration-style inclusion models for unaccompanied asylum-seeking and refugee children labelled as disabled in Rome, intersectionality (Crenshaw 1989) was largely an unknown concept in the field of education in Italy. At the same time, the Ministry of Education started grappling with the emerging numbers of migrant students labelled as disabled, across all sectors and specifically in secondary education (ISMU 2014; 2016). Statistical data collected from the Ministry of Education on 'non-Italian students' with disabilities were not disaggregated. Consequently, there was lack of clarity around the citizenship status of the targeted students (i.e., whether they were migrants, asylum-seekers, or refugees), as well as their types of disability. It became clear that the increasing numbers of migrant students labelled as disabled was a consequence of the implementation of the 2012 and 2013 Special Educational Needs (SEN) policies[1]. At the same time, the Ministry of Education did not offer any critical theoretical framework, pedagogical tool, or operational

---

1   In 2012 the Italian Ministry of Public Education introduced the macro-category of Special Educational Needs (SEN) through a three-tiered categorisation system that focuses on different types of provisions for learners. While the first sub-category (i.e., children with severe physical or intellectual impairments diagnosed by local health units in line with Framework Law 104/1992) is entitled to additional provisions and funding, the second and third sub-categories (i.e., children with learning difficulties certified by public or private clinical diagnosis – Law 70/2010, and students with cultural, linguistic, and socio-economic disadvantage without certified medical diagnosis but still requiring support) are only entitled to receive personalised support, including compensatory and dispensatory measures put in place by classroom teachers (D'Alessio 2014).

indication to classroom teachers, to support them in addressing this emerging phenomenon (Migliarini et al. 2019).

The articulation of the Disability Critical Race Studies (DisCrit) in education (Annamma et al. 2013; 2016), an intersectional and interdisciplinary framework focusing on racism and ableism as interlocking systems of oppression, pushed me to consider this theoretical tool as the lens to analyse the SENitization of forced migrant students, during the first year of my doctoral study (Migliarini 2017).

Expanding DisCrit with Butler's (1997) notion of subjectivation and performative politics, the doctoral study demonstrates how inclusion is conflated within ontologically different and exclusionary meanings of integration. A crucial finding of the study is that despite having a radical de-segregation policy (i.e., *Integrazione Scolastica*), asylum-seeking and refugee children are facing barriers such as ableism and racism. They are increasingly labelled as having Special Educational Needs, and constantly disabled, for them to receive quality education within mainstream, homogeneous and normative school settings. Discriminating discourses articulated by Italian professionnals' legitimate processes of SENitization and disablement. The study suggests the urgency to reform Italian educational and social reception policies and practices by adopting an intersectional and anti-racist stance.

By the end of my doctoral research project, in 2017, DisCrit had become internationally established. It was perceived to be useful to both those doing work in inclusive and special education, as it exposes the fault lines in ableist and deficit-oriented perspectives of disability, and it illustrates how disability interconnects with other socially constructed identities (e.g., class, gender, and sexual diversity). Lastly, it shows how race and ability are socially constructed and interdependent, and how ability is distributed and withheld in schools and classrooms (Annamma et al. 2016).

Since its original articulation in 2013, DisCrit has expanded significantly, crossing disciplinary boundaries and geographic borders (Gillborn et al. 2016; Handy 2018; Migliarini 2017). DisCrit's intellectual lineage reaches back to Anna Julia Cooper (1892), W.E.B. DuBois (1920), to more recent work explicitly questioning the connections between racism and ableism (Artiles 2013; Broderick/Leonardo 2011), and among emerging scholars who use DisCrit to critically analyse a range of topics including examining Positive Behavioral Intervention and Supports (PBIS) (Adams 2015); shifting teacher education for both white teachers (Beneke 2017; Siuty 2017) and teachers of colour (Kulkarni 2015); centring the voices of disabled scholars of colour (Cannon 2019; Hernandez-Saca 2017); and more. The dynamic landscape of scholarship taking up DisCrit reflect its role in fostering a transgressive space that has generated critical questions looking outward, inwards, and across divides (Annamma et al. 2022).

The present contribution serves as a reflection to understand how DisCrit is evolving and can contribute more thoroughly to reframe policy and practice of inclusive education in Italy, as well as transnationally. The contribution starts by illustrating the concepts of intersectionality and exploring the expansive tenets of DisCrit. This is followed by examples of doing DisCrit inclusion in the Italian context. Finally, the chapter reflects on the future of an expansive intersectional inclusion, in Italy and internationally.

2   Intersectionality and DisCrit in Inclusive Education Research

Intersectionality is a relatively recent concept, even if it has a very long history of elaboration, almost through all of modernity, since the emancipationist, anti-slavery movements of the American nineteenth century. It is a very important concept that has relevance in our present and specifically in Europe, where class has been for centuries the dominant social axes, generating social mobilisation. It is a concept characterised by three dimensions: epistemic, epistemological, and methodological. In its epistemic dimension, intersectionality includes a politics of positioning that comes from the context in which it originates, that is, the Black feminist movements and the feminist movements allied to the Black movement, and which critically analysed racial discrimination in the United States from the end of the 1970s to the end of the 1980s (Combahee River Collective 1978). In this context, intersectionality is used to build political agendas and anti-sexist knowledge in line with the objectives of the Black liberation movements. The epistemic dimension makes visible the position of privilege and advantage from which we speak, that is, the intersection of social dynamics that include race, sexuality, class, religion, disability, language, citizenship of the person speaking (Crenshaw 1989).

In its epistemological dimension, intersectionality produces knowledge towards dynamic forms of emancipation from any form of discrimination. It is attentive to the reproduction of power through the dynamics of power itself and to discursive practices that have to do with the reproduction of the norm, which supports the reproduction of power. The subject who speaks influences the thought that gets produced and claims that knowledge can never be considered neutral, and it has specific material and symbolic effects. If we claim knowledge as non-universal, non-objective, non-neutral, then we need to assume an intersectional methodology.

Within the methodological dimension of intersectionality, we cannot imagine a neutral, objective, universal political and educational practice, without asking ourselves who we are talking about and who are the subjects we are trying to understand and do research on, and what their position is with respect to the said social axes. Intersectionality for us white academics and researchers shouldn't be seen as a simple exercise to name our privilege or to reclaim our anti-racist positions. Intersectionality as a methodology implies, for us especially, a constant deconstruction that never reaches an end point. We need to deconstruct every institutional relationship to achieve a permanent decolonisation through a transformative political intervention. For example, in Europe, including the so-called more diverse countries like England and generally the UK, if we look at the number of non-white and marginalised students in the K-12 system, their academic achievement, and the possibility they have of acquiring higher education qualifications, and to work in academic institutions, we recognise that these institutions do not reward the analytical and thought-producing ability of non-white and multiply-marginalised students. Intersectionality has been at the heart of DisCrit design and articulation.

DisCrit exposes the limits of mainstreamed notions of inclusion and inclusive education, providing the justification as to why learning supports strategies for all students, and specifically for those from multiply marginalised communities, should operate intersectionally. Thus, by exploring the affordances of DisCrit for inclusive policies and practices, I attempt to recognise forced migrant students with disabilities in a more nuanced and accurate sense. DisCrit sheds light on the various forms of oppression that intersect in the daily lives of disabled forced migrant youth, and consequently affect their behaviour, academic performance, relationships, and how they 'navigate educational and social institutions with savvy and ingenuity' (Annamma et al. 2016: 22).

There are seven tenets of DisCrit that show the possibilities of re-imagining inclusive policies and practices; each tenet highlights why curriculum, pedagogy, and relationships are conceptualised in hegemonic ways and how they can be reimagined in generative ways for students and teachers (Annamma/Morrison 2018). First, DisCrit focuses on how racism and ableism are normal and interdependent (Collins 2011). These mutually constitutive processes are systemic and interpersonal and are often rendered invisible to restrict notions of normalcy to the desired and to marginalise those perceived as 'different' in society and schools (Annamma et al. 2016). Once a child is perceived and labelled as different from the norm (whiteness), they are then imagined as less capable in academic contexts (Annamma 2018). Inclusive education practices should tackle forms of racism and ableism together, not attempting to respond to one or the other form of oppression that students experience.

Second, DisCrit values multidimensional identities and troubles single notions of identities, such as race or disability. It acknowledges how experience with stigma and segregation often vary based on other identity markers intersecting with race and disability (i.e., gender, language, class) and how this negotiation of multiply stigmatised identities adds complexities. Multiply marginalised students have a clearer sense of the mutually constitutive processes of oppression, and how these processes are visible within segregated or dysfunctional inclusive spaces. As such, an approach to inclusive education that takes distance from the comfort-fantasy perspectives should consider the voices of multiply marginalised students to design inclusive practices.

Third, DisCrit rejects the understanding of both race and disability as primarily biological facts and recognises the social construction of both as society's response to 'differences' from the norm. Simultaneously, DisCrit acknowledges that these categories hold profound significance in people's lives, as it is evident in the marginalisation of students of colour or migrant students with disability labels, who are more likely to be segregated than their white peers with the same label (Fierros/Conroy 2002).

Fourth, DisCrit privileges voices of multiply marginalised students and communities traditionally missing in research (Matsuda 1987). Consequently, DisCrit recognises those who have been pushed outside of the educational endeavour through the discourse and practices of special segregated classrooms. DisCrit positions multiply marginalised students as knowledge-generators, capable of recognising interlocking oppressions and creating solutions to those systemic, interpersonal inequities, and comfort-fantasy ideas of inclusion.

Fifth, DisCrit considers how historically and legally whiteness and ability have been used to deny rights to those that have been constructed as raced and disabled (Valencia 1997). Schools have historically functioned as spaces to sort and fix multiply marginalised children, curing them of their disability or problematic behaviour (Margolis 2004). Through the present day, multiply marginalised students – especially (im)migrant students – often attend under-resourced schools where they have limited access to qualified teachers, engaging curriculum, and critical pedagogy (Fierros/Conroy 2002). Even when attending resourced schools, students of colour are often kept out of advanced placement/gifted classes, where creative thinking is valued (DeCuir/Dixson 2004).

Sixth, DisCrit recognises whiteness and ability as 'property', conferring rights to those that claim those statuses and disadvantaging those who are unable to access them (Adams/Erevelles 2016). Thus, when students are positioned as less desirable, they are barred access to engaging and accurate curriculum, culturally sustaining pedagogy, and relationships that are authentic (Leonardo/Broderick 2011). Whiteness and ability as properties operate also through teachers- biases and discriminatory attitudes that impact on students' well-being and participation in the classroom ecology (Ladson-

Billings 2001; Picower 200). The following section offers practical examples of doing DisCrit inclusion within the classroom and in the community in the context of Italy.

3   DisCrit Inclusion in Italian Classrooms

During the COVID-19 global pandemic, with colleagues from the United States and Italy, I conducted a qualitative pilot study in a comprehensive school in the centre of Rome, in response to classroom teachers' struggles to provide appropriate support to migrant students labelled as disabled (Migliarini et al. 2022). My colleagues and I conducted two focus groups with five teachers and one head teacher. We realised that teachers often use students' proximity to the white Italian norm and nondisabled status as a metric for ascertaining their ability or belonging in certain learning contexts. We have interpreted such attitudes as a reaction to the significant increase of migrant children in Italian classrooms (Italian Ministry of Education [MIUR] 2014). They also mirror the historical colour-evasive approach of the Italian society towards issues of race relations and racism in education (Migliarini 2018). Data collected during the focus groups were analysed through constructivist Grounded Theory method (Charmaz 2014).

The purpose of the study was to provide teachers with supporting strategies that can be used in reframing inclusive education practices through an intersectional and culturally relevant lens (Annamma et al. 2016; Annamma/Morrison 2018). We proposed DisCrit-informed strength-based approaches to help teachers in transforming the design and implementation of Individual Educational Programs (IEP henceforward) and Personalized Teaching Plan (*Piano Didattico Personalizzato- PDP* henceforward) into more radically inclusive tools, not reproducing deficit models of disability and diversity. Ultimately, the study explored the affordances of DisCrit to person-centred planning and strength-based practices, to centre multiply marginalised students, their families and communities in the design and implementation of IEP and PDP. The following section focuses on two DisCrit-informed strength-based practices and field tasks that we suggested to the teachers as a response to their struggles, Person-Centred Planning and Ecological Assessment (Migliarini et al. 2022).

3.1   Person-Centred Planning

The pilot study we conducted in Rome focuses on the implications of implementing MAPs (Vandercook et al. 1989), as one of the person-centred strategies, in the Italian context. When conducting MAPs, the teacher co-facilitates the meeting with another person scribing, and the following questions guide the discussion: (a) What is an MAP? (b) What is the story? (c) What is the dream? (d) What is the nightmare? (e) Who is the person? (f) What are their gifts, strengths, talents? (g) What are their needs? (h) What is the plan of action? The important implication of conducting MAPs is that it is proactive and helps forge authentic relationships with multiply marginalised disabled students and their families. This approach has been shown to increase the family's participation and satisfaction with the IEP process and increases teamwork and collaboration from the start (Weishaar 2010). Additionally, the MAPS process is foundational to the development of any inclusive education plan both in the U.S. and in southern countries (Elder/ Migliarini 2020). Additionally, the MAPs process can help teachers learn about the cultural complexities of families as well as establish a powerful, strength-based foundation for an IEP.

Although a non-school location would be best to increase parents' participation, in Italy meetings cannot be held outside the school settings, and IEP documents are not allowed to circulate for privacy reasons. Consequently, although, in the school, IEPs are constantly shared with parents and medical experts, their design is usually the result of the work of a single teacher and sometimes, class teachers, rather than a collaboration between parents and teachers. As deemed appropriate by the family, any stakeholders in the disabled student's life should be invited to the meeting, including but not limited to parents, siblings, aunts, uncles, cousins, friends, neighbours, social workers, therapists, and teachers. In the age of COVID-19, setting up virtual options is the safest approach, and if families have access to technology, this allows wide access to participation in virtual meetings (Migliarini et al. 2022).

3.2 Field Task #1: Conducting a Person-Centred Planning

For Field Task #1, the teacher would identify a multiply marginalised disabled student and connect to the family. The teacher would introduce the concept of PCP to the family and collaborate with them to set up a time and location for the meeting. The teacher would encourage the family to invite stakeholders to the meeting. During the meeting, the teacher would facilitate the meeting and work together to document the information shared during the meeting. Following the PCP, the teacher would write up a report that synthesises the information and share it with the family and stakeholders. See Appendix A for an example of what directions for conducting a PCP could look like (Migliarini et al. 2022).

3.3   Connections to DisCrit

Person-centred planning aligns well with DisCrit as it is a strategy centring the lived experiences of historically marginalised youth in schools. It is a tool that does not pretend to speak for marginalised students but aims at working together with families to dismantle structured inequities in the education system. This strategy acknowledges the legitimacy of different cultural heritages, constantly attempts to build significant connections between home and school, based on authentic solidarity, and integrate non-dominant cultural materials into the curriculum (Annamma/Morrison 2018). By using this strategy, teachers are offered an opportunity to know the interconnected forms of oppressions that students experience inside and outside the school.

3.4   Ecological Assessments

Promoting the use of ecological assessments is one way that schools can get organised and support multiply marginalised students who arrive at their school. An ecological assessment is an observation-based assessment meant to be used in different school-related settings over a period to get a more-accurate picture of what the student is good at and what they need to be successful in an inclusive setting (Downing et al. 2015). The assessment presumes an inclusive classroom and is meant to provide a holistic view of students and can be used in any environment. Ecological assessments help teachers to examine naturally occurring routines, what students without disabilities are doing, and whether and how students with disabilities are performing the same sorts of activities and actions (Migliarini et al. 2022).

3.5   Field Task #2: Conduct an Ecological Assessment

While conducting a PCP is a critical skill for teachers to learn, they also need to know how to analyse an inclusive environment and be able to identify existing supports that can be leveraged for disabled students. They need to determine the gaps in the environment which would pose barriers to supporting disabled students. To do this, the study suggests assigning teachers Field Task #2, which is an ecological assessment (Migliarini et al. 2022). The study suggests providing teachers the following steps to complete the field task: (a) Identify between 10-15 (more if needed) steps of the activity (e.g., How students without disabilities would engage with the lesson); (b) Identify the natural cues present in the environment (e.g., students line up when they hear the bell); (c) Identify the skills needed to perform the task; (d) Assess the student with a disability's performance of the task; (e) Identify the discrepancy analysis (e.g., Why the student did or did not complete the task, "The student may not have performed the task because they do not understand that the bell means to line up"); (f) Suggest an intervention (e.g., what skills you need to teach/supports you need to provide, teach a peer to remind the student with a disability that the bell has rung and they need to line up). See Appendix B for a sample filled-out ecological assessment and template (Migliarini et al. 2022).

3.6   Connections to DisCrit

Ecological assessment of classroom environment and of students aligns with the principles of DisCrit classroom ecology. DisCrit classroom ecology recognises classrooms as spaces that centre multiply marginalised students as valuable resources whose lived experiences and everyday knowledge must be built upon (Spratt/Florian 2015). Considering a DisCrit classroom ecology, this task helps teachers to refuse deficit-oriented master-narratives about learning, ability and behaviour of multiply marginalised students that animate dysfunctional classroom ecologies. The ecological assessment allows for the creation of trust relationships based in solidarity between students and teachers. Additionally, students' actions are perceived as strategies of resistance, often in response to interpersonal and state violence (Annamma/ Morrison 2018). Through ecological approaches and assessment teachers can teach students self-determination and self-knowledge (Annamma/Morrison 2018).

The following section of this contribution explores a further example of doing DisCrit inclusion in the Italian context, this time focusing on a community intervention.

4   DisCrit Inclusion in the Community

While gathering data for my doctoral research project, I noted that the refugee youth who participated in the research had a very close connection with Hip-Hop culture. Before our interviews, they would often sing along Hip-Hop or Afro Beat songs, or bang on the tables and chairs, creating and replicating beats. Some of them would walk along the corridors and rooms bobbing their heads and rhyming, mixing Italian words with those in Wolof or Mandinka and later showed pride in their latest song. Wolof is the language of Senegal and the Gambia, and the native language of the Wolof people. The Mandinka language or Mandingo is a Mande' language spoken by the Mandinka people of the Casamance region of Senegal, the Gambia,

Northern Guinea-Bissau, Guinea- Conakry, Côte D'Ivoire, and Mali. After each of these encounters, I realised that forced migrant youth were constructing master narratives about their migratory experience through Hip-Hop, and they were using beats and moves as learning mediators. However, this way of expressing themselves has never been validated by Italian school professionals or seriously considered as literacy (Migliarini 2017). The perceptions of Italian educators on refugee youth illiteracy serve to justify the migrants' racialisation and exclusion, in a society where inclusion corresponds also to the acquisition and performance of power majority languages (e.g., Italian, French, and English) (Migliarini/Cioé-Peña, under review). The need to contrast this manufacturing of deficit, along the lines of language, migratory status, race, and ability, by school professionals has been the driving force behind the community intervention inspired by DisCrit, Hip-Hop Pedagogy and the Krip-Hop movement[2].

Organised by You Artistry Collaborative (https://www.yacmovement. org/), a U.S. nonprofit promoting art through activism, in collaboration with other local youth organisations in Terni, "I am Hip-Hop: Beats, Rhymes and Culture" was designed as an inclusive intervention to facilitate socio-emotional learning for migrant students, while helping Italian youth recognise the creativity of the Black genius, that is excellence stemming from the African diaspora (Love 2015). Understanding Black cultural excellence is key for Italian youth since they live in a social context whereby the culture of the African diaspora is either devalued or exoticised (Migliarini 2017). The participants were offered a platform to (re)create meanings and identity, to showcase their talents, and to build a new and safe network of friendships. The president of YAC and myself were the research team that planned and organised the intervention, alongside members of local organisations, and we were involved in the process of data collection.

The intervention developed in two stages. During the first phase of the intervention, narrative observations of youth interactions with the MCs[3],

---

2   Krip-Hop nation is an international collective of Hip-Hop artists and other musicians that intends to address ableism in Hip-Hop, to challenge the charity model of disability, and align Hip-Hop to disability justice, national politics, language, and international solidarity (Moore 2020).

3   Master of Cerimonies (MCs) is the host of an event and their responsibilities consist of introducing speakers and maintaining the flow of an event (Adjapong 2017). The MC is the artist responsible for delivering musical content to an audience. Often when an MC is performing to an audience, they are accompanied by a fellow MC whose essential role is to be a professional in terms of knowing and understanding the musical content to provide support to successfully showcase meaningful performances for the audience. This element was adopted in the community intervention and performed by an Italian MC, leading the workshops on lyrical storytelling. The MC adopted the co-teaching strategy during the workshops; he delivered substantive instructions to a

peers, and members of the community were carried out by the organisers/ researchers during the two different workshops, to familiarise with youth and adult's everyday life experiences and relation to Hip-Hop culture. Parallel to this process, video recording of sections of the beat making, lyrical story-telling, and open mic sessions were carried out by the MCs, organisers, and members of the community. At the end of the workshop, a collective meeting was held in order to select the most relevant lyrical storytelling artifacts to be discussed with researchers and educational stakeholders.

In the second phase of the project, the selected video-fragments were watched and discussed collectively with educational stakeholders to explore ways of integrating Hip-Hop pedagogy and Krip-Hop within social and educational inclusive practices. The roles of the researchers during these collective discussions were to facilitate the process of problematisation of observed situations, the elicitation of implicit assumptions within enacted practices, and the co-construction of new meanings guiding pedagogical transformation (Bove/Cescato 2013). The future steps of the intervention entail elaborating action-research plans to apply Hip-Hop pedagogy to existing practices of inclusive education for all students, but especially for disabled migrant students.

A total of 55 participants attended the daily workshops, and about one hundred attended the evening block party. Among the 55 participants attend-ing the workshops, 30 were young Italians, five were adult educators, and 20 were young migrants and refugees. The Italian youth and adult participants were all from Terni and neighbouring towns in central Italy. All of them attended middle and secondary schools, and five of them attended primary schools. The adult educators were teachers in secondary schools in Terni. Migrant and refugee participants were mostly from West African countries, and three of them from South-East Asia. They were hosted in two major service agencies for forced migration in Terni. These services are part of the first/second reception systems. They offer educational and recreational activities to children and guarantee free health care specifically for forced migrants. Encouraging the 'social integration' of asylum-seeking and refugee children and youth appears to be their paramount objective. These services were deemed crucial to situate the research purposes. The migrant and refugee youth participants had different legal statuses: some had already obtained refugee protection, others were waiting for the final response from the local court, while others appealed against the refusal to be granted refugee

---

group of students with diverse learning needs (Cook/Friend 2017). In this way, he allowed the responsibilities for instructions to be shared between him and the partici-pants. The MC in the community event provided migrant and Italian youth with the opportunity to showcase their mastery of lyrical storytelling, as they supported peers in gaining the same mastery (Adjapong 2017).

status. Ten among the Italian and refugee youth participants had a certified disability, or already started the process of certification. Most of them were diagnosed with learning disabilities, emotional and behavioural disorders, and Post Traumatic Stress Disorders.

Considering positive research outcomes on Hip-Hop-Based-Education in the U.S. context (Hill/Petchauer 2013; Morrell/Duncan-Andrade 2002), and the complexities of being a Black migrant or refugee in Italy, the intervention intended to centre narratives of disabled and non-disabled migrant and Italian youth and other stories of marginalisation and incarceration. It was open for participation to teachers, parents or guardians and other adult members of the community. It took place on June 8th, 2019, at a community space in the city centre of Terni, in central Italy. The space was chosen for its key position in the city, and for being easily accessible for disabled and non-disabled participants. The city of Terni was chosen due to the high number of migrants and refugees residing there. Also, the need for the intervention was justified by the fact that some local refugee organisations have performed an assimilationist model of inclusion, not allowing the creativity of the youth to flourish, and not legitimising or recognising their cultures.

The programme of the community intervention was designed and executed by the research team and YAC organisers, local educational organisations, rapper and educator Amir Issaa, and music producer Rovion Rockmore Reed. Some local teachers and educators, with longstanding experience working in the community with young people, stepped in and helped us better frame the programme activities. Being a new type of intervention and considering the lack of knowledge about core values of Hip-Hop, attendance, participation, engagement and openness to produce creative writing were established as the measures of success of the workshops, and of the event in general. The workshops and event took place in Italian and English. Rovion Reed was provided with an Italian translator, while Amir was able to speak both Italian and English when needed. Considering the variety of backgrounds of the participants, bilingualism and multilingualism was highly encouraged in all activities, especially in the creative writing workshop. A breakdance battle took place after the workshop, facilitated by Hip-Hop Generation, and it was followed by a free concert and "open-mic" session, where migrant and Italian youth had the possibility of performing the song they had written in the afternoon. The workshops and concert were video-recorded and were made available for the public via YouTube channel (https://www.youtube.com/watch?v=UGb0FCvbBeY).

4.1 "Keepin' It Real": Youth Tales of Life and Migration

Figure 1 shows an artifact that was written by a young disabled migrant, who had been labeled as having behavioural issues in school, during the storytelling workshop. The first part of the artifact is written in Italian, and it talks about smoking and drinking. He believes that young people smoking is spoiling the party. He also wishes that those young people would "shut their mouth" (i.e., "chiudi la bocca"), and that he could throw some of them out ("ti mando fuori per forza"). These first lines in Italian speak about the cultural differences between Italian and migrant youth, most of whom come from religious families and therefore are not used to smoking and drinking habits.

The second part of the artifact is juxtaposed to the first part. It is written in Wolof, so we asked the participant to translate it into Italian and then English: "Where I come from is very far, the road was difficult, but thank God I arrived. I am not sitting around and waiting. I go to work. The things I get, I have. There are some people waiting for me. I do not wish to let them down. They trust me. All the way to Dakar". The participant turns to his own reality, he talks about the long and dangerous journey he had to face to arrive in Italy. He is not concerned with engaging in Italian party culture, he is focused on working and supporting his family back in Dakar. This artifact shows the complicated process of inclusion of migrant youth in Italian society, the challenges of peer relationships, and the aspiration and expectations of migrant youth. Also, it deconstructs the stereotype of the young male migrant who is perceived as living on welfare benefits and selling drugs to survive. It encapsulates the hopes of most young migrants, who come to Italy to work and support their families back in their home countries (Fig. 1).

This intervention intended to show how Hip-Hop pedagogy constitutes a call for educators to consider an innovative approach to teaching and learning that is connected to the culture of disabled migrant youth. Recognising young migrants who identify with Hip-Hop or Krip-Hop demonstrates educational stakeholders' understanding that they engage in a different culture than the dominant white Italian groups, and communicate differently than the dominant groups (Adjapong 2017). It encourages educators and students to consider how migrant and marginalised youth have historically been excluded from society and education, and consequently construct knowledge differently than the dominant group. This makes the call for an intersectional inclusive education characterised by innovative pedagogies increasingly urgent, both in the Italian context and internationally (Migliarini 2020).

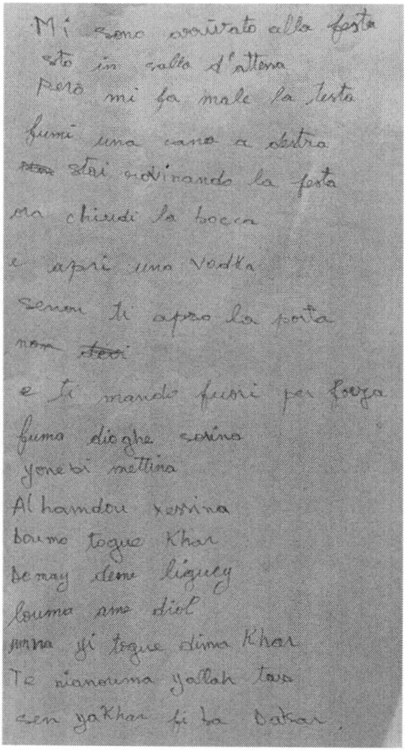
Mi sono arrivato alla festa
sto in sallo d'attena
però mi fa male la testa
fumi una canna a destra
stai rovinando la festa
ma chiudi la bocca
e apri una Vodka
senon ti apro la porta
non
e ti mando fuori per forza
fuma dioghe sokino
yone bi mettina
Al hamdou xessina
bouma togue Khar
Bemay deme liguey
louma ame diol
amna yi togue dima Khar
Te nianouma yallah tawa
sen yaKhar fi ba Dakar.

Figure 1

5 Conclusion: Towards a Transnational DisCrit Inclusion

This contribution reflected on the theoretical and geographical expansion of the Disability Critical Race Studies (DisCrit) in education. It drew the epistemological lineage of DisCrit, illustrating the origin and meaning of the concept of intersectionality. Then it demonstrated the affordances of DisCrit to reframe policy and practice of inclusive education in Italy. The first example showed the DisCrit-informed strength-based approach to support teachers in re-designing inclusive tools, such as IEP and PDP, to support the needs of migrant students labelled as disabled in the classroom. The second example highlighted the contribution of DisCrit, integrated into Krip-Hop and Hip-

Hop Pedagogy, to support intersectional inclusion of disabled migrants within the community of their host country. It showed the importance of translanguaging in understanding disabled migrant students' literacy skills.

This contribution makes the call for an intersectional inclusive education both in the Italian context and internationally. All teachers and educational stakeholders must acknowledge that the present definition of inclusive education, coupled with the monolithic approaches to teaching a Eurocentric curriculum, does not help students achieve or feel included in school and society. Intersectionality and DisCrit can bridge theory and practice to demonstrate pedagogical approaches that can be used to better reach disabled migrant and multiply marginalised students in the classroom (Annamma et al. 2022). DisCrit allows students to accept and affirm their identities and experiences while developing critical perspectives that challenge inequities in schools and society, which can be perpetuated by the traditional notion of inclusive education and curriculum.

I hope that the examples presented in this contribution are not only used by teachers in Italy, but that they are also critiqued and modified by others, in other contexts, who apply them. The implications of DisCrit for inclusive policy and practices in Italy, and elsewhere, are vast. DisCrit inclusion can help in promoting critical reflection and action for all teachers, while encouraging them to empower and embrace multiply marginalised students, their families, and their communities. For this reason, I have conceptualised this contribution as a reflection and an invitation for teachers, families, and researchers to reach out and share how they have applied DisCrit inclusion and what has been successful and challenging in this context.

References

Adams, D. (2015): Implementation of school-wide positive behavior supports in the neoliberal context in an urban elementary school. https://surface.syr.edu/etd/300/.

Adams, D. L./Erevelles, N. (2016): Shadow play: DisCrit, dis/respectability, and the carceral logics. In Annamma, S./Connor, D./Ferri, B. (eds.), DisCrit: Diability studies and critical race theory in education. New York, NY: Teachers College Press.

Adjapong, E. S. (2017): Bridging theory and practice in the urban science classroom: A framework for hip-hop pedagogy. In: Critical Education 8, 15, pp. 6–22.

Annamma, S./Connor, D.J./Ferri, B.A. (2013): Dis/ability critical race studies (Dis Crit): Theorizing at the intersections of race and dis/ability. In: Race Ethnicity and Education 16, 1, pp. 1-31.

Annamma, S./Morrison, D. (2018): DisCrit classroom ecology: using praxis to dismantle dysfunctional education ecologies. In: Teaching and Teacher Education 73, pp. 70–80. doi:10.1016/j.tate.2018.03.008.

Annamma, S./Ferri, B./Connor, D. (2022): DisCrit Expanded: Reverberations, Ruptures, Inquiries. Teachers College Press.

Artiles, A. J. (2013): Untangling the racialization of disabilities: An intersectionality critique

across disability models. In: Du Bois Review: Social Science Research on Race 10, 2, pp. 329-347.

Beneke, M.R. (2017): Race and Ability Talk in Early Childhood: Critical Inquiry into Shared Book Reading Practices with Pre-Service Teachers. ProQuest LLC (Doctoral dissertation).

Bove, C./Cescato, S. (2013): Cultures of education and rituals of transition from home to the infant toddler center: Observing interactions and professional development. Ricerche di Pedagogia e Didattica. In: Journal of Theories and Research in Education 8, 2, pp. 27–44.

Collins, K. M. (2011): Discursive positioning in a fifth-grade writing lesson. The making of a "bad, bad boy". In: Urban Education 46, 4, pp. 741–785. doi: 10. 1177/0042085911399339.

Cannon, M. A. (2019): Because I Am Human: Centering Black Women with Dis/ abilities in Transition Planning from High School to College. ProQuest LLC (Doctoral dissertation).

Charmaz, K. (2014): Constructing Grounded Theory. Second Edition. London: Sage.

Combahee River Collective (1978): The Combahee River Collective Statement.

Connor, D.J./Ferri, B.A./Annamma, S. (eds.) (2016): DisCrit: Disability Studies & Critical Race Theory in Education. New York: Teachers College Press.

Cooper, A. J. (1892/2017): A voice from the South: By a black woman of the south. Chapel Hill: The University of North Carolina Press. Retrieved June 14, 2019, from Project Muse database.

Crenshaw, K. (1989): Demarginalizing the Intersection of Race and Sex: A Black Feminist Critique of Antidiscrimination Doctrine, Feminist Theory and Antiracist Politics. In: University of Chicago Legal Forum 1, 8, pp. 139-167.

D'Alessio, S., (2014): Le normative sui bisogni educativi speciali in Europa e in Italia. Verso un'educazione inclusiva? La prospettiva dei Disability Studies in Patrizia Gaspari (Ed.) Pedagogia speciale e BES. Anicia: Roma, (pp. 217-244).

DeCuir, J. T./Dixson, A. D. (2004): "So when it comes out, they aren't surprised that it is there": Using Critical Race Theory as a tool of analysis of race and racism in education. In: Educational Researcher 33, 5, pp. 26–23. doi: 10.3102/0013189 X033005026.

Downing, J. E./Hanreddy, A./Peckham-Hardin, K. D. (2015): Teaching communication skills to students with severe disabilities (3rd ed.). Paul H. Brookes Publishing.

DuBois, W.E.B. (1920): Race intelligence. The Crisis. 20(3).

Elder, B./Migliarini, V. (2020): Decolonizing inclusive education: a collection of practical inclusive CDS- and DisCrit-informed teaching practices implemented in the global South. In: Disability and the Global South 7, 1, pp. 1852-1872.

Fierros, E. G./Conroy, J. W. (2002): Double jeopardy: An exploration of restrictiveness and race and race in special education. In Losen, D. J./Orfield, G. (eds.), Racial inequities in special education (pp. 39–70). Cambridge, MA: Harvard Education Press.

Gillborn, D./Rollock, N./Vincent, C./Ball, S. (2016): The black middle classes, education, racism, and dis/ability: An intersectional analysis. In Connor, D./Ferri, B./Annamma, S.A. (eds.) DisCrit: Critical Conversations Across Race, Class, & Dis/ability. New York, NY: Teachers College Press.

Handy, G. T. (2018): Examining Teaching Activities in War-affected Schools: Advancing Transformative Praxis. ProQuest LLC (Doctoral dissertation).

Hernández-Saca, D. I. (2017): Reframing the Master Narratives of Dis/ability at my Intersections: An Outline of an Educational Equity Research Agenda. In: Critical Disability Discourses/Discours critiques dans le champ du handicap, 8.

Hill, M. L./Petchauer, E. (eds.) (2013): Schooling hip-hop: Expanding hip-hop based education across the curriculum. Teachers College Press.

ISMU Fondazione (2014): Alunni con Cittadinanza non Italiana. L'eterogeneità dei percorsi scolastici. Rapporto nazionale A.S. 2012/2013. Milano: Fondazione ISMU.

ISMU Fondazione (2016): Alunni con Cittadinanza non Italiana. La scuola multiculturale nei contesti locali. Rapporto nazionale A.S. 2014/2015. Milano: Fondazione ISMU.

Kulkarni, S. S. (2015): Beliefs About Disability, Race, and Culture of Urban Special Education Teachers and their Retention Decisions. ProQuest LLC (Doctoral dissertation).

Ladson-Billings, G. (2001): Crossing over to Canaan: The journey of new teachers in diverse classrooms. San Francisco, CA: Jossey-Bass.

Leonardo, Z./Broderick, A. (2011): Smartness as property: A critical exploration of intersections between whiteness and disability studies. In: Teachers College Record 113, 10, pp. 2206-2232.

Margolis, E. (2004): "Looking at discipline, looking at labour: photographic representations of Indian boarding schools". In: Visual Studies 19, 1, pp. 54–78.

Matsuda, M. J. (1987): Looking to the bottom: Critical legal studies and reparations. In: Harvard Civil Rights Civil Liberties Law Review 72, pp. 30–164.

Migliarini, V. (2017): Subjectivation, agency and the schooling of raced and dis/abled asylum-seeking children in the Italian context. In: Intercultural Education 28, 2, pp. 182-195.

Migliarini, V. (2018): 'Colour-evasiveness' and racism without race: The disablement of asylum-seeking children at the edge of fortress Europe. In: Race Ethnicity and Education 21, 4, pp. 438–457. https://doi.org/10.1080/13613324.2017. 1417252.

Migliarini, V./Stinson, C./D'Alessio, S. (2019) 'SENitizing' migrant children in inclusive settings: exploring the impact of the Salamanca Statement thinking in

Italy and the United States. In: International Journal of Inclusive Education 23, 7-8, pp. 754-767, DOI: 10.1080/13603116.2019.1622804.

Migliarini, V./Elder, B.C./D'Alessio, S. (2022) A DisCrit-Informed Person-Centered Approach to Inclusive Education in Italy. In: Equity & Excellence in Education. DOI: 10.1080/10665684.2021.2047415.

Morrell, E./Duncan-Andrade, J. M. (2002): Promoting academic literacy with urban youth through engaging hip-hop culture. In: The English Journal 91, 6, pp. 88–92. https://doi.org/10.2307/821822.

Picower, B. (2009): The unexamined Whiteness of teaching: how White teachers maintain and enact dominant racial ideologies. In: Race Ethnicity and Education 12, 2, pp. 197-215, DOI: 10.1080/13613320902995475.

Siuty, M. E. (2017): (Re) Constituting Teacher Identity for Inclusion in Urban Schools: A Process of Reification and Resistance. ProQuest LLC (Doctoral dissertation).

Spratt, J./Florian, L. (2015): Inclusive pedagogy: From learning to action. Supporting each individual in the context of 'everybody.' In: Teaching and Teacher Education 49, 19, pp. 89–96. https://doi.org/10.1016/j.tate.2015.03.006.

Valencia, R. R. (1997): Conceptualizing the notion of deficit thinking. In Valencia, R. R. (ed.), The evolution of deficit thinking: Educational thought and practice. London, UK: Routledge Falmer, pp. 113–131.

Vandercook, T./York, J./Forest, M. (1989): The McGill Action Planning System (MAPS): A strategy for building the vision. In: Journal of the Association for Persons with Severe Handicaps 14, 3, pp. 205–215. https://doi.org/10.1177/154079698901400306.

Weishaar, P. M. (2010): Twelve ways to incorporate strengths-based planning into the IEP process. In: The Clearing House 83, 6, pp. 207–210. https://doi.org/10.1080/00098650903505381.

Adolescents' Attitudes Towards and Representations of Otherness

Anna Frizzarin

1   Introduction

Inclusion and equity are emphasised in the 2030 Agenda for Sustainable Development adopted by the United Nations in 2015 as laying the foundations for quality education. As stated in the declaration, this marks the commitment to guarantee *all* people, regardless of their differences (e.g., sex, age, race or ethnicity, disability, migratory background, etc.), equal learning opportunities and the chance to acquire the knowledge and skills required to fully participate in society (UNESCO 2015). This implies, in turn, addressing all forms of exclusion and marginalisation, disparities and inequalities in education. To do that, fostering the development of inclusive schools seems to be an indispensable prerequisite. All in all, inclusive education can be indeed seen as a process that seeks to identify and remove the barriers that may hinder the presence, participation, and achievement of *all* students, especially those at risk of marginalisation and exclusion in school (Slee 2018). Such emphasis on the contextual factors – instead of focusing on the categories where students may fall into – is what, according to Ainscow (2020), is required for the progress in relation to inclusion and equity. From the author's perspective, overcoming them constitutes indeed the most important means of developing forms of education that are effective for all.

Former research has identified peer attitudes as one of the main obstacles for students' participation in school (Bossaert et al. 2011; McDougall et al. 2004), showing that negative attitudes are likely to result in exclusionary and avoiding behaviours which, in turn, may hinder the participation of their targets. More specifically, given the compelling evidence in the international literature of biased peer attitudes towards and experiences of exclusion of various groups of students conceived as different like, for example, students with minority and/or migratory backgrounds, LGBTQ students, etc. (Burford/ Lucassen/Hamilton 2017; Henríquez et al. 2015; Priest et al. 2014; Santos/da Silva/Menezes 2018), the current study assumes that peer attitudes towards diversity/otherness may constitute a potential threat to inclusion. As we will see in the following section, identifying someone as different from oneself (i.e., as Other) may indeed result in prejudicial and negative attitudes which, in turn, can lead to his/her marginalisation and exclusion. In this process, the knowledge and the cultural models about otherness collectively shared in a given context play a crucial role, insofar as they are incorporated in single individuals' social representations which, in turn, influence their attitudes (Moscovici 1984).

From an inclusive perspective, it is thus pivotal to explore students' representations of and attitudes towards the conceived different ones and how they are linked with exclusionary patterns among peers in schools. So far, many studies have been conducted internationally on peer attitudes towards various groups of students. Yet, to the best of my knowledge, there are no instruments measuring peer attitudes towards otherness in its broadest sense from an inclusion/exclusion perspective. Therefore, the current chapter presents a self-reported instrument aimed to measure secondary school students' attitudes towards *otherness* (and their representations thereof) – here defined as 'attitudes towards the ones who are perceived as different and as such excluded by others'.

2   Diversity as social construct

In the literature, there are several theories and approaches dealing with the concept of diversity. The current study advocates a 'constructed' definition of otherness and refers to the social identity approach and to *othering* theories. Understanding diversity as a product emerging from social interactions means acknowledging that they don't have anything to do with the intrinsic characteristics of individuals but that they are instead the result of a collective process of signification which identifies some differences as salient in a specific social context (Burbules 1996).

In line with this idea, the social identity approach sees diversity as a social construct emerging in the process of identity formation (Bennett/Sani 2004). It is made up of two main theories: the Social Identity Theory (SIT; Tajfel 1972) and the Self-Categorization Theory (SCT; Turner et al. 1987). The former is focused on the psychological mechanisms (i.e., social identity, categorisation, and social comparison) underlying the distinction between *ingroup* and *outgroup* and, consequently, the emergence of prejudice and discrimination among members of different groups (Abrams/Hogg 2010; Dovidio et al. 2010). In turn, the SCT deals especially with social identity salience, that is how, in a particular context, some self-categories become salient while others remain in the background (Oaks/Haslam/Turner 1994). One of its core ideas is that individuals dispose of various identities and, depending on the specific self-category 'activated', they experience them-selves and others differently and behave accordingly (Hornsey 2008). In this sense, categories (and therefore difference) can be considered as transitional and context dependent.

In sum, the social identity approach identifies the psychological mechanisms upon which the social construction of diversity is grounded, recognising the crucial role of the social context in this process. However, it does not consider how the construction and the attribution of otherness itself are used to maintain existing social hierarchies and to justify the exclusion of the 'Others' (i.e., those who are recognised as different). In this sense, the concept of *othering* takes a step forward, designating the social and discursive practices through which otherness is constructed and ascribed to others and focusing on the consequences of this attribution process for those who are 'othered'.

Otherness can be defined as an imposed 'state of difference' (Udah 2019: 3) achieved through a process of self-other distancing based on binary and opposing categories such as us-them, ingroup-outgroup, etc. (Brons 2015). To fully understand the potential of othering processes, they must be contextualised within the broader dynamics of power formation/exercise and knowledge production (Canales 2000; Thomas-Olalde/Velho 2011). What is crucial here is that the subjects in the more powerful positions can 'construct otherness' by divulgating certain knowledge about the others that identifies them as *different* and *inferior*. In doing so, they are marking the border between inside and outside, between self and other, between ingroup and outgroup, legitimising such distinction as 'normal'. This produces a vicious circle, whereby the social hierarchy is reproduced and maintained, and the exclusion of the Others is legitimated basically through othering discourses (Thomas-Olalde/Velho 2011).

Against such theoretical background, *otherness* is here defined in its broadest sense, as all the differences/characteristics that may lead individuals to be conceived and labelled as different (and as such excluded) by others. Moreover, the willingness to not reproduce othering discourses and processes through the research resulted in the decision, in the present study, of adopting a *non-categorical* approach to diversity – thus avoiding any predefined category of difference.

3   Peer attitudes towards and representations of otherness

Attitudes are generally described as either a positive or negative evaluation of some object/entity (Eagly/Chaiken 1993). More specifically, the current study refers to Triandis (1971: 2), who described attitudes as 'an idea charged with emotion which predisposes a class of actions to a particular class of social situations'. This definition highlights the multidimensional structure of attitudes, which are assumed to be composed of an affective, a behavioural, and a cognitive component. Specifically, the affective component refers to people's feelings about an object, the behavioural component is linked to individuals' intentions to act in a certain way, and the cognitive component concerns beliefs/knowledge about the object. In the present study, the object are the students perceived as different and therefore excluded by their peers in secondary schools.

In the last two decades, a lot of research has been devoted to the study of peer attitudes towards inclusive schooling and especially towards students with disabilities – also in light of the difficulties encountered in their social participation in inclusive school settings (de Boer/Pijl/Minnaert 2012; Van Mieghem et al. 2020).

Attitudes are indeed thought to explain or even predict social behaviour, as postulated within the Theory of Planned Behavior (Ajzen 1991). Evidence supporting the role played by peer attitudes in shaping students' behaviour can be found in previous research: studies that sought to investigate the relationship between attitudes towards peers with disabilities and their social participation revealed a significant positive relationship between them both at the level of primary and secondary education (de Boer/Pijl 2016; Godeau et al. 2010; Petry 2018). These results suggest that negative peer attitudes are likely to give place to exclusionary or at least avoiding behaviours which, in turn, may hinder the participation of their targets. Moreover, former research also showed that there is compelling evidence of biased peer attitudes towards and experiences of exclusion of various groups of students conceived as different like, for example, students with minority backgrounds, LGBTQ students, etc. (Priest et al. 2014; Santos et al. 2018). All these findings seem to indicate that the inclusion of the students identified as 'Others' may be at risk and, therefore, that there could be a direct link between diversity/otherness and peer exclusion. This may be related to the representations of otherness held by students. As introduced above, othering discourses promote certain (collective) knowledge of the Others, which is then incorporated in individuals' social representations (Thomas-Olalde/Velho 2011). Such representations – that is, what people think and feel about a person/an object

– in turn influence their attitudes towards that person/object (Harma/Gombert/Roussey 2013).

So far, many instruments were developed internationally to measure children and adolescents' attitudes towards various groups of 'different' people (e.g., persons with disabilities, ethnic minorities, etc. – as defined by the respective authors[1]). Nevertheless, to the best of my knowledge, none of them measures adolescents' attitudes towards otherness in all its broad meaning and explores the representations of otherness held by students. As such, we do not know who constitutes the 'relevant Other' in the perspectives of the students and, consequently, which are the characteristics that are more likely to give place to exclusionary behaviours. To fill this gap, the current study presents a self-reported instrument combining a qualitative and a quantitative approach aimed to evaluate secondary school students' attitudes towards their perceived 'different' peers which strives to not (re)produce othering processes. Beside measuring their attitudes, the *Adolescents' Attitudes Towards Otherness Survey* (AATOS) also investigates students' representations of otherness. Specifically, such representations – as emerged from the validation study of the instrument – constitute the main focus of the present chapter.

4   The instrument

In the attempt to not reproduce othering processes through the research, the AATOS was designed avoiding the use of any predefined category of difference. To do that, a vignette for the definition of the target was created. Vignettes are short scenarios that can be developed in various forms (e.g., texts, images, etc.) whose purpose is to stimulate research participants' responses (Hill 1997). Typically, they are developed by researchers. Conversely, for the AATOS an 'open' vignette was designed (i.e., open to participants' definitions of otherness). At the beginning of the instrument, the respondents themselves are indeed asked to write the vignette after being prompted to describe a hypothetical boy or girl (Alex[2]) who, in their opinions, is excluded from his/her peers because perceived as 'different' (see Figure 1).

---

1   See, among others, the *Multi-Response Racial Attitude Measure* (MRA; Doyle/Aboud 1995), the *Chedoke-McMaster Attitudes Towards Children with Handicaps* (CATCH; Rosenbaum et al. 1986), the *Attitudes towards Religious Diversity Index* (ARDI, Francis et al. 2012).

2   In line with the non-categorical approach adopted, we chose a name for the target that could be attributed both to females and males. This allowed us to shirk the reproduction of a binary construction of gender. Moreover, using an international name (vs. an

Now think about a guy or a girl closer to your own age who, in your opinion, is excluded at school because of his/her diversity. (At this stage, try not to think about yourself and the times you may have felt excluded; you will be asked about that at the end of the questionnaire.)

This person can be fictional, someone you actually know or someone you have only heard about. You can choose who to describe, as long as this person is excluded at school because considered as different by others. You can also choose whether this person is a boy or a girl, in either case his/her name will be Alex.

Please describe Alex in the following box. You can describe his/her appearance, habits and/or behaviors, peculiarities, etc. The main thing is making clear how you imagine this person and how s/he differentiates from others.

Alex is...

_____
_____
_____ .

Please also explain why you think Alex is being excluded.

In my opinion, Alex may be excluded because/for...

_____
_____

Figure 1:   The initial open vignette.

All subsequent items/questions of the AATOS are then referred to Alex – the boy/girl that the participants described in the vignette (i.e., the person they designated as the target) – including the rating scale measuring participant's attitudes. The development process of the attitude scale is described in more detail in a previous paper (Frizzarin/Demo/de Boer 2022). In sum, the initial item pool was first created translating and adapting items of the affective and the behavioural subscales of the *Chedoke-McMaster Attitudes Towards Children with Handicaps Scale* (CATCH; Rosenbaum et al. 1986) and of the cognitive subscale of the *Multidimensional Attitude Scale Towards Persons with Disabilities* (MAS; Findler et al. 2007). The result is a multi-item scale covering all three attitude components (see Table 1).

Beside the open vignette and the attitude scale, the AATOS also comprises a self-constructed questionnaire tapping various variables (e.g., parti-

Italian one) was intended to not restrict the respondents' choice of the target in terms of nationality and cultural/ethnic backgrounds.

Table 1:   Overall structure and variables included in the AATOS.

Section	Variable(s)	Response format
Background information	— Gender — Age — School — Cultural background	— Free text — Free text — Multiple-choice (2 questions) — Free text (3 questions)
Vignette	— Representation of the Other and reasons for his/her exclusion — Target's perceived similarity/difference from oneself	— Free text (2 questions) — Likert-scale ranging from 0 ('very similar to me) to 10 ('very different from me')
Attitude scale	— 33-item scale tapping the affective (12), behavioural (12) and cognitive (9) components of attitudes	— Likert-scale ranging from 1 ('strongly disagree') to 5 ('strongly agree')
Contact Index	— Previous/current contact — Contact quantity — Contact frequency — Contact quality	— Yes/No — Multiple-choice — Multiple-choice (2 questions) — Multiple-choice (3 questions)
Open-ended questions	— Difficulties perceived in interacting with others — Presence of assimilative attitudes — Participants' perception of self-inclusion by peers — Motivations used by participants to explain their own exclusion by peers	— Free text — Free text — Likert-scale from 0 ('not included at all') to 10 ('very included') — Free text

cipants' background information, previous/current contact with people similar to the target, etc.) – built up based on the results of a systematic review conducted as preliminary stage of the project. Moreover, the AATOS includes a final section with some open-ended questions which are also meant to contribute to the evaluation of participants' attitudes. These concern: (a) the difficulties perceived in interacting with the Other; (b) the eventual presence of assimilative attitudes (i.e., thinking that the target should become more 'normal'/'like us', to be more accepted/included); and (c) the motivations used by students to explain their own experiences of exclusion in school. Table 1 summarises the overall structure and content of

218   Adolescents' Attitudes Towards and Representations of Otherness

the instrument[3]. The full text can be requested contacting the author per email.

In sum, the AATOS uses a combination of qualitative and quantitative data to integrate several aspects in the evaluation of respondents' attitudes. As mentioned above, in the current chapter we will focus on the responses provided to the initial vignette by participants in the validation study of the AATOS (conducted in the spring 2021), that is, their representations of otherness.

5   Method

5.1   Sample and administration procedure

In total, 543 students coming from two lower and three higher secondary schools located in different Italian regions (from North to South) constituted the convenience sample of the present study. For validation purposes, the aim was indeed to draw a sample including considerable variety in order to consider the developed instrument sound and robust across many individuals (DeVellis 2017). Due to missing or incomplete responses, some question-naires were excluded from data analysis, resulting in a final sample of 490 students (age range 11-20), distributed as follows: 268 students for the lower (N= 268, $M_{age=}$ 12,41; SD= 1,01; age range 11–15) and 222 students for the higher secondary school (N= 222; M_{age}=16,23; SD= 1,75; age range 14–20), respectively.

The survey was computer-based and was administered either at school or during distance-learning hours in the presence of a teacher. Adaptations to the procedure were needed depending on the local epidemiological situation (at the time of the study, some classes of the higher secondary schools were not attending school in presence due to the Covid-19 pandemic) and the resources of the single schools.

---

3   The structure presented in Table 1 refers to the version of the instrument used for data collection in the current study (i.e., the validation study of the AATOS). Based on the analyses and the outcomes of the quantitative part of the study (which are not the focus of this chapter), the instrument – and, specifically, the attitude scale – was further modified. This will be object of a subsequent paper.

Table 2:   Sample characteristics.

Participants' characteristics	Lower secondary school		Higher secondary school	
	N	%	N	%
Gender				
Males	147	54.9	57	25.7
Females	117	43.7	164	73.9
Other	3	1.1	1	0.5
Cultural background				
Born in Italy	241	89.9	206	92.8
Born in a foreign country	25	9.3	16	7.2
Both parents born in Italy	185	69.0	179	80.6
One parent born in a foreign country	26	9.7	22	9.9
Both parents born in a foreign country	55	20.5	21	9.5
School type				
Lyceum			194	87.4
Technical institute			27	12.2

5.2   Data analysis

The responses provided by participants to the vignette and the open-ended questions of the AATOS were analysed both with data- and concept-driven categories obtained through the method of Qualitative Content Analysis (Kuckartz 2014; Schreier 2012). Data-driven categories were inductively developed for: (a) participants' representation of the Other and the reasons for his/her exclusion (the two answers included in the vignette; see Fig. 1); (b) the motivations used by participants to explain their own experiences of exclusion (open-ended question). Conversely, concept-driven categories (i.e., developed deductively) were used to determine the eventual presence of assimilative attitudes (open-ended question, see Tab. 1). The emerged coding categories – first created for the pilot study of the instrument and then revised during the current study taking into account the new data – were included in the *Guide for the qualitative analysis of the AATOS*, a brief booklet providing the instructions and the categories for the analysis of the qualitative part of the survey.

To assure intersubjectivity in the analysis process (which is an aspect of the reliability of the coding categories; Schreier 2012), two rounds of estimation of intercoder agreement with two different independent coders were conducted. On both occasions, the agreement percentage was obtained at the document level, that is, if both coders assigned the same code(s) to a given participant (i.e., presence/absence of the code in the document; Kuckartz/Rädiker 2019). In the first round the agreement was calculated on about 10% (n= 50) of participants' responses. After discussing the disagreements emerged, the author adjusted the category systems included in the *Guide*. The second external coder was then asked to code about the 30% of the sample responses (n= 150) following the revised codebook. An overall agreement of 67.52% and 73.91% were obtained for the vignette responses in the two rounds respectively. However, in the current study, the percentage of agreement was not interpreted as a result *per se* but as a mean to improve the reliability and the quality of the coding categories included in the *Guide* (Schreier 2012). Once the codebook was deemed valid, the author coded the rest of the data.

6   Results

From students' responses to the vignettes, it emerged that they referred either to factors related to the target and his/her individual characteristics or to some external factors (i.e., that do not depend on the target but on others and/or the wider context) to represent Alex and to motivate his/her exclusion. Therefore, two main categories were identified: 'Factors related to the target' and 'External factors'. For each of them, several subcategories were developed to describe the *dimensions* to which participants referred to represent Alex (summarised in Table 3).

Before seeing in more detail the content and the frequencies of the single (sub)categories, it should be pointed out that the outcomes of the current study showed certain *multidimensionality* of students' representations of otherness. Respondents used indeed several combinations of characteristics and attributes to motivate why Alex is perceived as different (and as such excluded) by others. Only 13.7% of the sample used only one dimension (i.e., one subcategory) to describe the target in the vignette, while the others ranged from a minimum of 2 to a maximum of 8 dimensions/categories.

In the following, we will see the two main categories and their most frequently used subcategories.

Table 3:   Category system and frequencies for participants' responses to the vignettes.

Main category	Subcategories	Definition	N.
Factors related to the target	Physical appearance	All the characteristics referring to the target's physical appearance.	253
	Personality traits	All the characteristics referring to the personality of the target.	221
	Behaviours/ habits	All what the target does that is considered different/uncommon by others.	198
	Relationships with others	All what concerns the target's interactions and relationships with others.	147
	Culture/ ethnicity	All the characteristics and customs related to the target's different cultural/ethnic background.	119
	Opinions/ideas/ hobbies	All what concerns the target and his/her different ideas, hobbies and priorities.	99
	Skills/abilities	All what concerns the skills and abilities of the target (i.e., what s/he can/cannot do).	78
	Learning achievement	All what concerns the learning achievement and school life of the target.	51
	Gender identity/sexual orientation	All the characteristics related to the target's gender identity and/or sexual orientation.	50
	Disability	All the characteristics and/or difficulties related to the target's disability.	42
	Health conditions	All the characteristics referring to the health conditions (physical, psychological, etc.) of the target.	38
	Religion	All the characteristics and customs related to the target's different religion.	19
	SES	All the characteristics related to the target and/or his/her family SES.	5
External factors	Peers/others	All what the peers/other do that determine the perception of the target as Other and his/her exclusion.	77
	Society	All what concerns the society and its way to address diversity (prejudices, standards, common opinions, etc.) that determine the perception of the target as Other and his/her exclusion.	29

Main ca-tegory	Subcategories	Definition	N.
	Family	All what concerns the target's family that determine the perception of the target as Other and his/her exclusion.	17
	School	All what concerns the school and its struc-ture that determine the perception of the target as Other and his/her exclusion.	9
	Peer group	All what concerns the peer group that de-termine the perception of the target as Other and his/her exclusion.	8
	Other	Other external factors.	13

6.1   Factors related to the target

As displayed in Table 3, the main dimension 'factors related to the target' in-cludes both subcategories referring to Alex' more personal characteristics (e.g., personality traits, habits and behaviours, etc.) and to his/her group dimension, in terms of specific social groups/categories (e.g., culture, religion, etc.) s/he is identified with. In a previous stage of the study, such different 'levels' were clearly distinguished in two main categories ('Individ-ual characteristics' and 'Group characteristics/affiliations'; Frizzarin et al. 2022). Nevertheless, the disagreements emerged in the current study during the discussion following the first round of intercoder agreement calculation questioned a real 'qualitative' difference between those two dimensions (individual vs. group/social). The boundary between them was indeed very difficult to determine from participants' responses, and the frequent inter-sections between the respective subcategories seemed to indicate that what counted most was precisely the combination of certain characteristics rather than deciding at what 'level' they pertained. Therefore, the two old main categories were merged into one ('Factors related to the target'). In this way, it was possible to adhere completely to participants' responses – and to pre-serve their complexity – without imposing on them preconceived and simplistic categories.

What concerns more specifically the content of participants' responses, the most widely used subcategory (51.63%) to describe Alex was related to his/her physical appearance. This category includes statements about specific physical characteristics (e.g., not conforming to beauty standards, being overweight, etc.), but also personal care (e.g., not being clean-cut, not paying attention to one's image, etc.) and look/style of the target (i.e., what Alex wears, if s/he follows the trends, etc.). Moreover, it was also used to code all the responses referring to Alex' skin colour. Such cases were therefore characterised by the overlap of the categories 'Physical appearance' and 'Culture/ethnicity'.

'Looking at him you cannot say that he is a good-looking guy, but he is not ugly, neither. [...] But since he doesn't take care of his image and has "no style", he is a loser in his peers' eyes'. (M, 19)

'(Alex) is different from the others also for his physical appearance, his skin is caramel coloured'. (F, 14)

The subcategory 'personality traits' was also frequently used by participants (45.10%) to describe the different and excluded Other. This category includes all the characteristics that refer to the personality of Alex. Nevertheless, most respondents portrayed the target as someone who is very shy, withdrawn, insecure, who does not talk a lot, etc.

'(Alex is) is a quiet person, who doesn't talk a lot, she doesn't participate to the discussion and never does the first step (that is, she doesn't come to you and start talking with you)'. (F, 14)

A variety of behaviours and habits were also cited by the participants (40.41%) to explain Alex' exclusion. This category encloses all what the target *does* and that defines him/her as Other. Among them, we can mention, for example, having strange habits and behaviours in general, but also transgressive, non-conforming and annoying behaviours. Also in this case, sometimes participants described habits and customs related to the target's culture and/or other group affiliations. In such cases, the subcategories 'Behaviours/habits' and the respective 'group' subcategory overlapped.

'He always talks over others and makes impertinent comments that are annoying. (Alex may be excluded) for his strange behaviours and his attitude'. (M, 13)

'Alex has different customs compared to ours, and for this reason is not able to integrate'. (F, 18)

Several respondents (30%) also mentioned the difficulties encountered by Alex in interacting and building relationships with others, which, in their opinion, contribute to his/her perception as Other. Moreover, such difficulties were often linked to the personality traits described above (i.e., being shy, withdrawn, etc.).

'(Alex may be excluded because) [...] he is very introverted, and therefore can't become friends with new people'. (F, 14)

Alex' ethnic and cultural background was the 'group' characteristic most cited in the current study (24.29%). In their descriptions, participants referred indeed to a variety of attributes like different nationalities, physical charac-teristics (e.g., different skin colour), customs (e.g., food, clothes, etc.), language difficulties, etc.

'(Alex is) a person with a different skin colour. He has African origins, but he was born in Italy. […] He is excluded because of his different skin colour'. (M, 12)

Participants also frequently described Alex in terms of his/her individual opinions (20.20%). The target was indeed often portrayed as someone who has different ideas and/or ways of thinking and seeing things. Moreover, this subcategory was used to code all those responses concerning what Alex likes, his/her preferences and priorities, but also his/her hobbies and interests.

'He doesn't talk with anyone because he can't find someone who shares his interests. He finds useless the topics his peers find entertaining'. (F, 17)

The result of the current study also showed that Alex was sometimes described in terms of his/her skills and abilities, that is, what s/he can(not)/is (not) able to do (15.92%). This includes statements referring to how good/ bad Alex is at carrying out certain activities (e.g., at school, in sports, etc.), but also different kinds of difficulties related, for example, to other characteristics such as a disability, specific health conditions, etc. (overlap of the subcategories 'Skills/abilities' and 'Disability' or 'Health conditions'). Moreover, this subcategory was used to code all the answers describing the difficulties of the target with the second language (overlap of the subcategories 'Skills/abilities' and 'Culture/ethnicity').

'Because, unlike his peers, Alex can't go out and play or just hang out with his friends. He always has to be accompanied by an adult'. (F, 18)

'Alex can't speak Italian and doesn't understand what others say'. (F, 13)

Less mentioned subcategories were: learning achievement (10.41%), gender identity/sexual orientation (10.20%), disability (8.57%), health conditions (7.76%), religion (3.88%) and SES (1.02%).

6.2   External factors

The second main category developed for the vignette responses covers all statements referring to some external factors to describe Alex and to motivate his/her exclusion. We called them 'external' because such factors have nothing to do with the target and they do not depend directly on his/her characteristics.

Under this main dimension, the most used argument was related to Alex' peers or in general to others (i.e., the people surrounding him/her) and the way they behave and react toward him/her. Some students (15.71%) indeed motivated the target's exclusion in terms of others' characteristics/limits (e.g., being superficial, having prejudices towards the target, etc.) and their difficulties in interacting with him/her (e.g., they do not know how or do not want to interact with him/her), thus attributing the 'problem' to those that exclude Alex.

'(Alex may be excluded because) there are people who are not open-minded and tend to exclude the persons who are not like them instead of integrating them in the group'. (F, 12)

'His classmates perceive his diversity as a burden and instead of including him in the group and making him feel part of class, they exclude him and make him feel even more different not allowing his integration'. (F, 18)

Also the wider context and the society in general were mentioned by participants (5.92%) as a determinant factor for the perception of Alex as Other and for his/her exclusion. This subcategory includes all what concerns the society and its way to address diversity like, for example, common prejudices and stereotypes, standards (e.g., beauty standards, gender roles, etc.), popular opinions, etc.

'(Alex may be excluded because) the society we live in, sadly, often sees diversity as a danger and not as something to embrace and discover'. (F, 14)

'Nowadays, if a girl is a bit chubby, she is immediately targeted because the standards of the modern society don't accept curvy girls'. (M, 18)

Less mentioned subcategories regarded: the family of the target and its characteristics (3.47%), the school context and its organisation (1.84%) and the peer group and its 'rules' (1.63%).

7   Discussion

The current chapter described some results from the validation study of the *Adolescents' Attitudes towards Otherness Survey*, a self-reported instrument combining a qualitative and a quantitative approach in the evaluation of secondary school students' attitudes towards their conceived different and therefore excluded peers. Specifically, the focus here was on participants' representations of otherness.

In line with the broad definition of otherness embraced in the present study, the main purpose of the vignette placed at the very beginning of the instrument was to let participants decide who the target of the instrument would be (i.e., the object of the attitudes being measured) in order to avoid the use of any predefined category of difference (and therefore the activation of othering processes). Categories are indeed increasingly seen as problematic in social research (Gillespie/Howarth/Cornish 2012) – insofar as, when unchallenged, they tend to reproduce the differences under study strengthening existing status hierarchies and social inequalities (Baez 2004). Moreover, in this way, it was possible to explore participants' representations of otherness and thus to gain insight on who is actually at risk of being excluded because conceived as different by peers.

Overall, the findings showed that the excluded Other in school can be embodied in and represented by a wide range of characteristics. These regarded both the personal and the group/social dimension of the target, indicating that otherness is linked not only with different social groups/ categories (e.g., students with disabilities, minority backgrounds, etc.), but also with a wide range of attributes concerning the single individual. Actually, in the present study, individual characteristics (like physical appearance, personality traits, etc.) were the most cited to describe Alex in the vignette. Conversely, the 'personal' dimension is typically neglected in attitude research, which is mainly focused on *intergroup* attitudes and relations. Moreover, from the content analysis of the vignettes it emerged strongly the *multidimensionality* of students' representations of otherness – as highlighted by the number of intersecting dimensions used by them to describe Alex and to motivate his/her exclusion. Respondents indeed used mostly several attributes to depict the target, demonstrating a far more complex representation of otherness than the one conveyed by a simple label/category traditionally employed in attitude instruments. This confirms the inadequacy of the use of fixed and deterministic categories which are not able to reflect the complex crossways of identities, roles and situations that the participants experience in their daily life interactions (Sapon-Shevin 2014).

Furthermore, from an inclusive perspective, research focused on *some* specific categories of students is not compatible with a broad definition of inclusion – which calls for a focus on *all* learners, no matter their individual differences. As highlighted by Messiou (2017), such a way of doing research not only reproduces a 'narrow' idea of inclusion but also risks being harmful both for the students identified with those categories and the ones that do not fall in any group which is considered to deem special attention – but still experience learning difficulties and/or marginalisation. In the first case, the focus on *some* students/categories is associated with the risk of stigma and devaluation, as evidenced by the *dilemma of difference* (Norwich 2013; Terzi 2005). In the second case, the focus on certain groups of students risks excluding from the inclusive discourse all those that do not fall into such predefined categories, putting them at greater danger of being marginalised (Messiou 2012). Even though among the characteristics used to describe the excluded Other in school in the current study some more commonly studied groups/categories do emerge (like disability, ethnicity, gender identity, etc.), the most cited dimensions used to represent Alex in the vignette were related to aspects usually neglected in the inclusive research field (i.e., all the characteristics concerning the 'individual' dimension). All this reiterates the importance of adopting a broader approach to diversity – such as the one proposed in this study – which does not restrict the focus only to certain specific categories of students but is instead able to take into account all the individual differences (and their respective intersections) that could lead to consider the Other as different and, in turn, to his exclusion and marginalisation.

Nevertheless, the current study does not aim to deny the usefulness and the inevitability of social categories, first and foremost in research. Especially in the inclusive research field, it must be recognised the need to identify (and therefore to name) the differences which expose students to a greater risk of exclusion and marginalisation in certain educational contexts, to define, consequently, where compensatory actions must be implemented by schools (but not exclusively) in order to guarantee their full inclusion. Problematising the use of categories in research does not imply rejecting them; instead, the aim is to encourage the adoption of more critical and reflexive stances (Gillespie et al. 2012). In this sense, the current study tries to make a 'positive' use of such categories, insofar as it does not impose any *a priori* defined category, letting them emerge from the responses of the participants themselves and problematising their use in its theoretical framework. From this point of view, such a use may be fully compatible with a broad idea of inclusion, given that investigating students' representations (and categories) of otherness – far from reproducing an individual and deficit-oriented model of diversity – might constitute a fundamental step in the process of identification and removal of the barriers to an effective inclusion of *all*. Identifying the differences considered as relevant according to students' experiences and perspectives (as allowed by the initial open vignette of the AATOS) might be indeed interpreted as the starting point for actions and interventions aimed at targeting existing discrimination and thus favouring inclusive processes.

8   Conclusion

The instrument proposed in this chapter sought a paradigm shift in research on peer attitudes and exclusion, moving the focus from specific categories of 'different' students (such as students with disabilities, students with different cultural backgrounds, etc.) to 'otherness' itself – understood as the product of a social (collective) process of construction. The AATOS was therefore designed so as to include all the characteristics that, in a given context, may lead individuals to be recognised and labelled as Other. At the same time, given the willingness to not give place to othering processes, it was developed avoiding the use and the (re)production of any predefined and fixed category of difference. This led to the creation of the open vignette for the definition of the target which, ultimately, can be considered the most innovative part of the instrument.

Nevertheless, at least two limitations linked with the initial vignette should be mentioned at this point. Firstly, in some responses it was difficult to distinguish between more general/contextual characteristics (i.e., provided for purely descriptive purpose – like, for example, Alex' age, hair/eye color, etc.) and attributes that were instead directly linked with the target's diversity (in participants' perspective). Therefore, it is possible that also non-(or not so)-relevant characteristics were coded during the content analysis of the vignette answers and are thus represented in the study results. This, together with the fact that the sample of the current study was not a representative one, requires certain caution when interpreting and generalising the study outcomes. Secondly, from a wider perspective, the qualitative component of the AATOS (vignette and open-ended questions) demands more time for data analysis compared to "common" attitude instruments. Even though the *Guide for the qualitative analysis of the AATOS* was thought to make the analysis process easier for researchers who may want to use the AATOS in the future, employing it to carry out surveys with large samples might be challenging due to research time and resource constraints.

Despite these shortcomings, it can be concluded that the open vignette constitutes the key element for implementing the paradigm shift mentioned above. Through it, it was indeed possible to avoid not only deterministic and simplistic categories but also too generic terms (such as 'others', 'different peers/students', etc.) to describe the target, allowing instead participants' representations of otherness to emerge. This is crucial to understand the potential of the AATOS which, on the one hand, consists in an extremely broad and open tool (therefore applicable to a variety of contexts) and, on the other hand, is precise with respect to the representation of its target (as described in the words of research participants themselves). As such, the instrument proposed here may constitute an important asset both for researchers and school practitioners who are interested in the relation between otherness and exclusionary patterns among peers in schools.

References

Abrams, Dominic/Hogg, Michael A. (2010): Social Identity and Self-Categorization. In: Dovidio, John F./Hewstone, Miles/Glick, Peter/Esses, Victoria M. (eds.): The SAGE Handbook of Prejudice, Stereotyping and Discrimination. London: Sage Publications, pp. 179-193.

Ainscow, Mel (2020): Promoting Inclusion and Equity in Education: Lessons from International Experiences. In: Nordic Journal of Studies in Educational Policy 6, 1, pp. 7-16.

Ajzen, Icek (1991): The Theory of Planned Behavior. In: Organizational Behavior and Human Decision Processes 50, pp. 179-211.

Baez, Benjamin (2004): The Study of Diversity: The "Knowledge of Difference" and the Limits of Science. In: The Journal of Higher Education 75, 3, pp. 285-306.

Bennett, Mark/Sani, Fabio (2004): Introduction: Children and Social Identity. In: Bennett, Mark/Sani, Fabio (eds.): The Development of the Social Self. New York: Psychology Press, pp. 1-26.

Bossaert, Goele/Colpin, Hilde/Pijl, Sip J./Petry, Katja (2011): The Attitudes of Belgian Adolescents towards Peers with Disabilities. In: Research in Developmental disabilities 32, 2, pp. 504-509.

Brons, Lajos (2015): Othering, an Analysis. In: Transcience: A Journal of Global Studies 6, pp. 69-90.

Burbules, Nicholas C. (1996): Deconstructing 'Difference' and the Difference this Makes to Education. Retrieved from https://lchcautobio.ucsd.edu/wp-content/uploads/2015/08/Burbules-1996-Deconstructing-%e2%80%9cDifference%e2%80%9d.pdf (accessed February 17, 2020).

de Boer, Anke A./Pijl, Sip J. (2016): The Acceptance and Rejection of Peers with ADHD and ASD in General Secondary Education. In: The Journal of Educational Research 109, 3, pp. 325–332.

de Boer, Anke A./Pijl, Sip J./Minnaert, Alexander (2012): Students' Attitudes towards Peers with Disabilities: A Review of the Literature. In: International Journal of Disability, Development and Education 59, 4, pp. 379-392.

Canales, Mary K. (2000). Othering: Toward an Understanding of Difference. In: Advances in Nursing Science 22, 4, pp. 16-31.

DeVellis, Robert F. (2017): Scale Development: Theory and Applications (4th ed.). Thousand Oaks, CA: Sage.

Dovidio, John F./Hewstone, Miles/Glick, Peter/Esses, Victoria M. (2010): The SAGE Handbook of Prejudice, Stereotyping and Discrimination. London: Sage Publications.

Doyle, Anna B./Aboud, Frances E. (1995): A Longitudinal Study of White Children's Racial Prejudice as a Social Cognitive Development. In: Merrill-Palmer Quarterly 41, pp. 210-229.

Eagly, Alice H./Chaiken, Shelly (1993): The Nature of Attitudes. In: Eagle, Alice H., and Chaiken, Shelly (eds.): The Psychology of Attitudes. Fort Worth: Hartcourt Brace College Publishers, pp. 1-21.

Findler, Liora/Vilchinsky, Noa/Werner, Shirli (2007): The Multidimensional Attitudes Scale toward Persons with Disabilities (MAS): Construction and Validation. In: Rehabilitation Counseling Bulletin 50, 3, pp. 166-176.

Francis, Leslie J./Croft, Jennifer S./Pyke, Alice/Robbins, Mandy (2012): Young People's Attitudes to Religious Diversity: Quantitative Approaches from Social Psychology and Empirical Theology. In: Journal of Beliefs and Values 33, 3, pp. 279-292.

Frizzarin, Anna/Demo, Heidrun/de Boer, Anke A. (2022): Adolescents' Attitudes towards Otherness: The Development of an Assessment Instrument. In: European Journal of Special Needs Education. DOI: 10.1080/08856257.2022.2037822.

Gillespie, Alex/Howarth, Caroline S./Cornish, Flora. (2012): Four Problems for Researchers Using Social Categories. In: Culture & Psychology 18, pp. 391-402. DOI: 10.1177/1354067X12446236.

Godeau, Emmanuelle/Vignes, Céline/Sentenac, Mariane/Ehlinger, Virginie/Navarro, Félix/Grandjean, Hèlén/Arnaud, Catherine (2010): Improving Attitudes towards Children with Disabilities in a School Context: A Cluster Randomized Intervention Study. In: Developmental Medicine & Child Neurology 52, 10, pp. 236-242.

Harma, Kahina/Gombert, Anne/Roussey, Jean-Yves (2013): Impact of Mainstreaming and Disability Vsibility on Social Representations of Disability and Otherness Held by Junior High School Pupils. In: International Journal of Disability, Development and Education 60, 4, pp. 312-331.

Henríquez, Susan V./Moltó, Cristina C./Carrillo, Miguel C. (2015): Understanding Elementary and Secondary Students' Representation of Cultural Differences as Reflected in the Process of Intercultural Communication in School Contexts. In: Nordic Psychology 67, 1, pp. 65-86.

Hill, Malcolm (1997): Research Review: Participatory Research with Children. In: Child and Family Social Work 2, pp. 171-183.

Hornsey, Matthew J. (2008): Social Identity Theory and Self-Categorization Theory: A Historical Review. In: Social and Personality Psychology Compass 2, 1, pp. 204-222.

Kuckartz, Udo (2014): Qualitative Text Analysis: A Guide to Methods, Practice & Using Software. London: Sage Publications.

Kuckartz, Udo/Rädiker, Stefan (2019). Analyzing Intercoder Agreement. In: Kuckartz, Udo and Rädiker, Stefan (eds.): Analyzing Qualitative Data with MAXQDA: Text, Audio, and Video. Springer International Publishing, pp. 267-282.

McDougall, Janette/DeWit, David J./King, Gillian/Miller, Linda T./Killip, Steve (2004): High School-Aged Youths' Attitudes Toward their Peers with Disabilities: The Role of School and Student Interpersonal Factors. In: International Journal of Disability, Development and Education 51, 3, pp. 287-313.

Messiou, Kyriaki (2012): Confronting Marginalisation in Education: A Framework for Promoting Inclusion. London: Routledge.

Messiou, Kyriaki (2017): Research in the Field of Inclusive Education: Time for a Rethink? In: International Journal of Inclusive Education 21, 2, pp. 146-159.

Moscovici, Serge (1984): The Phenomenon of Social Representations. In: Farr, Robert and Moscovici, Serge (eds.): Social Representations. Cambridge: Cambridge University, pp. 289-309.

Norwich, Brahm (2013): Addressing Tensions and Dilemmas in Inclusive Education: Living with Uncertainty. London: Routledge.

Oakes, Penelope J./Haslam, Alexander S./Turner, John C. (1994): Stereotyping and Social Reality. Oxford: Blackwell.

Petry, Katja (2018): The Relationship between Class Attitudes towards Peers with a Disability and Peer Acceptance, Friendships and Peer Interactions of Students with a Disability in Regular Secondary Schools. In: European Journal of Special Needs Education 33, 2, pp. 254-268.

Priest, Naomi/Perry, Ryan/Ferdinand, Angeline/Paradies, Yin/Kelaher, Margaret (2014): Experiences of Racism, Racial/Ethnic Attitudes, Motivated Fairness and Mental Health Outcomes Among Primary and Secondary School Students. In: Journal of Youth and Adolescence 43, 10, pp. 1672-1687.

Rosenbaum, Peter/Armstrong, Robert/King, Susanne (1986): Children's Attitudes toward Disabled Peers: A Self-Report Measure. In: Journal of Pediatric Psychology 11, pp. 517–530.

Santos, Hugo/da Silva, Sofia M./Menezes, Isabel (2018): From Liberal Acceptance to Intolerance: Discourses on Sexual Diversity in Schools by Portuguese Young People. In: Journal of Social Science Education 17, 1, pp. 55-65.

Sapon-Shevin, Mara (2014): How we Respond to Differences – And the Difference it Makes. In: Lawrence-Brown, Diana and Sapon-Shevin, Mara (eds.): Condition Critical: Key Principles for Equitable and Inclusive Education. New York: Teachers College Press, pp. 86-101.

Schreier, Margrit (2012): Qualitative Content Analysis in Practice. Thousand Oaks: Sage Publications.

Slee, Roger (2018): Defining the Scope of Inclusive Education. Think Piece Prepared for the 2020 Global Education Monitoring Report Inclusion and Education. Retrieved from: http://disde.minedu.gob.pe/handle/MINEDU/5977

Tajfel, Henri (1972): Social Categorization. In: Moscovici, Serge (ed.): Introduction a la psychologie sociale, Vol. 1. Paris: Larouse.

Terzi, Lorella (2005). Beyond the Dilemma of Difference: The Capability Approach to Disability and Special Educational Needs. In: Journal of Philosophy of Education 39, 3, pp. 443-459.

Thomas-Olalde, Oscar/Velho, Astrid (2011): Othering and Its Effects – Exploring the Concept. In: Ydesen, Christian and Niedrig, Heike (eds.): Writing Postcolonial Histories of Intercultural Education. Frankfurt am Main: Peter Lang, pp. 27-51.

Triandis, Harry C. (1971): Attitudes and Attitude Change. New York: Wiley.

Turner, John C./Hogg, Michael A./Oakes, Penelope J./Reicher, Stephen D./Wetherell, Margaret S. (1987): Rediscovering the Social Group: A Self-categorization Theory. Oxford: Blackwell.

Udah, Hyacinth (2019): Searching for a Place to Belong in a Time of Othering. In: Social Sciences, 8,11, pp. 297-313.

UNESCO (2015): Transforming Our World: The 2030 Agenda for Sustainable Development.

Van Mieghem, Aster/Verschueren, Karine/Petry, Katja/Struyf, Elke (2020): An Analysis of Research on Inclusive Education: A Systematic Search and Meta Review. In: International Journal of Inclusive Education 24, 6, pp. 675-689.

Individual Education Plans as Instruments and Practices for Inclusion: Problems and Dilemmas

Petra Auer, Rosa Bellacicco, Dario Ianes[1]

1 Introduction

The Individual Education Plan (IEP), and with it the nowadays internationally widespread phenomenon of individual planning (Alves 2014, 2018), took its origins within the *Education for All Handicapped Children Act* (Public Law 94–142, 1975; cfr. Shaddock 2002), which was prompted by the U.S. civil rights and enacted to recognise the democratic rights of all individuals to a free and appropriate education (Goodman/Bond 1993). Starting from then, the elaboration of an IEP in many nations had the purpose to ensure meeting the individual educational needs of students with disabilities (or other difficulties and disadvantages in learning). Therefore, the IEP is discussed to be one of the key tools educational settings have to be able to provide the necessary support for students with Special Educational Needs (SEN; Blackwell/Rossetti 2014). Since this beginning almost 5 decades ago, IEPs became "ubiquitous" because, even though under various names, they can be found in most countries around the globe (Mitchell/Morton/Hornby 2010). Even though these documents and the related practices do not share the exact same use and status in each national context, what they have in common is that they are the key element of special education provisions as a measure for children with SEN. Moreover, most national legislations foresee that the document is elaborated and designed in a multi-professional team, uniting representatives of different institutions such as school, health services, and the family, making the IEP an interinstitutional document (Blackwell/ Rossetti 2014; Müller/Venetz/Keiser 2017). Over the course of time and with more recent and international policies and movements (e.g., Salamanca Statement UNESCO 1994; UN Convention on Rights of Persons with Disabilities [UN CRPD] 2006; Agenda 2030 and Sustainable Development

---

1 The design of the text is equally attributable to all three authors. As far as the drafting is concerned, Petra Auer is responsible for the paragraphs 1, 2, 3, 3.1.1, 3.1.3, 3.1.4, 3.1.5 and 5, Rosa Bellacicco for the paragraphs 3.1.2, 3.2 and 3.3, whereas Dario Ianes bears responsibility for paragraph 4.

Goals as laid down by UN 2015), the development went into a direction where inclusive and quality education in schools *for all pupils* have been the objective (Alves 2018). This implied that schools around the globe have been confronted with the task of developing inclusive cultures, policies, structures, and practices (Ainscow/Booth/Dyson 2006; Powell et al. 2019). Behind this laid above all a change in the mindset that can be clearly interpreted as a transformation in the notion of education for children and students with disabilities into the direction of a social justice model (Hernández-Torrano/ Somerton/Helmer 2020). Within such a shift of the state of mind, the IEP, on the one hand, undoubtably can be understood as an instrument aimed at attaining the goal of inclusive education, guaranteeing the fundamental human right of access to education for everyone (Article 26, Universal Declaration of Human Rights [UDHR]; UN 1948), and trying to realize equitable educational institutions. On the other hand, seen from exactly the same perspectives of inclusion and educational justice, individual planning can also be seen from a critical perspective as running counter some of the key aspects of these principles. By elaborating some of the prevailing challenges and critical aspects surrounding the IEP as found in the scientific literature, as both a document and an instrument, the present contribution tries to discuss how these challenges hinder the IEP being an inclusive instrument and, on the other hand, how they could instead be turned into potentials making the IEP an instrument and practice for inclusion.

2   Procedure

A non-systematic international literature review constitutes the groundwork of the present contribution. In line with the overarching aim underlying the major investigation of bringing together different national perspectives, literature in English, German, and Italian language was considered. In a first step we searched different databases (ERIC, Google Scholar, *FIS-Bildung*) as well as the university library catalogue for English literature. We used the following combinations of search terms using boolean operators (i.e., AND, OR): *Individual education plan, Individual education program, IEP, Individual planning, Personalized Learning Plan* (1) on their own and combined with (2) *inclusion, inclusive* or (3) *tensions, contradiction, dissonance, paradox, ambiguities, dilemma of difference, trilemma of inclusion*. Besides limiting the results for the respective language, we did so for the date range from 2010 to 2021 since conventionally, a decade is the timeframe needed to observe certain consistent trends. Additionally, we also adopted the snow-balling approach, that is, we checked the bibliography of the publications which were very close to our work and took note of recurring citations to find further relevant works. For this second search approach, we extended the date range by setting January 2000 as the start date for the case the publication seemed to be highly related to the topic. We included journal articles, book chapters, monographs, and reports and considered both theoretical and empirical works. The contributions can be assigned to a broad range of national perspectives (i.e., Portugal, Italy, Switzerland, Germany, UK, Sweden, Norway, Ireland, Canada, U.S., New Zealand, Australia), while some also take an international viewpoint. What followed was an in-depth reading to elaborate possible problems and/or dilemmas, which then were summarised into thematic categories by two researchers. The results of the literature review and the identified categories were then presented and discussed in the larger research group and succeeded by a follow-up literature review aimed at clarifying open questions as well as extending to Italian and German publications. For this purpose, corresponding search terms and databases in the respective language were used and the results were then incorporated. Overall, after screening the abstracts of more than 1,500 hits and the results from the snowball-approach, 73 documents built the groundwork of the non-systematic literature review and the results presented in this contribution.

3   Problems and dilemmas found in the literature review

Overall, the literature review revealed two broad categories of challenges: IEP-related *problems* and *dilemmas*. We speak of a problem when there can be one or even several different and combinable solutions to the challenge. Problems are situated on an applicative level. A dilemma, instead, is a situation in which there are two or more solutions, but each choice excludes the other solution, leading to the fact the situation can never be completely resolved (Boger 2017; Norwich 2008; VandenBos 2015). In contrast to the problems, dilemmas are located on a structural level. After combining equivalent categories, five categories of problems (i.e., *accessibility, gender differences, collaboration in the multi-professional team, students' and parents' participation, IEP as an administrative tool*) and three categories of dilemmas (i.e., *recognition of difference through identification, recognition of difference through curriculum goals, role of specialised professionals assigned on the basis of a diagnosis*) emerged, which are illustrated hereafter. For the sake of a better understanding, it should be pointed out that all the categories are intertwined, which inevitably leads to an overlapping. Accordingly, the categories cannot always be clearly distinguished from each other, but rather the transitions from one category to another tend to be blurred.

3.1　Problems

3.1.1　Problems of accessibility of IEP

Within a first category of problems, we summarised all those which were related to aspects of access of the IEP. Several publications addressed the low accessibility from the student's and/or parents' side as owed to the language and style used in the document and the processes around it (e.g., Mitchell/ Morton/Hornby 2010; Royer 2016). Müller, Venetz and Keiser (2017), for instance, in their overview of research literature on the usefulness of IEPs, report that in a fair amount of the cases students and parents do not comprehend it. Similarly, Royer (2016), points to the fact that students do not understand the language used in their IEP meeting or even feel intimidated by the professional jargon used by the other members. Some authors (e.g., Shaddock 2002; Royer 2017) provide possible solutions to counteract such a problem, arguing that the accessibility of an IEP can be promoted through personalisation of the document itself as well as through an age-appropriate language and style. In this line, Elder, Rood and Damiani (2018) advocate for the use of a strength-based writing style since in the end the language used in the IEP frames the teachers' thinking and expectations about the students and, or consequently, translates to the didactic offers and provided educational opportunities. But it is not only students and parents who might encounter problems regarding the accessibility of this interinstitutional document. The diagnostical part of the IEP can be challenging for teachers to fully understand it and therefore the medical language can create a barrier. Müller, Venetz and Keiser (2017) also address it as a "scientific-systematic overload" referring to the fact that IEPs often are based upon scientific category systems, which could lead to a sense of incompetence among teachers.

3.1.2　Problems arising from gender differences

Some researchers have drawn attention to the gendered aspects in IEPs. While the fact that more boys than girls receive special support in schools seems to be a pattern existing in most Western countries, on the basis of our review only two pieces of research approached "overwhelmingly" the issue of gender bias among the pupils receiving IEPs. Hirsh (2012), for example, explored 379 IEPs from grades three (9-year-olds), five (11-year-olds) and eight (14-year-olds) of Swedish compulsory school. The author noted that IEPs seemed primarily a document shaping pupils' personalities at the expense of learning targets. Moreover, whilst the distribution of *learning targets* was similar for boys and girls, boys received more *being targets* related to personality and, in particular, associated to disturbance, inefficiency and carelessness/disorderliness than girls. The authors suggest that this poses a serious equity problem as it contributes to reproduce and reinforce dichotomous categories in which boys appear to have negative behaviour and attitudes, which are forbidden by prevailing norms (as deviating from the image of the ideal pupil), while girls appear less vulnerable in those fields and, even if lacking in other features (e.g., self-confidence and verbal expressiveness), they do not receive IEP *being targets*. The second study by Andreasson and Wolff (2015) – carried out again in Swedish schools – analysed the quality of IEPs in terms of designed investigations or interventions. They found that while there was higher frequency of boys than girls (68% versus 32%) who had IEPs, there were no substantial differences in the quality of IEPs between girls and boys. However, a key difference was that boys' IEPs comprised more negative statements about their personal characteristics, with no link to their difficulties. The authors discuss that this skewed gender distribution can imply an impact on boys' future learning, self-confidence, and motivation.

3.1.3 Problems related to the collaboration in the multi-professional team

Even though most jurisdictions worldwide contain the standard that the development of an IEP needs to be considered as a process of collaboration between the different professionals and other figures involved to ensure addressing the students' needs (Mitchell/Morton/Hornby 2010), it was found that different aspects related to the IEP-team collaboration seem to be problematic. In detail, the literature review revealed several studies addressing the different professionals' lack of or low participation in the IEP meetings and the elaboration of the IEP (Blackwell/Rossetti 2014; Cioè-Peña 2020; Chiappetta Cajola 2007; Mitchell/Morton/Hornby 2010; Shaddock et al. 2009) as well as in its implementation in everyday practice (Ní Bhroin/King 2020; Rose et al. 2012). First, IEP meetings seem to be realised more as a production of the document rather than a real collaborative act. For instance, Cioè-Peña (2020), through an ethnographic study on the perceptions and beliefs regarding disability, bilingualism, and motherhood of Latinx mothers of Emergent Bilinguals Labelled as Disabled (EBLADs), found that in moments where all members of the multi-professional team are present the encounter turns into a check-off of administrative points. Each member working individually on the IEP, according to the author, implies the risk that the subjective perspective of each member prevails, and consequently the student is not addressed in a wholistic manner, which would necessitate the mutual consideration of all team members' perspectives. In the case schools mainly pursue the elaboration of an IEP rather than interprofessional collaboration, the document turns into multiple fragmentary processes (Cioè-Peña 2020). Also, Blackwell and Rossetti (2014) in their literature review on the IEP development found that one critical aspect of IEP meetings consists in certain team members not expressing their opinion and, based on their role, contributing only to a limited extent. In contrast, Lee-Tarver (2006), through a survey among 123 curricular teachers, came to the result that the majority of them considered the elaboration of the IEP as a process of the whole team wherein key information resulted from collaboration. Such a result is supported by the findings reported by Ní Bhroin and King (2020), who in a mixed methods design study found that curricular and special teachers report collaboration taking place in the elaboration of the IEP. However, the findings also clearly reveal that when it comes to the implementation of the document in the everyday school practice, the weight mainly lies on the shoulders of one professional – the special teacher – and takes place in push- and pull-out situations.

3.1.4   Problems related to students' and parents' participation

Closely connected to and intertwined with the category outlined above, we found several problems addressed in the literature which can be summarised in the category related to the participation of students and parents. Overall, many of the authors (Albers 2012; Andreasson/Asp-Onsjö/Isaksson 2013; Blackwell/Rossetti 2014; Goepel 2009; King/Ní Bhroin/Prunty 2017; Kurth et al. 2019; Mitchell/Morton/Hornby 2010; Singh/Keese 2020; Weishaar 2010; Williams-Diehm et al. 2014) discuss or report missing or low participation of students and/or their parents in the elaboration of the IEP. Different contributions point to the passive role that students and parents generally assume in the IEP meetings and the elaboration of the document, which some also address to as *symbolic participation* with reference to Skrtic (2005; e.g., Andreasson/Asp-Onsjö/Isaksson 2013; King/Ní Bhroin/Prunty 2017). In their literature review, Blackwell and Rossetti (2014) summarise that parents cannot be considered as equal partners in the development of the IEP as intended by the legislation, but that (special) teachers are those who control the IEP meeting and with that also the elaboration of the IEP. Further, family characteristics such as income or ethnic background seem to influence the grade of participation. Such a result is sustained by the already above cited empirical work of Cioè-Peña (2020), which was able to identify some possible problems related to parents' participation in the field of inter-sectionality (i.e., disability and ethnic minority). According to her findings, meetings were realised in a way hindering mothers' agency, the participating mothers were treated as listeners instead of active contributors and in part were unaware of the power of their role in an IEP meeting. Instead, Goepel's (2009) qualitative study can be considered as taking a further step, since it not only revealed missing participation of the parents and students but was also able to show some possible consequences of it. She found that IEP targets were decided overall by the adults and that in the case the child did not identify with them, a disengagement from learning and missing willingness to comply with them could be observed. On the contrary, when children valued the targets and consequently their IEP, they approached learning positively. Similarly, Blackwell and Rossetti (2014) cite some studies reporting positive effects of student-led IEP meetings and showed a positive relationship between student participation and academic outcomes.

3.1.5   Problems related to IEP as an administrative rather than pedagogical tool

The last category of problems identified within the present literature review relates to the predominant use of the IEP as an administrative document instead of exploiting its pedagogical potential. Such problems in part stem from the fact that, in daily practice, the IEP embodies many different and sometimes even contradictory roles (e.g., educational, legal, resource allocation etc.; Müller/Venetz/Keiser 2017), which in turn are a result of its intersectional nature. That is, the IEP is conceptualised as an interinstitutional document located in the intersections of school, family, policy (Blackwell/ Rossetti 2014), and in many countries also the health services (e.g., Ianes/ Demo/Dell'Anna 2020). On the one side, we found critical reflections on the IEP as an instrument lacking a proper translation from policy into practice (e.g., Andreasson/Asp-Onsjö/Isaksson 2013), which leads to the fact that compliance often becomes the first goal practitioners fulfil (Cioè-Peña 2020). That is, the instrument, due to different reasons such as lack of time, resources, or clear guidelines, is not used as intended and laid down by international and national legislations. Instead, the production of the IEP as a required document is simply fulfilled. On the other side, some authors argue that the IEP can be seen as a mere bureaucratic response to increasing diversity (e.g., Shaddock 2002; Breitenbach 2019). As argued by Alves (2014, 2018), following such an understanding, IEPs are used to circumvent a reform of the school system. While society changed into the direction of diversification, schools have remained largely static in terms of their organisation over decades and the IEP can therefore be seen as an add-on solution to an "obsolete" system. Overall, such a use of the IEP as an administrative rather than pedagogical and didactical tool is reflected critically within the scientific literature (e.g., Andreasson/Asp-Onsjö/Isaksson 2013; Ní Bhroin/ King 2020), with some authors arguing that by doing so a crucial opportunity for the development and implementation of meaningful educational experiences for students will be missed (Blackwell/Rossetti 2014). In other words, as laid down by Pavone (2014), preserving the use of the IEP from bureaucratic and administrative constraints would give it its full educational value as one of the fundamental guidelines for inclusive design.

3.2   From problems to dilemmas

The fact that the field of inclusive education poses some dilemmas is not a new matter (Croll/Moses 2000; Dyson 2001; Ho 2004; Minow 1990). Before addressing the dilemmas reproduced by the IEPs as identified in the present literature review, there is a need to disclose and examine the assumptions and values embedded in these dilemmas that fundamentally reside in the concept of inclusive education. In fact, while inclusion is a global phenomenon (Hernández-Torrano/Somerton/Helmer 2020), at the same time, it is a concept hard to define and lacking universally agreed interpretation (Artiles et al. 2006; Artiles/Kozleski/Waitoller 2011; Florian 2014; Loreman/Forlin/Sharma 2014; Wolff et al. 2021). The divergent definitions noted in the research literature (e.g., Göransson/Nilholm 2014) "reflecting complementary ideas about inclusion that were developing simultaneously in different parts of the world offer an explanation for why the field is considered a conceptual muddle" (Florian 2014: 293). Notably, the declination of a definition in "special" – the narrowest interpretation – or in "inclusive" education, – the broadest interpretation – often misleadingly used as synonyms, is considered a challenge for practice. In this regard, one of the challenges going beyond the notion of placement and mainstreaming is the pertaining question of who is in the focus, that is, what pupil groups are supposed to be "included" (Magnússon 2019). In the attempt to "decouple" the two concepts (Florian 2019), one can argue that special education concerns students with disabilities or special educational needs and focuses on individual assessment and planning and specialised instruction (Salend 2011). Inclusive education, instead, engages a broader idea of inclusion and is understood as increasing the participation and learning of *all* students. Consequently, fully inclusive education requires a "more systemic approach to changing schools so that they might better educate each and every student" (Ferguson 2008: 110) and encompasses a process of school transformation by restructuring policies, practices, and school cultures to respond to student diversity (Ainscow/Booth/Dyson 2006; Loreman/Deppeler/Harvey 2011; Slee 2011).

Both special and inclusive education concepts have received substantial critiques in the scientific literature. As Kauffman and Hornby (2020) have pointed out, special education emphasises engagement in a programme of instruction that is meaningful and appropriate for students with SEN instead of focusing on being physically present in mainstream classrooms. According to the authors, full inclusion is impossible to achieve in practice since mainstream settings are unable to be flexible enough to grant no limits in the accommodation of students even with severe special educational needs. On the other hand, special education has been criticised for its focus on the perceived deficits of the individuals. By referring to a normal distribution, special education still divides students into the normal and those who fall outside the margins of the bell curve, which leads to proving the latter with specialised support the others do not need (Florian 2019; Richardson/Powell, 2020). Consequently, its practices can result in labelling children with SEN, thereby stigmatising and excluding them (Vislie 2003; Messiou 2017). As long as educational difficulties are viewed as results of individual factors rather than contextual factors, marginalisation of vulnerable pupil groups risks deepening (Ainscow 1998). Therefore, a special or inclusive view implies a diverse conceptualisation of difference: in negative terms in special education as representing lower status, or positively in inclusive education as a celebration of individuality and an ordinary aspect of human development (Kerins 2014). These basic tensions related to how to recognise differences have been referred to as the "dilemma of difference" by Norwich (2008, 2013) since both options have some risks associated with stigma, devaluetion, rejection, or denial of opportunities. In detail, he found that such dilemmas exist in the areas of placement (i.e., to what extent students with SEN learn in mainstream schools/ordinary classes or not), identification (i.e., whether to identify and how or not), curriculum (i.e., how much of a common curriculum was relevant). This dilemmatic perspective, in part, provides the framework for the discussion of findings in this section about IEP use.

3.3   Dilemmas

3.3.1   Dilemmas related to the recognition of difference through identification in the IEP

Although it is clear that the identification of SEN marks pupils out as different from others in some way, also the supporters of inclusive education recognise that there is a dilemma: if children are identified as having SEN, there is a risk of negative labelling and stigma, while if they are not, there is a risk that they will not get the necessary teaching and their special educational needs will not be met (Norwich 2008). These conflicting priorities are played out daily in schools through the IEP and related processes as, for instance, can be seen in the work of Alves (2014, 2018). In 2014, the author presents a comparative study on the use of IEPs in England and Portugal. The results indicate that in both countries, despite the context of the promotion of inclusion for all, the implicit assumption of diversity as a challenge and a problem persists. Despite the use of differentiated instruction or whole class plans targeted at all pupils, questions raised by the dilemma of identification remain evident because only students considered as different, "with pro-blems", or at the "bottom end of the continuum of ability" are regarded as needing an IEP or being entitled to an IEP. This allows the allocation of resources, which, however, involves a limited, pre-existing, repertoire of responses aimed at making "diverse" students the closest possible to the targets expected. A subsequent and more general reflection by the author (2018) reiterates the argument that the IEP mostly is addressed to pupils who do not "fit the norm" and are associated with the provision of something additional or different from what is provided to the rest of the (still relatively homogeneous) pupil population.

These results are generally consistent with an earlier picture by Ianes and Demo (2017) on the IEP in inclusive schools in Italy. On the one hand, the IEP is conceived as the ideal instrument for interweaving the focus on the student population and the focus on the needs and potentials of one single child. It can be the planning instrument through which the class team makes the school and class curriculum accessible and adapted for this child. On the other hand, because it is linked to a diagnosis and extra resources, the authors warn that the IEP identifies the pupil as "special" and "different". Therefore, according to authors' reflection, the IEP may reinforce the focus on this specific child as a special child, and it risks weakening the focus on the aspects that the child has in common with other children. The authors posit also a few possible consequences for children and teachers. For instance, for the latter, it could lead to the idea of teaching in two groups: the majority of relatively homogeneous pupils who "learn without difficulties" and a minority of differentiated special learners. This, in turn, would result in a weak professional orientation to the diversity addressed to the whole class group.

3.3.2   Dilemmas related to the recognition of difference through curriculum goals in the IEP

Norwich (2008) presents the curriculum dilemma as being about the consequences of having, or not having, a common curriculum for all students. If all pupils with SEN are offered the same learning experiences as their peers, there is the possibility that some will be denied the learning experiences that are significant to their needs and potentials. If they are not provided with the same learning experiences, issues relating to equity of provision arise. A certain kind of detrimental implications in trying to ensure students with SEN access to the general education curriculum emerge from the studies by Andreasson and Carlsson (2013) and Andreasson, Asp-Onsjö and Isaksson (2013). In their analysis of IEPs of pupils with SEN in Swedish schools, they discuss students' individual progress or achievement in the documents. They draw attention to the IEPs' underlying discourse, which seems to rely on assumptions of the identity of a "normal child". However, as the children with SEN "defective" in some ways, it emerges that, ultimately, the purposes of IEPs are to reconstruct desired, ideal children. In terms of curriculum, it means to legitimise a certain type of objectives considered necessary and appropriate for developing "good" school pupils and members of society, academically, socially, behaviourally, and physically adjusted (e.g., academically, that is, working towards and reaching the target on time; behaviourally, that is, focused, with the right equipment, on time, in place). The authors conclude that the documents are permeated by a "normalizing" mentality and a hegemonic discourse that constitutes a systematic exercise of power.

In a somewhat different direction, survey data by Ní Bhroin and King (2020) highlight that while students' IEP targets are typically incorporated in special teachers' plans, class teachers' plans do not specifically refer to individualised learning targets. Moreover, while special teachers strategically address individualised learning needs with alternative curricula offered to pupils, the same does not hold for class teachers, despite their awareness of the SEN students' priority learning goals. The authors conclude that extending the IEP targets into class teachers' plans and having a real alignment between IEP targets and curriculum goals may ensure that there is not an overemphasis on the individual and their deficits, thus making IEPs a pedagogical tool across the school. Similarly, Martinez and Porter (2020) observed scarce blending of lesson plans for the whole class with the personalised needs of students as laid down in the IEP or Personal Learning Plan (PLP) in inclusive schools of a province in Canada. They reported that teachers typically design a lesson plan for all students who follow the regular curriculum, while the integration of the variation demanded by SEN students' diverse needs is most often a "peripheral" or "secondary" action (Martinez/ Porter 2020: 1556). Despite the attempts to use differentiation strategies in daily practices, instructional planning for students with IEP often remains based on a separate curriculum and instructional strategies distinct from those for the whole class.

3.3.3 Dilemmas related to the role of specialised professionals assigned on the basis of the diagnosis

Finally, we have identified another type of dilemma, which is closely related to the problems of collaboration between teacher colleagues already described above. The question is whether the fact that additional and specialised personnel resources for inclusive teaching and learning like special teachers, Special Education Needs Coordinator [SENCos], or education assistants are tied to students with a diagnosis and the IEP may emphasise the tensions with class teachers when it comes to a shared responsibility for both the differentiated teaching for students with SEN and the teaching for the overall class.

Mitchell et al. (2010), in their review, noted that SENCos face considerable challenges in coordinating the writing of IEPs. It was also apparent that, primarily in secondary schools, it appeared difficult to establish a rapport with the subject teacher. Concerns have been expressed that many secondary class teachers are likely to not keep in mind the targets set for the pupils with SEN and do not have time to provide the adapted teaching as outlined on their IEPs, undermining the IEP efficacy. A common thread reported in all selected studies is the need that class teachers regularly discuss with SENCos and integrate SEN planning into whole-class planning, allowing SENCos to become their consultants. In the same vein, two studies by King, Ní Bhroin and Prunty (2017) and Ní Bhroin and King (2020) were conducted to explore the impact of professionalisation on teachers' learning related to the IEP process and, particularly, on collaborative practices. The evidence suggests that the development of the collaboration between class and special teachers reflects the interdependence of these two roles. There is also a widespread agreement that the need for their joint involvement is closely correlated to the phase of planning and teaching and the interweaving of individualised targets with the general curriculum. As outlined in the preceding dilemma, data from Ní Bhroin and King (2020) found that this very often is not the case since individualised learning targets could be found only in special teachers' plans who are also the ones who address these targets. The authors suggest that further shared responsibility with class teachers is needed to avoid special teachers working in a vacuum and vice versa. In the same vein, the study by Martinez and Porter (2020) identified a clear differentiation between the role and responsibilities of the teacher and the Educational Assistant (EA) in the classroom. A limited integration of the EA support as part of the classroom team has also been outlined. This is evident, for example, in the missing reference of the work or duties of the EA in lesson plans. The authors recommend the creation of a school culture that provides clarity in professional roles and responsibilities and encourages the EAs to become a support for the professional decision-making of the class teacher through collaborative consultation, as well as coaching, co-teaching, co-planning, and so forth.

4   Discussion

Regarding the Individual Education Plan and its practices, the literature review has highlighted two types of issues that necessarily need to be kept distinguished. The category of problems is often linked to implementation difficulties. Consequently, if these are solved, the practices would become effective, being "good" practices, accurate and in no way distorting or risky. Instead, the category of dilemmas is not solved by merely improving the conditions of implementation of practices but by overcoming some distortive structural conditions, which force tough and ambivalent decisions. The most evident cluster of problems is the one related to participation/collaboration in the development and implementation of the IEP. The parents of pupils with disabilities should be active partners in the definition and management of the

IEP, but this is not always the case. Further, all too often, pupils with disabilities themselves are not involved, leading to the most serious short-coming of the unheard student voice. In Italy, a new model of IEP has been in force on the state level since 2020 (Ianes/Cramerotti/Fogarolo 2020), which, for secondary schools, foresees the active participation of students with disabilities in the design of their IEP. However, our very recent survey (Fogarolo/Cramerotti/Ianes 2022) found that only in 27% of the cases student's voices were consulted. Further, and still related to the same area of problems, the collaboration between teachers and other professionals appears also difficult. Difficulties stem not only from the fact that they belong to different institutions (education and health services) but also from a different language or vocabulary use as well as divergent models of analysis and understanding of the human functioning of students with disabilities. These diverse ideas on the person underlying the definition of an IEP (i.e., pedagogical model, medical model, biopsychosocial model, ICF model) partly also explain the difficulties highlighted in the cluster of accessibility problems, which are not only caused by linguistic aspects. In this field of problematic aspects related to the access of the IEP by the various actors of the inclusive processes, we must also consider increasing complexities caused by the various state legislations protecting the privacy of pupils with disabilities regarding sensitive data (e.g., diagnosis, health conditions, etc.). The category of problems defined as the coexistence of pedagogical and administrative functions might also be approximated to the dilemma situations. It is clear and desirable that the IEP should be a tool for inclusive co-planning between teachers, parents, and professionals. Conversely, the referenced literature shows that its bureaucratic use is inversely proportional to the quantity and quality of the time dedicated to didactic and educational co-planning. In other words, in kindergarten and primary school, where teachers have greater pedagogical competence and more time to plan together, the IEP is less bureaucratic and more like a real working tool. Instead, in the subsequent school levels, where didactic and pedagogical competence is very low and where there is no time for joint planning between teachers, the tendency towards bureaucratisation is much more pronounced. Within this tension between being a pedagogical or bureaucratic tool, we should also bear in mind an element playing a significant distorting role: in the IEP, the necessary hours of additional personnel resources (i.e., special teacher/teacher assistant) are indicated. The indication "obliges" the school to provide that number of hours or type of support: in the case of non-com-pliance, the administrative courts ground their judgement on the IEP document, being the only one with legal value, even superior to any local government budget limit. This clearly shows the instrumental value the IEP has in addition to its pedagogical value, a structural situation that leads many families to have legal disputes with schools.

As regards the dilemmatic situations, well identified by Brahm Norwich in his famous works, within the present literature review, they have been clustered in three areas. In the first area, there is a tension, not only attributable to the IEP but to all the various forms of identification of difficulties. These are, on the one hand, necessary to recognise modes of functioning and rights but, on the other hand, are stigmatising and labelling. In the case of the IEP and the corresponding individualisation practices, the necessity/right of the pupil clashes with the fact that they are the only ones having an IEP. Having an IEP is an unequivocal sign of disability, a definite stigma of negative diversity. This situation is evident in those standard teaching methods where the class group follows a one-size-fits-all approach and only the disabled pupil is provided with individualised teaching, maybe partially or even fully outside the classroom. In this cluster of dilemmas, the distorting structural factor is, in fact, the standard teaching method for all except some: if the teaching method would be open, flexible, personalised, and universal for all (e.g., Open Learning, Universal Design for Learning), the conditions for this type of dilemma would not arise because it would be normal for everyone to have an at least partially individualised learning pathway.

The second dilemmatic area is based on two other problematic questions. First, in the case of more severe disabilities, the development and learning needs force the definition of individual goals, which are very different and distant from those of the classmates. They are necessary but once again run the risk of becoming a stigma and separator. Here the distorting structural factor lies in the idea of human functioning underlying the IEP: an idea consisting only of functions (e.g., cognitive, motorial, communicative, autonomy, etc.) or considering the pupil's social participation in the various dimensions of interaction and relationship with their classmates? The first type of idea is more likely to lead to a separating technical approach, while the second seeks to coordinate objectives linked to functions with those related to participation in activities for the whole class. Instead, a biopsychosocial idea like the ICF could hold both planning orientations together. The second question concerns the "target group": for whom is the IEP made? An inclusive IEP, which succeeds in escaping the second dilemmatic tension, is intended for both the disabled pupil and the whole class to improve its degree of inclusiveness. This occurs when specific didactic strategies enter the joint learning routines of the classroom context and modify its inclusiveness in the sense of "special normality". For instance, through the use of augmentative and alternative communication (AAC), visual aids, visual diaries for the succession of events, social stories, systems of symbolic reinforcement of pro-social behaviour, and so forth for the whole class.

The third dilemmatic area, which is related to specialised professionals (e.g., special teachers) assigned to pupils with disabilities, is particularly emblematic of another distorting structural factor: a special pupil must correspond to a special teacher. This special teacher is generated only by that specific pupil's diagnosis and often has to operate in a special environment (e.g., resource room) with special teaching strategies. The force of this structural culture related to this medical model in education has led – and still leads – to this third type of dilemma: additional human resources that are necessary but at the same time at high risk of creating segregation. Over-coming this third type of dilemma seems to lie within the deconstruction of the "special-pupil-special-teacher-link" through the diffusion of special characteristics necessary for specific learning within the normality of the educational contexts of all. In this way, the latter are enriched with specific competencies – without delegating inclusion only to special teachers, who become enabling professionals – and become responsive to the differences of all pupils.

5   Conclusions

As the discussion of the results of the present literature review made evident, in conclusion it can be said that the IEP by its mere existence, elaboration or implementation as a document or as an instrument can not be seen as a tool or practice making inclusion a reality. On the contrary, it can even become a means of stigmatisation or marginalisation. To be in line with the shift of the state of mind of inclusion from an understanding originating from the concept of disability of individual pupils towards an understanding making education systems responsible to provide education for everybody, thus an understanding in the sense of social justice (Hernández-Torrano/Somerton/Helmer 2020), it seems that the focus needs to be put on the *how*. The way the document is conceptualised within the national legislation, the way the IEP is elaborated and written, the way the IEP-meetings are realised, the way students and teachers are involved, the way the document is implemented into practice, the way lessons are planned by its use on an everyday basis, the way the instrument is seen and used by practitioners in the field … All these *hows* in the end will make the difference and have the potential to turn the IEP into an instrument and practice for inclusion.

References

Albers, Timm (2012): Individuelle Entwicklungspläne (IEP) in inklusiven Settings. Internationale Befunde zur Partizipation von Kind und Familie im Prozess der schulischen Förderplanung. In: Vierteljahresschrift für Heilpädagogik und ihre Nachbargebiete 82, 3, pp. 202–212.

Ainscow, Mel (1998): Would it work in theory? Arguments for practitioner research and theorising in the special needs field. In: Clark, Cathrine/Dyson, Alan/Millward, Alan (eds.): Theorising Special Education. London: Routledge, pp. 7–20.

Ainscow, Mel/Booth, Tony/Dyson, Alan (2006): Improving schools, developing inclusion. London: Routledge.

Alves, Ines F. (2014): Responding to diversity, constructing difference. A comparative case-study of individual planning in schools in England and Portugal. Diss. Manchester: The University of Manchester.

Alves, Ines F. (2018): The Transnational Phenomenon of Individual Planning in Response to Pupil Diversity: A Paradox in Educational Reform. In: Hultqvist, E. Lindblad, S./Popkewitz, T. (eds.): Critical Analyses of Educational Reforms in an Era of Transnational Governance. Educational Governance Research. Cham: Springer International Publishing, pp. 151–168.

Andreasson, Ingela/Wolff, Ulrika (2015): Assessments and Intervention for Pupils with Reading Difficulties in Sweden. A Text Analysis of Individual Education Plans. In: International Journal of Special Education 30, 1, pp. 15–24.

Andreasson, Ingela/Asp-Onsjö, Lisa/Isaksson, Joakim (2013): Lessons learned from research on individual educational plans in Sweden. Obstacles, opportunities and future challenges. In: European Journal of Special Needs Education 28, 4, pp. 413–426.

Artiles, Alfredo J./Kozleski, Elizabeth B./Dorn, Sherman/Christensen, Carol (2006): Learning in Inclusive Education Research. Remediating Theory and Methods with a Transformative Agenda. In: Review of Research in Education 30, pp. 65–108.

Artiles, Alfredo J./Kozleski, Elizabeth B./Waitoller, Federico R. (2011): Inclusive Education. Examining Equity on Five Continents. Cambridge: Harvard Education Press.

Blackwell, William H./Rossetti, Zachary S. (2014): The Development of Individualized Education Programs. In: SAGE Open 4, 2, 215824401453041.

Boger, Mai-Anh (2017): Theorien der Inklusion – eine Übersicht. In: Zeitschrift für Inklusion, 1. https://www.inklusion-online.net/index.php/inklusion-online/article/view/413.

Breitenbach, Erwin (2019): Diagnostik: Eine Einführung. Wiesbaden: Springer.

Chiappetta Cajola, Lucia (2007): L'impiego funzionale degli strumenti di integrazione scolastica. Diagnosi funzionale, Profilo dinamico funzionale e Piano educativo individualizzato In: Canevaro, Andrea (ed.): L'Integrazione scolastica degli alunni con disabilità. Trent'anni di inclusione nella scuola italiana Trento: Erickson, pp. 221-247.

Cioè-Peña, María (2020): Planning Inclusion. The Need to Formalize Parental Participation in Individual Education Plans (and Meetings). In: The Educational Forum
84, 4, pp. 377–390.

Croll, Paul/Moses, Diana. (2000): Ideologies and utopias. Education professionals'
views on inclusion. In: European Journal of Special Educational Needs 15, 01,
pp. 1-12.

Dyson, Alan (2001): Special needs in the twenty-first century: Where we've been
where we're going. In: British Journal of Special Education 28, 1, pp. 24-29.

Elder, Brent C./Rood, Carrie E./Damiani, Michelle L. (2018): Writing strength-based
IEPs for students with disabilities in inclusive classrooms. In: International Journal of Whole Schooling 14, 1, 116–155.

Ferguson, Dianne L. (2008): International trends in inclusive education. The conti-
nuing challenge to teach one and everyone. In: European Journal of Special
Needs Education 23, 2, pp. 109–20.

Florian, Lani (2014): What counts as evidence of inclusive education? European
Journal of Special Needs Education 29, 3, pp. 286-294.

Florian, Lani (2019): On the necessary co-existence of special and inclusive education. In: International Journal of Inclusive Education 23, 7-8, pp. 691-704.

Fogarolo, Flavio/Cramerotti, Sofia/Ianes, Dario (Eds.) (2022): Questionario sul GLO.
Report e analisi dei dati quantitativi. Trento: Erickson.

Goepel, Janet (2009): Constructing the Individual Education Plan: confusion or
collaboration? In: Support for Learning 24, 3, pp. 126–132.

Goodman, Joan F./Bond, Lori (1993): The individualized education program. A retro-
spective critique. In: The Journal of Special Education 26, 4, pp. 408–422.

Göransson, Kerstin/Nilholm, Claes (2014): Conceptual diversities and empirical
shortcomings. A critical analysis of research on inclusive education. In: European
Journal of Special Needs Education 29, 3, pp. 265-280.

Hernández-Torrano, Daniel/Somerton, Michelle/Helmer, Janet (2020): Mapping
research on inclusive education since Salamanca Statement. A bibliometric
review of the literature over 25 years. In: International Journal of Inclusive
Education. https://doi.org/10.1080/13603116.2020.1747555

Hirsh, Åsa (2012): The individual education plan: a gendered assessment practice? In:
Assessment in Education: Principles, Policy & Practice 19, 4, pp. 469–485.

Ho, Anita (2004): To be labelled or not to be labelled, that is the question. In: British
Journal of Learning Disabilities 3, 1, pp. 86-92.

Ianes, Dario/Cramerotti, Sofia/Fogarolo, Flavio (2020): Il nuovo PEI in prospettiva
bio-psico-sociale ed ecologica. I modelli e le Linee guida del Decreto inter-
ministeriale n. 182 29/12/2020 commentati e arricchiti di strumenti ed esempi.
Trento: Erickson.

Ianes, Dario/Demo, Heidrun (2017): Il Piano Educativo Individualizzato. Luci e
ombre di quarant'anni di storia di uno strumento fondamentale dell'Integrazione
Scolastica in Italia. In: L'integrazione scolastica e sociale 16, 4, pp. 415-426.

Ianes, Dario/Demo, Heidrun/Dell'Anna, Silvia (2020): Inclusive education in Italy. Historical steps, positive developments, and challenges. In: Prospects 49, pp. 249–263.

Kauffman, James M./Hornby, Gary (2020): Inclusive vision versus special education reality. In: Education Sciences 10, 9, 258.

Kerins, Pauline (2014): Dilemmas of difference and educational provision for pupils with mild general learning disabilities in the Republic of Ireland. In: European Journal of Special Needs Education 29, 1, pp. 47-58.

King, Fiona/Ní Bhroin, Orla/Prunty, Anita (2018): Professional learning and the individual education plan process. Implications for teacher educators. In: Professional Development in Education 44, 5, pp. 607–621.

Kurth, Jennifer A./McQueston, Jessica A./Ruppar, Andrea L./Toews, Samantha Gross/Johnston, Russell/McCabe, Katie M. (2019): A Description of Parent Input in IEP Development Through Analysis IEP Documents. In: Intellectual and Developmental Disabilities 57, 6, pp. 485–498.

Lee-Tarver, Aleada (2006): Are Individualized Education Plans a Good Thing? A Survey of Teachers' Perceptions of the Utility of IEPs in Regular Education Settings. In: Journal of Instructional Psychology 33, 4, 263-273.

Loreman, Tim/Deppeler, Joanne/Harvey, David (2011): Inclusive Education. Supporting diversity in the classroom (2nd ed.). Crows Nest: Allen & Unwin.

Loreman, Tim/Forlin, Chris/Sharma, Umesh (2014): Measuring indicators of inclusive education. A systematic review of the literature. In: Forlin, Chris/Loreman, Tim (ed.): Measuring Inclusive Education (Volume 3), pp. 165–187.

Magnússon, Gunnlaugur (2019): An amalgam of ideals: Images of inclusion in the Salamanca Statement. In: International Journal of Inclusive Education 23, 7-8, pp. 677-690.

Messiou, Kyriaki (2017): Research in the field of inclusive education. Time for a rethink? In: International Journal of Inclusive Education 21, 2, pp. 146-159.

Minow, Martha (1990): Making all the difference. Inclusion, exclusion and American law. Ithaca: Cornell University Press.

Mitchell, David/Morton, Missy/Hornby, Gary (2010): Review of the literature on individual education plans. New Zealand Ministry of Education.

Müller, Xenia/Venetz, Martin/Keiser, Christian (2017): Nutzen von individuellen Förderplänen: Theoretischer Fachdiskurs und Wahrnehmung von Fachpersonen in der Schule. In: Vierteljahresschrift für Heilpädagogik und ihre Nachbargebiete 86, 2, pp. 116–126.

Ní Bhroin, Órla N./King, Fiona (2020): Teacher education for inclusive education. A framework for developing collaboration for the inclusion of students with support plans. In: European Journal of Teacher Education 43, 1, pp. 38–63.

Norwich, Brahm (2008): Dilemmas of difference, inclusion and disability. International perspectives on placement. In: European Journal of Special Needs Education 23, 4, pp. 287–304.

Pavone, Marisa (2014): L'inclusione educative. Indicazioni pedagogiche per la disabilità. Milan: Mondadori Education.

Powell, Justin J. W./Merz-Atalik, Kerstin/Ališauskienė, Stefanija/Brendel, Michelle/ Echeita, Gerardo/GuÐjónsdóttir, Hafdís et al. (2019): Teaching Diverse Learners in Europe. Inspiring Practices and Lessons Learned from Germany, Iceland, Lithuania, Luxembourg, Spain and Sweden. In: Schuelka, Matthew/ Johnstone, Christopher/Thomas, Gary/Artiles, Alfredo J. (eds.): The Sage Handbook of Inclusion and Diversity in Education. London: SAGE, pp. 321–337.

Richardson, John G./Powell, Justin J. W. (2020): Comparing special education. Origins to contemporary paradoxes. Stanford: Stanford University Press.

Rose, Richard/Shevlin, Michael/Winter, Eileen/O'Raw, Paul/Zhao, Yu (2012): Individual Education Plans in the Republic of Ireland. An emerging system. In: British Journal of Special Education 39, 3, pp. 110–116.

Royer, David J. (2017): My IEP. A Student-Directed Individualized Education Program Model. In: Exceptionality 25, 4, pp. 235–252.

Salend, Spencer J. (2011): Creating Inclusive Classrooms. Effective and reflective practices (7th ed).. Boston: Pearson.

Shaddock, Anthony. J. (2002): An Unplanned Journey into Individualised Planning. In: International Journal of Disability, Development and Education 49, 2, pp. 191–200.

Shaddock, Anthony/MacDonald, Nancy/Hook, Julie/Giorcelli, Loretta/Arthur-Kelly, Michael (2009): Disability, diversity and tides that lift all boats. Review of special education in the ACT. Chiswick: Service Initiatives.

Singh, Shailen/Keese, Jeffrey (2020): Applying systems-based thinking to build better IEP relationships. A case for relational coordination. In: Support for Learning 35, 3, pp. 359–371.

Skrtic, Thomas M. (2005): A Political Economy of Learning Disabilities. In: Learning Disabilities Quarterly 28, 2, pp. 149–155.

Slee, Roger (2011): The Irregular School. Exclusion, schooling and inclusive education. London: Routledge.

United Nations (UN) (1948): Universal Declaration of Human Rights [UDHR], Article 26. https://www.un.org/sites/un2.un.org/files/udhr.pdf.

United Nations (UN) (2006): Convention on the Rights of Persons With Disabilities. New York: United Nations.

United Nations (UN) (2015): Transforming our world. The 2030 Agenda for Sustainable Development. https://sdgs.un.org/2030agenda.

United Nations Educational, Scientific and Cultural Organization (UNESCO) (1994): The Salamanca statement and framework for action on special needs education. New York, NY: United Nations.

VandenBos, Gary R. (ed.). (2015): APA Dictionary of Psychology. Washington: American Psychological Association.

Vislie, Lise (2003): From integration to inclusion. Focusing global trends and changes in the Western European societies. In: European Journal of Special Needs Education 18, 1, pp. 17–35.

Weishaar, Phillip M. (2010): Twelve Ways to Incorporate Strengths-Based Planning into the IEP Process. In: The Clearing House 83, 6, pp. 207–210.

Williams-Diehm, Kendra L./Brandes, Joyce A./Chesnut, Pik Wah/Haring, Kathryn A. (2014): Student and parent IEP collaboration: A comparison across school settings. In: Rural Special Education Quarterly 33, 1, pp. 3–11.

Wolff, Charlotte E./Huilla, Heidi/Tzaninis, Yannis/Magnúsdóttir, Berglind Rós/Lappalainen, Sirpa/Paulle, Bowen/Seppänen, Piia/Kosunen, Sonja (2021): Inclusive education in the diversifying environments of Finland, Iceland and the Netherlands. A multilingual systematic review. In: Research in Comparative and International Education 16, 1, pp. 3-21.

Conclusion – The Challenge of Integrating Antinomies Around Inclusive Education

Heidrun Demo

1   Antinomies and dilemmas in inclusive education

Reflections on tensions, antinomies and dilemmas in education, and specifically in the field of inclusive education, are not new (Croll/Moses 2000;
Dyson 2001; Ho 2004; Judge 1981; Minow 1990). They arise each time
different values or approaches seem to be contrasting but equally valuable.
Because of the contrast, a choice is necessary in the name of coherence; at the
same time, because of the comparable value, the same necessary choice
implies some kind of loss.

Looking at the philosophical pedagogical tradition, the Italian *Problematicism* has identified in antinomies an antidote to dogmatism. *Problematicism*
rejects the possibility for mankind to attain absolute knowledge and drawing
on metahistorical truths or principles (Baldacci 2003). In this awareness, it
does not end up in nihilisms but states the heuristic nature of antinomies and
recognises in their analysis the source for at least temporary meaningful
solutions (Trebisacce 2012).

Taking into consideration antinomies in education can be seen as relevant
for reflecting on what counts as progress or improvement. Norwich (2002)
puts forward the idea of "ideological impurity", the understanding that
"pursuing single value positions to their full application can undermine other
important values" (Norwich 2002: 483). For that reason, a set of policies and
practices that can be traced back to a fully coherent set of values on all levels
in education is limited in the possibility to capture all what we consider
worthy. The recognition of the value of impurity requires instead a complex
balancing between different, maybe also contradicting positions.

For the field of inclusive education, the core dilemma is the so-called
dilemma of difference that describes the unavoidable choice between, on the
one hand, identifying individual characteristics at right of receiving specific
provisions with the risk of labeling and, on the other hand, offering common
provisions to all with the risk of not making available what is necessary to
some (Terzi 2005).

The dilemma implies the intertwining of two dimensions: a theoretical
and political one. Both of them have been addressed also in the different

chapters of these books, some exploring more a conceptual definition of it, others looking at the issues of provisions and organisation of learning settings.

In this concluding chapter, a possible way to think dilemmas in a heuristic way will be discussed, relying on the *dialogic* as described in Edgar Morin's work: an opportunity to integrate antinomies without overlooking the essentially conflictual co-existence of the two antagonisms. In doing so, I strongly refer to Ianes', recently also updated, work (Ianes 2006; Ianes/ Demo 2022), who in his book *Speciale Normalità − Special Normality* introduces the idea to use the *dialogic* to move forward in the theory and policies of inclusive education.

2   The dispositive of the *dialogic*

Morin's major work is the *Method*, a six volume opus, in which he defines what knowledge is and how it is constructed, describing an approach to inquiry that aims at recognising and doing justice to the complexity of life. In this series of books, the philosopher discusses the idea that authentic comprehension is not possible with the current fragmentation of knowledge in scientific disciplines and, instead, argues for a reform of thinking, based on the idea of complex thinking. From his point of view, the structure of disciplines that fosters compartmentalised and monodisciplinary knowledge represents an obstacle for comprehension. In fact, intellectual comprehension of a complex structure, as the world we live in is, is not possible with a reductive or simplifying mental structure. The principle of reduction becomes not only limiting, but even un-human if applied not to intellectual but to human comprehension. It hinders the development of an awareness of human complexity, the deep understanding that in every human being there is the possibility of the best and the worst, and that life events strongly impact the way (the best or worst) potentials are developed. In this framework, knowledge is not understood as a linear connection of separated pieces of information, but much as the relationship between the whole and its parts where it is "impossible to know the parts without knowing the whole, or to know the whole without knowing the parts in detail" (Pascal 1669: 25).

Against this background, Morin has identified some connecting concepts, logical dispositives that support complex thinking which aims at reconnecting the fragmentation resulting from disciplinarity. One of those is the notion of *dialogic*. It can be understood as a form of dialectic but not in the reducing Hegelian sense of thesis and antithesis overcome by a synthesis. The *dialogic* is based on the complementary co-existence of antagonisms (thesis/antithesis), which are logically re-connected without negating their opposition.

No harmonic synthesis occurs, instead a generative conflict is conserved, a constant search for useful connections, also accepting contradictions. In the book *Einseigner à vivre* (Morin 2014) the couple life–death is used to exemplify the dialogic: the two notions are antagonisms and at the same time interconnected in several manners, as, for example, in ecosystems where the death of some living beings represents a source of life for other living beings.

In this chapter, the dispositive of the *dialogic* will be used to discuss a possible integration of some antinomies of inclusive education, both on a theoretical level and on the level of educational policies and practices.

3   The antinomy of the subjects of learning in Inclusive Education: Equality vs. Recognition of Difference

The first antinomy addresses the perspective on learners within inclusive education. Do we see them as all the same because they are all children and young people with the right for high-quality education that applies to everyone, *or* do we think that we need to identify learners exposed to a higher risk of exclusion and underachievement in order to understand the barriers they are facing?

The first perspective stresses sameness among all learners. It becomes visible, for example, in the International Forum celebrating in 2019 the 25th anniversary of the Salamanca World Conference on Special Needs Education that was organised with the theme "Every learner matters". With that choice, UNESCO reaffirmed the broadened notion of inclusion that in the last at least 20 years has moved from the idea of serving children with disabilities within general educational settings towards the principle to strengthen equal access to quality learning opportunities for all learners (Ainscow 2020). The idea has a twofold meaning. First, it regards the equal value of all human lives. It is well described in one of the values that Tony Booth puts at the basis of the Index for Inclusion: "Equality" understood as each life and each death being equally worthy (Booth/Ainscow 2016). Second, it implies the recognition of the same rights for everyone, in line with the international UN Universal Declaration of Human Rights (UDHR). Art. 25 affirms that "everyone has the right to education" and that "education shall be directed to the full development of the human personality and to the strengthening of respect for human rights and fundamental freedoms". Furthermore, Art. 28 of the UN Convention on the Rights of the Child states the State's duty to "make primary education compulsory and available free to all" and "make higher education accessible to all on the basis of capacity by every appropriate means".

Summarising, the principle of *equality* in inclusive education affirms the sameness of all learners' intrinsic value and rights.

The second perspective clearly recognises learners' differences in terms of learning opportunities. This point of view stresses the fact that the personal characteristics of some learners imply a higher risk of failing in learning within the current educational system. This is the reason why, for example, alongside the UN Declaration of Human Rights, the Convention of Rights for Persons with Disabilities (CRPD) was ratified in 2006. Art. 24 affirms the states parties duty to ensure an inclusive educational system that grants "a. the full development of human potential and sense of dignity and self-worth, and the strengthening of respect for human rights, fundamental freedoms and human diversity; b. the development by persons with disabilities of their personality, talents and creativity, as well as their mental and physical abilities, to their fullest potential; c. enabling persons with disabilities to participate effectively in a free society". As visible in comparing the extracts reported in this section of the CRPD-Art.24 and of UDHR-Art.25, the CRPD does not introduce different rights for this group of persons but aims at ensuring the full enjoyment of human rights by means of specific measures reserved for persons with a disability. Following that logic, on a national level, most of the European countries provide for the identification of students considered at risk, often defined as students with Special Educational Needs, and for special measure for them in terms of resources and/or placement (Meijer/Watkins 2019). From a pedagogical point of view, these policies mirror the need for a specific emphasis on those groups of learners regarded to be at risk of marginalisation, exclusion or underachievement, which has been highlighted in several works where inclusive education is defined in terms of equity (Ainscow 2016). Summing up, the principle of the *recognition of difference* emphasises the importance of the identification of learners at risk in order to prevent and/or address exclusion.

Both principles are supported, as seen above, by reasonable arguments; at the same time, they both imply risks. In fact, the stress on learners' sameness connected with the principle of equality can lead to overlooking some forms of injustice some learners are experiencing (Norwich/Koutsouris 2017; Shakespeare 2016). And precisely for that reason, the principle of the recognition of difference has been discussed. At the same time, identifying learners at risk by means of socially constructed categories like the SEN category also involves the risk of labelling (Algraigray/Boyle 2017).

Using the dispositive of the dialogic, the two both valuable principles can coexist and be integrated in a manner that reduces the risks that emerge when one is considered stand-alone. We are imagining here the possibility to re-connect the recognition of learners' sameness in terms of value and rights with the recognition of their difference. To say it in terms of inclusive policies, the challenge is constituted by the search for a way to identify learners at risk without constructing them as different, as it happens with labelling mechanisms. The proposal I put forward is that the challenge can be addressed with an understating of humankind (anthropological model) that responds to two criteria:

1. It adopts a relational understanding of learning and participation: The model interprets risk and development in learning and participation as the result of the interaction between individual characteristics and environmental factors.
2. It can be applied to all learners: The model is not reserved to describe risk and development of a specific group of students, but it looks at learning and participation potentials and risks for all in a global manner.

Concretely, the anthropological model of human functioning provided by the International Classification of Functioning, Disability and Health (ICF; WHO 2001) can represent a good starting point. Its bio-psycho-social definition of functioning is an example of relational understanding of what a learner can and cannot do in terms of learning and participation. This understanding limits the threat of labelling because risk and development are seen as the result of the encounter of the learners' personal physical and psychological characteristics with the learning context, with the consequence that the context is recognised in its role of potential facilitator or barrier, and the risk of failure is not interpreted as a responsibility of personal characteristics. In the interpretation and use proposed by the WHO, ICF should be only adopted for the description of the functioning of persons with a disability; adaptations of the model for a broader use have already been discussed and could represent a basis for further development (Griffo 2009).

4 The antinomy of the ways and objects of learning in Inclusive Education: Special vs. General Education

The second presented antinomy refers to the level of interventions, of the organisation of the educational offer in inclusive education. Should the educational offer of inclusive education be focused on supporting learners identified as at risk of failure with specific interventions or should it instead be focused on making the general education offer more flexible, varied, and accessible to everyone?

Special education has aimed at developing effective responses for some of the students we have defined as at risk of failure, which in this field are identified as students with special educational needs: special education comprehends any kind of "educational intervention and support designed to address special education needs" (Florian 2014: 10). It has produced important knowledge, for example, about teaching and learning sign language or Braille, around alternative communication systems that integrate verbal and iconic symbols or on a rich variety of methods to support the development of self-regulation and self-determination. On the other side, the idea itself that "additional support is defined by what is not generally available to all" (Florian 2020: 5) has historically connected the special education offer with some forms of segregation, as it is conceived as separated from what is offered to everyone. This is true for educational systems where special schools and classes exist but is reproduced also in mainstream settings where push- and pull-out phenomena take place with the idea to effectively respond to the students' specific needs. Furthermore, the existence of special education implicitly affirms that some learners need something different that cannot be ensured in the offer of general education (Florian 2014). Summing up, the construction of theory and practices to support learners at risk of special education has produced some useful knowledge for the development of learning, but it is intrinsically connected with segregating vectors.

To some extent, inclusive education was initially built exactly on the idea of overcoming the segregation produced by special education. Placement in mainstreaming for all – but between the lines one could read for students with disabilities – was at its heart. In countries that developed towards mainstreaming for students with disabilities, the importance of rethinking the general education context in terms of accessibility, plurality and flexibility became clear quite soon. From this awareness, the proposals around the idea of Universal Design have grown (e.g., Rose 2000). The challenge is to create learning environments that remove barriers and grant accessibility to all by means of plurality: multiple means of representation, expression and engagement ensure access to information and the possibility to follow self-determined paths of learning within a shared and common context. Although the idea of a school without barriers and obstacles is a powerful source of inspiration, capable of pointing the direction for various actions for change, it is important to relativise its strength on a theoretical level, as it presents some problematic issues (Shakespeare 2016). A critical issue concerns the possible incompatibility between different measures of reducing and/or breaking down barriers. Thinking from a systemic perspective, to create a single school environment where all the barriers everyone might encounter are removed can be highly challenging because, if aggregated in the same environment, measures to overcome different barriers may conflict with each other. Furthermore, there is an economical issue related to plurality: in a context with limited resources, the creation of a large plurality of means might conflict with other meaningful priorities. In brief, the idea of creating universal learning environments by means of plurality opens interesting perspectives for making general education accessible to all but also poses some problems.

By means of the dispositive of the dialogic, the apparent incompatibility of inclusion understood as interventions for students at risk and of inclusion seen as accessible general education for all will be critically discussed. With Florian (2020), I put forward the idea that special and inclusive education "are both imperfect practices with scope for future development that support the equity agenda" (11). Scopes of both can be realised if inclusion becomes a value, very similar to equity, that orients the theory and practice of general education, similarly to what happens within the framework of Universal Design. At the same time, the need of finalising towards priorities, the expenditure of limited resources and the awareness that the same set of plural means can advantage some but hinder others require a more individuals-sensitive perspective. In this sense, some measures are activated not *a priori* but because of the presence of one or the other learner facing a specific risk of underachievement. From this perspective, knowledge and competencies developed within special education can be a resource for a general education oriented towards inclusion, but only if the intrinsic segregating character described above is overcome. As long as special education intervention is interpreted as specialist, done in specific places by specific professionals, it will lead to some forms of segregation. But if the knowledge, competencies and instruments of special education are shared in a general education offer and become part of a set of plural means, then they acquire a different meaning. They are embedded in a context where differences are assumed as the norm for learning and expand the borders of what is assumed as the normal educational offer for specific groups of learners. This can happen when special education knowledge is shared among professionals and seen as a useful means to enhance the quality of the learning environment of the whole group. From this perspective, special education could enrich the possible means general education offers, if it is committed to inclusion and equity.

Finally, specific knowledge developed in special education is in fact not the only need to ensure that the general educational offer is able to address the risk of exclusion and underachievement that some learners experience. It is enough in this sense to recall the work of intercultural education or of linguists in relation to multilingualism, or the sociologists of education who have explored the relations of inclusion and exclusion with respect to differences of census. For this reason, a general education committed to inclusion and equity is necessarily declined as an interdisciplinary field of investigation that requires the collaboration of different disciplines with general and specific outlooks, where special education is just one among many others.

5   The Antinomy of Inclusive Education Research: Generation of Theory vs. Development of Practices

The third antinomy regards research in education more in general, but it is discussed here because it implies consequences also for the field of inclusive education. It addresses the choice between rigorous research that contributes to generalisable theories of education on one side and research aimed at knowledge relevant for a specific context in terms of development and improvement.

The attempt to look at this antinomy with a dialogical perspective that reconnects the antagonisms is not new. Already in the 20th century, the idea of connecting theoretical and practical work has led to the development of action research (Lewin 1946), which flourished around the 1970s and 80s. It was a first effort to overcome the traditional distinction between basic and applied research in the field of social sciences (McKenney/Reeves 2021). Nevertheless, at the end of the last century, action-research and the family of approaches grown around it have often been represented as limited in their scientific rigour. More recently, a narrow understanding of the discourse around *evidence-based*, a concept that gained more and more attention at the beginning of the new millennium, emphasised the perceived scientific limitedness of these approaches. At the same time, critical voices arose. Mitchell (2012) suggests that for educational processes that can hardly be described with a linear and causal input-output model, the notion of evidence should be broadened and extended from only randomised experimental studies to include all qualitative and quantitative rigorous research. And Biesta (2007) criticises the notion that educational decisions can be reduced to effectiveness and efficiency. He claims, on the contrary, that besides effectiveness, the issue of desirability plays an essential role. For not all effective pedagogical actions are clearly desirable.

On this background, an interesting perspective comes from the approach of Educational Design Research (EDR), "a genre of research in which the iterative development of solutions to practical and complex educational problems also provides the context for empirical investigation, which yields theoretical understanding that can inform the work of others" (McKenney/ Reeves 2019: 39). At the heart of the proposal, there is the idea of a research approach that can, at the same time, contribute to a meaningful development of learning settings and to credible theories that can inform others on learning processes.

EDR has in common with the large bunch of approaches grown around action-research the involvement in forms of inquiry that aim at developing practice and the combination of reflection and action to promote change in educational contexts (Chapman/Ainscow 2021; Kemmis 2010; Reason/Brad-bury 2001). Its peculiarity lies in accompanying the engagement for change with rigorous research in order to contribute simultaneously to school development in specific contexts and to knowledge production that can be generalised. This means, for example, that the analysis of the initial problem/issue goes beyond an informal exploration of the field and implies the collection of formally documented evidence in relation to a framework informed by literature. Or that the evaluation of the activated strategies is both formative and summative with the aim not only to orient further deci-sions for the context development, but also to produce new knowledge useful for other situations that address similar issues (McKenney/Reeves 2019). Summing up, EDR is concerned with structuring research processes in a rigorous manner so that the results can inform the work of others and at the same time address issues that are perceived as relevant in the professional fields. This can contribute to a culture of evidence that ensures desirability (Biesta 2007) by means of proximity to the educational field and scientific rigour through methodological accurateness.

6   Conclusive thoughts

Looking back at this chapter but also more in general at the whole book, the connection between the different presented lines of thoughts, experiences and backgrounds can be found in the red thread of a welcoming attitude towards antinomies and dilemmas. In the wave of this though, I propose the image of border-crosser to represent the role of inclusive education.

This means, as discussed in this text, that inclusive education can assume the role of reconnecting knowledge that has been split in different intellectual traditions, often seen opposed to each other, moving beyond ideological walls, as, for example, in nourishing a generative relationship between special and general education.

In a scenery that is only touched on in this book but needs to be de-veloped further in the future, it also means that inclusive education can be the framework where reflections around quality and equitable education en-counter and can be woven together by valuing different forms of knowledge and passing the borders of isolating specialised languages and methodologies.

For the specific context of the Province of Bolzano where we are writing from, the border-crosser role also has an intercultural sense. This volume collects many contributions that have their roots in the discourses around inclusive education in the German and Italian speaking countries. Traditio-nally, they have often been published and disseminated in the respective contexts. Reconnecting them in a joint book that places them in reciprocal dialogue and dialogue with other international traditions in the shared English language offers a space for a common understanding of some key concepts of inclusive education.

Finally, taking the border-crosser position assumes a political meaning in regard of the relationship between education, research, and society. For research within the academic community, it means to recognise the necessity to build on collaboration, both within and across disciplines; and this implies a positioning that firmly contains the pressures of constant evaluation and competition in the name of a meritocratic culture. It also means the openness to see research in strict connection with the educational field and society more in general. Approaches like EBR as described above require to cross the boundaries and listen to different voices, for example, the voice of practitioners that deal with everyday challenges and problems, the voice of students and children that experience the way policies and practices are implemented, the voice of parents and their expectations for education, the voice of school leaders as they seek to move their school forward, the voice of local authorities that take responsibility for policies, the voice of researchers that pose questions informed by evidences and theories.

In this sense, I would like to express a wish to all the readers committed to inclusive education opportunities for a constant growth in listening and dialogue: we will meet in crossing our borders!

References

Algraigray, Hatim/Boyle, Christopher (2017): The SEN label and its effect on special education. In: The Educational and Child Psychologist 34, 4, pp. 70–79.

Ainscow, Mel (2016): Diversity and Equity: A Global Education Challenge. In: New Zealand Journal of Educational Studies 51, 2, pp. 143–155.

Ainscow, Mel (2020): Promoting inclusion and equity in education. Lessons from international experiences. In: Nordic Journal of Studies in Educational Policy 6, 1, pp. 7–16. DOI: 10.1080/20020317.2020.1729587.

Baldacci, Massimo (2003): Il problematicismo. Dalla filosofia dell'educazione alla pedagogia come scienza. Lecce: Milella.

Biesta, Gert (2007): Why "what works" won't work. In: Educational Theory 57, 1, pp. 1–22.

Booth, Tony/Ainscow, Mel (2011): Index for Inclusion. A Guide to School Development Led by Inclusive Values. Bristol: CSIE.

Chapman, Christopher/Ainscow, Mel (eds.) (2021): Educational equity. Pathways to success. London: Routledge.

Dyson, Alan (2001): The Gulliford lecture. Special needs in the twenty-first century. Where we've been and where we're going. In: British Journal of Special Education 28, 1, pp. 24–29.

Florian, Lani (2014): Reimagining Special Education. Why New Approaches are needed. In: Florian Lani (ed.), The SAGE Handbook of Special Education. Los Angeles: SAGE, pp. 9–22.

Florian, Lani (2019): On the necessary co-existence of special and inclusive education. In: International Journal of Inclusive Education 23, 7–8, pp. 691–704.

Florian, Lani/Black-Hawkins, Kristine/Rouse, Martyn (2017). Achievement and Inclusion in Schools. London: Routledge.

Griffo, Giampiero (2009): La convenzione delle Nazioni Unite sui diritti delle persone con disabilità e l'ICF. In: Borgnolo, Giulio/de Camillis, Romolo/Francescutti, Carlo/Frattura, Lucilla/Troiano, Raffaella/Bassi (eds.): ICF e Convenzione ONU sui diritti delle persone con disabilità. Trento: Erickson, pp. 13–23.

Ho, Anita (2004): To be labelled or not to be labelled. That is the question. In: British Journal of Learning Disabilities 32, pp. 86–92.

Ianes, D. (2006): La speciale normalità. Trento: Erickson.

Ianes, Dario/Demo, Heidrun (2022): specialità e normalità? Trento: Erickson.

Judge, Harry (1981): Dilemmas in education. In: Journal of Child Psychology and Psychiatry 22, pp. 111–116.

Kemmis, Stephen (2010): What is to be done? The place of action research. In: Educational Action Research 18, 4, pp. 417–427.

Meijer, Cor J. W./Watkins, Amanda (2019): Financing special needs and inclusive education – from Salamanca to the present. In: International Journal of Inclusive Education 23, 7–8, pp. 705-721. DOI: 10.1080/13603116.2019.1623330.

McKenney, Susan/Reeves, Thomas C. (2019): Conducting Educational Design Research. New York: Routledge.

McKenney, Susan/Reeves, Thomas C. (2021): Educational design research. Portraying, conducting, and enhancing productive scholarship. In: Medical Education 55, 1, pp. 82–92.

Minow, Martha (1985): Learning to live with the dilemma of difference. Bilingual and special education. In: Law and Contemporary Problems 48, 2, pp. 157–211.

Mitchell, David (2013): What really works in inclusive and special education. New York: Routledge.

Morin, Edgar (2014): Enseigner à vivre. Manifeste pour changer l'éducation. Arles: Actes Sud/Play Bac.

Norwich, Brahm (2002): Education, inclusion and individual differences. Recognising and resolving dilemmas. In: British Journal of Educational Studies 50, 4, pp. 482–502.

Norwich, Brahm/Koutsouris, George (2017): Addressing dilemmas and tensions in inclusive education. In: Oxford research encyclopedia of education.

Pascal, Blaise (1669): The Thoughts of Blaise Pascal. London: George Bell and Sons.

Reason, Peter/Bradbury, Hilary (eds.) (2001): Handbook of Action research. Participative inquiry and practice. London: Sage.

Rose, David H. (2000): Universal design for learning. In: Journal of Special Education Technology 15, 3, pp. 45–49.

Shakespeare, Tom (2006): Disability rights and wrongs. London: Routledge.

Terzi, Lorella (2005): Beyond the dilemma of difference. The capability approach to disability and special educational needs. In: Journal of Philosophy of Education 39, 3, pp. 443–459.

Trebisacce, Giovambattista (2012): Dal razionalismo critico al problematicismo pedagogico. Considerazioni e spunti di ricercar. In: Studi sulla formazione 15, 2, pp. 93–101.

World Health Organization (WHO) (2001): International classification of human functioning, disability and health. Geneva: WHO. https://www.who.int/standards/classifications/international-classification-of-functioning-disability-and-health.

About the Authors

Alessandra Imperio, Postdoctoral Research Assistant, Faculty of Education/ Cognitive and Educational Sciences Lab (CESLab), Free University of Bozen-Bolzano, Italy. Main research interests: Active learning approaches for inclusion and the development of critical-thinking competence and life skills in general, inclusive and fair assessment, teacher training.

Anja Tervooren, Full Professorship for Education and Childhood Studies, Institute of Education, University of Duisburg-Essen, Germany. Main research interests: Theories of difference, childhood and intersectionality, qualitative research methods, gender and disability studies.

Anna Frizzarin, Postdoctoral Research Assistant, Competence Centre for School Inclusion, Free University of Bozen-Bolzano, Italy. Main research interests: Inclusion in educational settings, students' attitudes and social representations in relation to perceived diversity, participation opportunities and processes inside and outside the school.

Catalina Hamacher, Postdoctoral Research Assistant, Institute of Educational Science, University of Duisburg-Essen, Germany. Research interests: Inclusion and educational justice, childhood research, institutionalization of the pedagogical, reconstructive social research.

Dario Ianes, Past Professor for Inclusive Education, Faculty of Education/ Affiliated Member, Competence Centre for School Inclusion, Free University of Bolzano-Bozen, Italy; Co-founder of the Publishing House Erickson. Main research interests: Analysis of the Italian inclusive school system, organization of support in inclusive education, Individual Education Plan based on the ICF Model.

Francesca Berti, Postdoctoral University Researcher with fixed-term contract (Type A), Faculty of Education, Free University of Bozen-Bolzano, Italy. Research interests: Primary education research with focus on didactics, play-based learning, heritage education.

Heidrun Demo, Associate Professor for Inclusive Education, Faculty of Education/Competence Centre for School Inclusion, Free University of Bozen-Bolzano, Italy. Research interests: Analysis of inclusive school systems also in a comparative perspective, inclusive school development, inclusive classroom, teacher professionalization for inclusive education.

Joanne Banks, Assistant Professor in Inclusive Education, School of Education, Trinity College Dublin, Ireland. Main research interests: Inclusive and special education, educational disadvantage, Universal Design for Learning, student experience.

Mai-Anh Boger, Postdoctoral Researcher, Faculty of Humanities, University of Ratisbon, Germany. Research interests: Philosophies of alterity and difference, psychoanalysis (of internalized oppression), inclusion/diversity.

Michaela Kaiser, Assistant Professor in Art Education, Department of Art and Visual Culture, Carl von Ossietzky University of Oldenburg, Germany. Research Interests: Inclusive education, achievement, difference and inequalities, art and art education.

Petra Auer, Postdoctoral University Researcher with fixed-term contract (Type A), Faculty of Education, Free University of Bozen-Bolzano, Italy. Research interests: Inclusion in educational settings, values in primary school age children, socialization in the school context, acculturation of ethnic minority children and youth.

Rosa Bellacicco, Postdoctoral University Researcher with fixed-term contract (Type B), Department of Philosophy and Education Sciences, University of Turin; Affiliated member, Competence Centre for School Inclusion, Free University of Bozen-Bolzano, Italy. Research interests: Students with disabilities in school and higher education and their transition to employment.

Silver Cappello, Postdoctoral Research Assistant, Competence Centre for School Inclusion, Free University of Bolzano-Bozen, Italy. Research interests: Inclusion in educational settings, didactics in primary education, school disaffection and teaching-learning processes.

Rune Hausstätter, Professor in Special Education, Faculty of Education, Inland Norway University of Applied Sciences, Norway. Main research interests: Theories of special education, inclusion, professional development and comparative special education research.

Simone Seitz, Full Professorship for General Didactics and Inclusive Education, Faculty of Education/Competence Centre for School Inclusion, Free University of Bozen-Bolzano, Italy. Main research interests: Inclusion and educational justice, primary education and extended learning, didactics and achievement, professionalization.

Valentina Migliarini, Assistant Professor in Education Studies, Department of Education and Social Justice, University of Birmingham, UK. Research interests: Equity & inclusive education, race, migratory status and disability intersections in education, linguistic ableism, abolitionist teaching.

Index of Terms